The Great Migration
in Historical Perspective

Blacks in the Diaspora
Darlene Clark Hine, John McCluskey, Jr., and David Barry Gaspar
GENERAL EDITORS

The Great Migration in Historical Perspective

New Dimensions of Race, Class, and Gender

EDITED BY

Joe William Trotter, Jr.

INDIANA UNIVERSITY PRESS
Bloomington and Indianapolis

. **Library of Congress Cataloging-in-Publication Data**

The Great migration in historical perspective : new dimensions of
race, class, and gender / edited by Joe William Trotter, Jr.
     p.   cm. — (Blacks in the diaspora)
     Includes index.
     ISBN 0-253-36075-7. — ISBN 0-253-20669-3 (pbk.)
     1. Afro-Americans—Migrations.   2. Migration, Internal—United
States—History—19th century.   3. Migration, Internal—United
States—History—20th century.   4. United States—Population—
History—19th century.   5. United States—Population—History—20th
century.   I. Trotter, Joe William, date.   II. Series.
E185.86.G65   1991
305.996'073—dc20   91-4379

1 2 3 4 5   95 94 93 92 91

For African-American migrants to industrial America and for John and Lois Brinson and family, in memory of our aunt, Nonia Zinnerman

CONTENTS

FOREWORD

by Nell Irvin Painter

Were Africans who had been forcibly transported from Africa to the Americas immigrants? Making historical comparison with immigrant Europeans to a land already peopled by Native Americans, the historian is tempted to answer in the affirmative. Africans in the Americas spoke the pidgins and forged the creole languages that everywhere characterized the early interaction of different cultures. Generational differences also underscored the African-ness of the African immigrants and the American-ness of their American-born children. Africans' creole children, born into a triracial society, inhabited a different social and psychological world from their parents. American-born generations of African decent also experienced a sex ratio different from that of the immigrant generations, which were heavily male. No matter how much love and familial connection drew the generations together, to American-born children their African-born parents and grandparents seemed like immigrants, culturally and linguistically foreign.

As is related in slave narratives, Africans in the Americas enjoyed a special kind of prestige: they had been born free. Though enslaved in this country, they had not always been slaves: by this token their status in the slave quarters increased. Their stature made them less immigrants than captives: they had left a promised land for hell. This is not the classic saga of American immigrants.

Asians and Europeans coming to the United States voluntarily had lovely names for this country. In the nineteenth century, Chinese immigrants called it the "Golden Mountain," and others have coined their own phrases to designate the "land of opportunity." African-Americans over the generations of detention could hardly evoke such terminology. They were slaves—defined by the status of "involuntary servitude"—in the very same land in which, as the old joke went, a Jew could be Czar. In this sense, the African immigrant generation had little in common with European and Asian counterparts. To use the word "immigrant" for Africans, as well as for voluntary immigrants, strips language of symbolic meaning.

Although we do not use the word "immigrant" for the people who, in the late nineteenth and twentieth centuries, left the southern countryside for northern and southern cities, they, more than their African ancestors, deserve the term. Leaving the sexual abuse, poverty, and multifaceted disabilities that plagued them, the women and men who made the break from their bad "Old Country"—the rural South—were seeking their fortune (with all the meanings of the word in folklore) in the way of other immigrants to the United States. Southern migrants exercised their freedom and reached a better land.

While white Americans have celebrated liberty for more than two centuries, freedom has been the key to black Americans' quest. Freedom comes in many versions: the freedom attained against great odds by the fugitive; the freedom purchased by one's self or one's family member; or the freedom represented by the rumor or the fact of the Union Army in the neighborhood, the Emancipation Proclamation, the Confederate defeat, and the several triumphs (lasting or illusory) over Jim Crow. After emancipation in 1865, former slaves tested their freedom and walked about, leaving their erstwhile places of employment (if we can call it employment when the worker is not paid). They sought family and free air, and, as Exodusters in 1879, they left a South in which they feared they would be reenslaved with the end of Reconstruction. These were acts of freedom, whether the destination lay ten or one thousand miles away.

In this sense, the Great Migration of the early twentieth century represents for African-Americans both immigration and freedom. These were voluntary movements, initiated by the individual or the family, in pursuit of what they saw as their own best interests. Motives were mixed: my own Hosea Hudson left sharecropping in Wilkes County, Georgia, in 1923, leaving a touchy relationship with his brother-in-law, cotton culture devastated by the boll weevil, and a rural culture of churchy morals and racial etiquette that he found confining. In the city—first Atlanta, then Birmingham—Hudson found paid work, gained skills in which he took great pride, and joined a political party that promised to fulfill his hope for radical social and economic change. As a working-class black Communist, Hudson was hardly representative of his generation, yet he is as one with the many thousands who saw migration as a decisive step toward personal autonomy.

Urbanization brought another engine of twentieth-century American life—commercial entertainment—into contact with the fertile ground of southern black culture. However much rural geniuses, like bluesman Robert Johnson, might become legendary after death, they could only reach masses through the radio and recording industries that blossomed in the 1920s. Whether sacred or secular (and secular is a mild word for much that is in the blues), the black southern music that has so fundamentally influenced American popular culture depended on migration. Without that first step, without reaching the radio or the recording studio, the Muddy Waterses, the Thomas Dorseys and the Ma Raineys would have remained mere local talent. In this sense, black migration represents a basic component of twentieth-century American culture.

In the realm of politics, too, the migration that took black southerners out of the South and brought them within reach of the ballot box had revolutionary consequences. Disfranchised in the South, African-Americans were able to exercise their citizens' rights and pursue their political interests in only the most constricted and indirect manner. Without black constituents, southern politicians had little reason to embrace issues of importance to those who were the victims of racial and economic oppression. Only when large numbers of blacks were voters—which meant only when large numbers of blacks had left the South—did the Federal Government begin to support black civil rights. If it remains true that the Civil Rights movement could not have succeeded without federal support, it must also be remembered that, by the 1940s, black voters in the North and West had already made civil rights an issue worth a politician's embracing. As voters, black southerners outside the South led Harry S. Truman, John F. Kennedy, and Lyndon Johnson to the issue of civil rights. In turn, the movement and the legislation the movement inspired remade the Jim Crow South.

Since the Civil Rights movement dismantled the worst of white supremacy in the South, another migration has been taking place, which is sometimes called reverse migration. Now people who left the South at mid-century are returning—going home. They are retiring rustbelt workers who, tired of dirt and cold and crime, are going back to their own Carolina. With their savings and their hopes for a real New South, they build far nicer houses than those they left and send their grandchildren to decent schools. They are not returning to the "bad Old Country" that they left, for many swore never again to set foot in the white man's South; but they still see themselves as southerners, sometimes even as rural southerners, and they are reclaiming their southern identity.

In this homecoming, southern black migrants resemble the immigrant sojourners of industrial America who made their pile and went back to China or Italy. The parallel, however, goes only so far: black "immigrants" remain within the same society and the same economy, whether rural or urban, northern or southern. Through their "immigrant" experience they have profoundly altered the culture that all late twentieth-century Americans share.

PREFACE

This volume brings together recent scholarship on the Great Migration in historical perspective. It examines black migration to Norfolk, Pittsburgh, Chicago, Richmond, California, southern West Virginia, and, accenting the gender dimension, to a variety of cities in the urban Midwest. The collection not only documents the usual sources, causes, and consequences of black population movement, but also the dynamic role of black kin, friend, and communal networks in the process. Thus, the essays locate black migration within the South, situate it within the changing political economy, and emphasize the role of blacks in shaping their own migration experiences.

While the essays emphasize the effect that southern blacks had on their own migration, they also illuminate contrasts in the sources, magnitude, and impact of black migration on different cities. Essays by James R. Grossman, Peter Gottlieb, and Shirley Ann Moore illuminate black migration to the urban North and West. They suggest that black migrants responded to cities with very different economic opportunities. Although blacks entered a variety of jobs in each city, they were especially attracted to meat-packing in Chicago, steelmaking in Pittsburgh, and shipbuilding in Richmond.

Black migration to these northern and western cities was often preceded by a series of stops in several southern and non-southern cities and small towns. Thus, many southern blacks who migrated to Chicago, Pittsburgh, and Richmond were better prepared for life in urban America than we are accustomed to believing. As sociologist Carole Marks argues in her recent study on the subject (although she perhaps overstates the claim), " A majority of the migrants of the Great Migration were urban, nonagricultural laborers, not the rural peasant usually assumed."[1]

By carefully situating their studies within the context of southern black culture, family, and community life, Grossman, Moore, and Gottlieb also modify the causal dynamics of black population movement. More specifically, they transcend the often mechanistic portrait of push-pull forces as causes of black migration. Grossman treats the Great Migration to Chicago as a grassroots social movement, fueled by its own leadership and information networks. Similarly, Gottlieb analyzes the black migration to Pittsburgh as "a process of self-transformation." For her part, Moore argues that black migrants to Richmond "were not passive victims pushed and pulled in a drama beyond their control."

According to essays by Earl Lewis and Joe Trotter, black migration to Norfolk and southern West Virginia developed unique characteristics. The seaports and navy yards of Norfolk and the coalfields of southern West Virginia represented the final destination points for many southern migrants. As Lewis notes, "South to North migration has been confused with rural to urban migration." More blacks migrated to southern cities between 1900 and 1920 than to northern ones, and they continued to migrate to those southern cities through World War II. Moreover, as Trotter notes, black migration to southern West Virginia was neither rural to rural nor rural to urban, but rather rural to rural-industrial. By focusing on southern destinations of black migrants, Lewis and Trotter show that the southern economy offered diverse industrial attractions of its own. Nonetheless, like black migration to the urban North and West, black kin and friendship networks played an important role in black population movements within the South.

Black men and women often had different reasons for moving to the new industrial environment. In her ground-breaking essay on the gender dimension, social historian Darlene Clark Hine challenges us to examine the role of black women in the travel and communications networks: she urges us to unravel the complicated gender-specific threads of black migration from the peculiarly racial and class components. In migration research, she argues, scholars need to pay more attention to "the non-economic motives propelling black female migration." For many black women left the South "to escape from sexual abuse at the hands of southern white, as well as black, men." Thus, although linked by common threads, the essays show varieties of black migration experiences.

Finally, this collection suggests the maturation of black migration studies within the larger field of black urban history. Closely intertwined with the development of black urban history, studies of black migration stress its impact on the nature of black-white social contacts, racial segregation in the urban environment, and the transformation of rural blacks into a new industrial working class. Yet, unlike the essays in this volume—based upon the imaginative use of oral interviews, company records, newspapers, manuscript collections, and a variety of statistical accounts—few studies systematically analyze the role of blacks in shaping their own geographical movement. Therefore, in order to illuminate the dimensions of this problem in urban historical research, this volume includes a critique of the black migration literature, pinpoints strengths and weaknesses therein, and suggests a framework for essential discussion, reconceptualization, and new research. Indeed, taken together, these essays should facilitate the crystallization of black migration studies as a new subfield.

NOTE

1. Carole Marks, *Farewell—We're Good and Gone: The Great Black Migration* (Bloomington: Indiana University Press, 1989), p. 3.

ACKNOWLEDGMENTS

To my colleagues and contributors to this volume, I owe a huge debt. They persevered over the past three years and helped to bring this book to full fruition. The contributors to this volume did more than submit individual essays. By offering critical comments on my own contributions, they helped to transform this book into a truly collaborative enterprise. I especially wish to thank Earl Lewis, James Grossman, and Darlene Clark Hine for their thoughtful comments on my essays. I owe a special debt to Darlene Clark Hine, who encouraged me to submit the manuscript to Indiana University Press (for consideration in the Blacks in the Diaspora Series), and to the anonymous reader who enthusiastically recommended publication.

For helping to strengthen the manuscript and improve its reception by the scholarly community, I wish to thank my colleagues Kenneth Kusmer of Temple University and August Meier of Kent State University, both of whom offered thoughtful comments on the manuscript. The book also benefitted from the ongoing interest of editors Frederick Hetzel and Maurine Greenwald at the University of Pittsburgh Press. They reviewed the manuscript, offered helpful feedback, and encouraged the book from the early stages, and to them, I also say thanks. Graduate and undergraduate students also contributed to this project, through their thoughtful comments, enthusiasm, and keen interest. I am particularly indebted to my graduate assistants Lori Cole and John Hinshaw.

This volume had its genesis in the Carnegie Mellon University conference on the black migration which was co-sponsored by the University Libraries and the Department of History. Held in conjunction with the Smithsonian Institution's traveling exhibition ("Field to Factory: Afro-American Migration, 1915–1940"), the conference program included four scholarly papers; an oral history panel, moderated by historian Laurence Glasco of the University of Pittsburgh; and critical comments from social historian and conference chair Nell Irvin Painter of Princeton University. To my colleagues, panelists, and co-workers on this event, I extend a collective thanks.

For helping to make the initial event possible, I am grateful to project Co-director Sylverna Ford, Assistant to the Director, Hunt Library; Thomas Michalak, Director of University Libraries; Peter N. Stearns, chair, Department of History; Mary Catherine Johnsen, Special Collections; Roye Werner, Reference Librarian; and the members of the Pittsburgh Center for Social History. I especially thank Spencer Crew and the staff of the Smithsonian Institution, and our sponsors for the "Field to Factory'' project: Duquesne Light Company, Mellon Bank, the Pennsylvania Ethnic Heritage Center, the Pittsburgh Foundation, and Westinghouse Electric Corporation.

Finally, as in other projects of this nature, I am grateful to my wife LaRue. She not only provided the co-directors with a model for planning and publicizing the ''Field to Factory'' project, she encouraged the publication of this volume at every stage of the process. She believed that this volume could make a difference. Her faith in this book was reinforced by my mother, sisters, brothers, cousins, and an expanding number of nephews and nieces. This book owes its existence, however, to millions of southern blacks who migrated to industrial America, seeking a better life for themselves and their families, and, therefore, I dedicate this book to them and to my cousins, John and Lois Brinson and family, in memory of our aunt, Nonia Zinnerman, who taught us the meaning of extended kinship and community networks.

The Great Migration
in Historical Perspective

Introduction
Black Migration in Historical Perspective
A Review of the Literature

Joe William Trotter, Jr.

Since the arrival of Africans on slave ships in the early seventeenth century, migration has been an enduring theme in African-American history. Yet, only with the advent of World War I did blacks make a fundamental break with their rural past and move to cities in increasing numbers. Since the early twentieth century, the nature, causes, and consequences of that momentous population movement have engaged the labors of scholars from a variety of disciplines. In order to place the essays in this volume within a broader scholarly context, this chapter explores the diverse and changing modes of treating the mass migration of blacks to American cities between the two World Wars.

The literature on black migration during the early twentieth century unfolded within the larger context of three distinct, but interrelated, conceptual orientations in black urban history. The first of these, the race relations model, emerged at the turn of the twentieth century, peaked during the early 1930s, and persisted in varying degrees through the 1950s. Mainly sociological and social anthropological in approach, the race relations model took a variety of forms, including urban community studies, special case studies, and general syntheses of existing knowledge. It elaborated the socioeconomic push-pull explanation of black population movement, and analyzed black migration as a pivotal element in changing race relations. Although such studies examined black migration within the larger context of preceding patterns, black migration as a historical phenomenon was a secondary, rather than a primary, theme in most of the race relations literature.[1]

The ghetto model of black urban history emerged during the early 1960s and dominated scholarship on the subject through the late 1970s. Primarily the work of historians employing interdisciplinary techniques, the ghetto model treated the black migration as a historical process, incorporated the push-pull explanation of the pattern, and, most of all, analyzed its impact on the process of ghetto formation, i.e., the rise of largely segregated black housing and community life in the urban environment. While the ghetto framework moved the dynamics of historical change to the fore of research on black migration and urban community development, it paid insufficient attention to the role of blacks in shaping their own migration experience, underplayed the impact of migration on the black class structure, and paved the way for the emergence of an alternative class analysis of black migration during the late 1970s and early 1980s.[2]

Building upon the ghetto model, the proletarian approach analyzes the black migration as a historical process. It also assesses a range of forces undergirding the phenomenon. Unlike the ghetto and race relations approaches, however, it examines the impact of migration on class formation, paying particular attention to the rise of the urban industrial working class. Yet, much like earlier models, the proletarian framework, as employed by some writers, gives inadequate attention to the roots of black migration in the southern black experience, including the role of black kin and friendship networks.[3]

Thus, despite its importance in a variety of approaches to black urban history, until recently, few scholars explored the historical dynamics of black migration itself. This essay examines the various scholarly traditions, highlights the strengths and weaknesses therein, and, based upon the essays in this volume, suggests the gradual emergence of black migration studies as a new scholarly subfield.

The Race Relations Model and Black Migration:
The Pre-World War I Era

Studies of black migration from rural to urban America had roots in the pre–World War I era. In 1899, in his pioneering study *The Philadelphia Negro*, W. E. B. Du Bois emphasized migration as a key element in black population growth and community development. Focusing on the late nineteenth century migration of blacks to Philadelphia, a series of questions guided his research. "Whence came these people?" he asked; and "How far are they native Philadelphians, and how far immigrants, and if the latter, how long have they been here?" No questions concerning the effects of northern city conditions on blacks, he said, "can be intelligently answered until we know how long these people have been under the influence of given conditions, and how they were trained before they came."[4]

Du Bois noted the predominance of young black women, the prevalence of blacks from the Upper South states of Virginia and Maryland, and the often circuitous and indirect nature of black migration to the city. "Much of the immigration to Philadelphia is indirect; Negroes come from country districts to small towns; then go to larger towns; eventually they drift to Norfolk, Va., or to Richmond. Next they come to Washington, and finally settle in Baltimore or Philadelphia."[5] Although Du Bois included little data on the causes of black migration in the study itself, in order to gain a greater appreciation for the southern background of Philadelphia blacks, for two months during the summer of 1897, he studied blacks in rural Virginia, which resulted in the publication of "The Negroes in Farmville, Virginia" (1898).[6]

Commissioned by the Sociology Department of the University of Pennsylvania, *The Philadelphia Negro* aimed first and foremost to help solve contemporary problems in race relations. It used research as a tool for social reform.[7] Thus, despite the highly empirical nature of his research and his penetrating insights into the nature of black migration as a process of step-by-step movement from rural and small town America to the big city, Du Bois perceived the black migrant in largely pathological terms as a social problem. His research on the southern background notwithstanding, the migratory movement of blacks from country district, to small town, and finally to the big city resulted in training for what he called the "criminal class" in the "slums of Seventh and Lombard streets."[8] To be sure, Du Bois modified his viewpoint by noting many exceptions to the rule. He also emphasized the role of racial discrimination in limiting the opportunities of black migrants. Yet he failed to probe deeply the positive character and impact of black southern rural life on migrants. *The Philadelphia Negro* leaves the impression that the southern Afro-American culture and experiences had little to offer blacks in the move from country to city.[9]

Moreover, although Du Bois offered substantial historical discussion of the black migration from the seventeenth through the late nineteenth centuries, his interest in the issue was mainly as background for the elucidation of conditions in 1896 and 1897. He was not interested in a detailed historical analysis of black migration. Indeed, as the imperatives of problem solving gained sway over the research agenda, the dynamics of historical change received correspondingly less attention.

Like Du Bois, in his study of blacks in late nineteenth and early twentieth century Boston, John Daniels placed his treatment of black migration within a race relations framework. *In Freedom's Birthplace: A Study of the Boston Negro* (1914) grew out of Daniels's involvement with a black branch of the South End Settlement House for European immigrants. It shifted the attention of white reformers from blacks in the South to blacks in the North. In his original introduction to the book, Robert A. Woods, the pioneer Boston Settlement leader, noted that "large sums of money were annually contributed to . . . improvement among colored people in the South, while practically no specific attention was paid to the serious problem of the steadily increasing Negro population in Boston."[10]

Daniels like Du Bois viewed the black migration into and out of Boston in largely negative terms. Most migrants, he said were "ignorant, deficient in practical ability, and almost entirely lacking in any training" above unskilled labor and menial service.[11] He noted that black population movement was affected by the same forces which caused shifting "among any element of the population." Yet, unlike Du Bois, Daniels believed that black geographic mobility and the poor economic status of the migrant was "inherent in the negro character."[12]

Daniels' study was not only racist, it was also less rigorous in methodology and more descriptive, rather than analytical, in presentation than the *Philadelphia Negro*. While *In Freedom's Birthplace* reflected the race relations approach to black migration, it had little influence over subsequent research on the topic. More influential in the scholarly discourse on the subject was a series of essays in the *Annals of the American Academy of Political and Social Science, Charities: A Review of Local and General Philanthropy*, the *New York Age*, the *Nation*, the *Southern Workman*, and a limited number of other newspaper and journal outlets.[13]

In charting and explaining prewar patterns of black migration, some of the essays not only complemented, but also exceeded the monographs of Du Bois and Daniels. R. R. Wright, a research fellow in Sociology at the University of Pennsylvania, for example, identified the precise geographical origins and destination of early migrants. He observed that blacks from the southern Atlantic states traveled up the seaboard to the northern Atlantic states, while blacks from the south central division moved up the Mississippi Valley to the north central states. Others from both southern divisions migrated west; some traveled up the Mississippi and then crossed over through Missouri and Kansas, whereas others migrated to the west coast "around the Southwest through Texas."[14] Moreover, using the economist's push-pull model, Wright emphasized the comparative economic, social, and political developments in the North and South, acknowledged the importance of black kin, friend, and community networks, and warned his counterparts against overemphasis on pathology in research on urban blacks.[15]

For Wright and other prewar analysts, however, the reform goal nonetheless remained paramount. Bending to the imperatives of racial reform, Wright concluded that the migrants were not "the best negroes," but the "ill-adjusted."[16] Without an emphasis on the pathological dimensions of black life in cities, Wright and his contemporaries feared, as did George Edmund Haynes of the New York Urban League, that the blacks' "economic and social difficulties may be less generally known; his migrations and concentrations in cities, North and South . . . given less attention."[17] Despite important shortcomings, prewar research nonetheless helped to shape black migration studies during World War I and its aftermath.

The Race Relations Model and Black Migration:
World War I to Early 1930s

Beginning with *Negro Migration in 1916–17* (published in 1919 by the U.S. Department of Labor, Division of Negro Economics) studies of the Great Migration proliferated between World War I and the early 1930s.[18] They included the books of Carter G. Woodson, *A Century of Negro Migration* (1918); Emmett J. Scott, *Negro Migration during the War* (1920); Thomas J. Woofter, *Negro Migration: Changes in Rural Organization and Population of the Cotton Belt* (1920); Charles S. Johnson (for the Chicago Commission on Race Relations), *The Negro in Chicago:*

A Study of Race Relations and a Race Riot (1922); Louise V. Kennedy, *The Negro Peasant Turns Cityward: Effects of Recent Migrations to Northern Cities* (1930); Edward E. Lewis, *The Mobility of the Negro* (1931); and Clyde V. Kiser, *Sea Island to City: A Study of St. Helena Islanders in Harlem and Other Urban Centers* (1932).[19] These studies pinpointed the changing characteristics of black migration, emphasized the push and pull of economic factors, and, compared to their prewar counterparts, de-emphasized the pathological dimensions of the process. Much as in the prewar era, however, the race relations imperative (and, during the war years, the national security imperative) retained its sway over wartime and postwar scholarship. Thus, black migration as a historical process, including the dynamic role of black kin, friend, and communal networks, received inadequate attention.

To be sure, contemporary scholars placed black migration within a larger historical context. Francis D. Tyson, T. J. Woofter, and other Labor Department analysts, for example, acknowledged the relationship between black population movement from the underground railway before the Civil War to the widespread migration of 1916–17. In their research on the subject, Charles S. Johnson, Emmett Scott, and Louise V. Kennedy reinforced the same point. The wartime and postwar studies documented the increase of southern black migration to the North from no more than three hundred thousand in 1910 to nearly one million during the war years. Whereas prewar studies had shown how the Upper South and women dominated the spatial and gender sources of black migration, the newer studies illuminated the growing predominance of Deep South blacks and young men.[20]

Yet, much like the *Philadelphia Negro*, the war and postwar studies did not explore the historical connection in substantial detail. Prewar developments served as a brief backdrop. They helped to analyze changes in the volume, sources, and direction of the movement during World War I. As Kennedy stated in her study, the movements during the war and postwar years "were especially significant because they revealed a decided increase in the volume of migration and a peculiar change in the major direction and the length of the moves which were made."[21]

While such studies failed as historical treatments, they succeeded quite well as cross-sectional analyses. They not only documented the growing predominance of young men from the lower South, they also identified the precise subregional and occupational dimensions of the process. Various studies of the states of Georgia, Florida, Alabama, Mississippi, and Louisiana, carefully pinpointed the specific sections of these states with the heaviest out-migration.[22] According to T. J. Woofter, for example, black farm laborers migrated from the boll weevil infested areas of southeastern Georgia, while large numbers of common laborers left the cities and small towns of Macon, Waycross, Albany, and especially Savannah's turpentine and sawmill gangs.[23]

As contemporary studies pinpointed the precise regional, subregional, and occupational characteristics of black migrants, they also clarified the issue of destinations, utilizing the notion of secondary migration. As R. H. Leavell stated in his study of black migration from Mississippi, the mere fact that a black "moved out of his former [southern] home" was no evidence "that he [had] moved to a northern city." Southern cities like New Orleans, Birmingham, Jacksonville, Savannah, and Memphis among others "became concentration points." Birmingham and Bessemer served as the major distribution points for blacks going north from Alabama. The Southern, Louisville, and Nashville, the St. Louis and San Francisco, and the Illinois Central Railroads all travelled northward from Birmingham and Bessemer. T. J. Woofter identified cities in Georgia like Columbus, Americus, and Albany as distribution points for blacks leaving from west Georgia and east Alabama, while Valdosta, Waycross, Brunswick, and Savannah served as distribution centers for blacks leaving the depressed agricultural counties of southern and southeastern Georgia. To blacks migrating from Mississippi, Arkansas, Alabama, Louisiana, and Texas, "Chicago was the logical destination," while "the North" meant Pennsylvania, New Jersey, New York, Boston, and other New England cities to blacks coming from Florida, South Carolina, Virginia, and Georgia.[24]

Upon arrival in northern cities, black population movement often flowed into additional migratory streams. Wartime and postwar scholars of black population movement documented the process. "All of the arrivals here did not stay," Emmett Scott observed of the black migration to Chicago. "They were only temporary guests awaiting the opportunity to proceed further and settle in surrounding cities and towns." In Philadelphia, he also noted, black migration "broke bulk, scattering itself into the various industrial communities desiring labor." Within about one hundred miles of Philadelphia, cities like Wilmington, Delaware, and Lancaster, Pottsville, York, Altoona, and Harrisburg, Pennsylvania, all received black migrants who first migrated to the City of Brotherly Love.[25]

In his study of St. Helena, a South Carolina Sea Island, Clyde V. Kiser traced the movement of black migrants to what he called "the feverish and congested cities of the North." He documented the Sea Islanders' movement to Philadelphia, Boston, and especially Harlem, New York, via southern cities like Savannah, Georgia and Charleston, South Carolina. In the urban North, Kiser documented the migrants' intermetropolitan movement. Somewhat contrary to Du Bois, he also concluded that few St. Helenians reached the big cities through "intermediate residence in a village or a small town."[26] Blacks from St. Helena Island tended to leave their small rural surroundings for cities of substantial size, first in the South and then in the North.

Black migration studies of the wartime and postwar years included discussions of a range of precipitating push factors on the southern end, pull forces on the northern end, and, to some extent, the role of black family and kinship networks on both ends. However, within this framework, contemporary studies stressed the primacy of economic forces. In his analysis of the black migration between 1919 and 1924, Edward E. Lewis noted fluctuations in black population movement over brief periods of time, but he explained the pattern by the " 'pull' of industrial demand for labor" in the North and the " 'push' of agricultural disorganization in the Cotton Belt."[27] Writing during the late 1920s, Kennedy linked the Great Migration to prewar patterns, noted a brief postwar decline, and then specified a sharp resurgence during the mid-1920s. Emphasizing forces "which are 'driving' and those which are 'beckoning,' " Kennedy nonetheless concluded that the latest movements possessed much the same characteristics as observed from 1916 to 1920.[28] In the U.S. Department of Labor study, James B. Dillard summarized the major components of the push-pull model as applied to black migration:

> That the lack of labor at the North, due mainly to the ceasing of immigration from Europe, was the occasion of the migration all agree. The causes assigned at the southern end are numerous: General dissatisfaction with conditions, ravages of boll weevil, floods, change of crop system, low wages, poor houses on plantations, poor school facilities, unsatisfactory crop settlements, rough treatment, cruelty of the law officers, unfairness in courts, lynching, desire for travel, labor agents, the Negro press, letters from friends in the North, and finally advice of white friends in the South where crops had failed. All of these causes have been mentioned, and doubtless each cause mentioned has had its influence in individual cases. . . . However the influence came, and whatever concurrent causes may have operated all will agree . . . that 'better wages offered by the North have been the immediate occasion for the exodus'."[29]

By emphasizing the primacy of economic forces, the wartime and postwar studies also stressed the role of external forces like labor agents. During the war years, they sometimes portrayed the migrants as irrational actors in a drama beyond their control. Northern labor agents entered southern communities offering work at higher wages. Migrants allegedly left hurriedly, giving little thought to employers, families, or friends. As the movement gained momentum, the most thoughtful of men were swept up into the migration "fever." Emmett Scott's study offers perhaps the most extreme illustration of this viewpoint:

> In the first communities visited by the representatives of northern capital, their offers created unprecedented commotion. Drivers and teamsters left their wagons standing in the street. Workers, returning home, scrambled aboard the trains for the North without notifying their employers or their families.[30]

Although the wartime and early postwar writers emphasized the primacy of external forces like labor agents, "migration fever," most agreed, soon gave way to the thoughtful role of black kin, friend, and communal networks. Few of these scholars ignored the hand that blacks took in shaping their own migration experience. Despite his illustrations to the contrary, for example, Emmett Scott elevated the role of mass discussion to a prominent position among the list of forces stimulating the black migration. In the barber shops, grocery stores, and churches, blacks articulated their grievances, exchanged good news from the North, and formed migration clubs, pooling their resources in a communal approach to movement North. Deeply enmeshed in black kin and friendship networks, Scott suggested that black women played a conspicuous role in helping to organize the migration process.[31]

In his study of St. Helena Islanders, Clyde V. Kiser elevated the role of kin and friendship networks to a key place, and sharply modified the usual emphasis on the role of socioeconomic push-pull forces. Kiser emphasized the persistence of important cultural linkages between life in the city and life at home.[32]

Perhaps Kiser's emphasis on the role of black kin, friend, and communal networks was inevitable given the nature of his research project and the unique characteristics of the people he studied. *Sea Island to City* grew out of a larger project on St. Helena Island, initiated in 1928 under the direction of T. J. Woofter. Funded by the Social Science Research Council and the Institute for Research in Social Sciences at the University of North Carolina, a team of scholars spent months "studying various phases of the Island's culture." The project resulted in the publication of Woofter's *Black Yeomanry: Life on St. Helena Island* (1930).[33] Drawing heavily upon *Black Yeomanry*, Kiser expanded his analysis toward the urban destinations of the migrants.

Black life on St. Helena Island was unique: blacks on the Island were landowners, rather than landless sharecroppers, renters, or laborers; they lived in relatively isolated island communities; and they experienced relatively few face to face interactions with neighboring whites. Moreover, compared to blacks elsewhere in the South, the Sea Islanders' culture reflected high levels of social and cultural links to slavery and African backgrounds. Indeed, according to Kiser, many of the complaints of Islanders against whites developed after they left the Island. Life in the northern cities intensified the contrasting situation in the South and clarified the forces which had led them to move.[34]

As suggested by the foregoing emphasis on the role of blacks in shaping their own migration experience, the wartime and postwar writers tended to view migratory black workers in more positive terms than had their prewar counterparts like Du Bois and Daniels. Driven by the labor demands of the national defense program, the Department of Labor studies viewed the black workers as a valuable asset. The United States confronted a labor shortage both in agriculture and industry. "On the whole," historian Carter G. Woodson concluded, "these migrants are not lazy, shiftless and desperate as some predicted that they would be." Likewise, despite the eruption of a violent race riot, the Chicago Commission on Race Relations concluded that black labor had "made a satisfactory record." For her part, Louise Kennedy placed the black migration within a broader national and global context: "Their migration is linked with the trend from the open country, which has been characteristic of all peoples in recent decades."[35]

Nonetheless, even as the wartime and postwar analysts of black migration transcended the negative perspective of their prewar counterparts, the pathological interpretation retained a powerful grip on the new studies. In the pioneering work of sociologist E. Franklin Frazier, the social disorganization framework gained its most prominent postwar expression. According to Frazier, the Great Migration resulted in the uprooting of southern black rural folk from a moral (even if paternalistic and racist) order, which ensured the stability of black families as viable mechanisms in the progress of the race. Massive black migration to cities like Chicago disrupted the old mores, and brought in its wake a host of problems; black migrants swelled the crime, divorce, and illegitimate birth rates on the one hand, while deflating African-American urban social, cultural, and institutional affiliations on the other. While Frazier presented the most extreme view of the city as a corrosive agent in the lives of black migrants, much of the contemporary scholarship reinforced his viewpoint.[36]

Indeed, as the research of E. Franklin Frazier suggests, although the studies established a basis for understanding the black migration as a social process, the treatment of these issues was limited, as in the prewar years, by insufficient attention to the role of blacks in their own movement, an attenuated historical perspective, and the larger race relations framework. While wartime and postwar scholars acknowledged the importance of black kin, friend, and communal networks (and in Kiser's case gave unusual attention to it), most emphasized the primacy of external forces. Such a framework, while useful, prevented a fuller explication of how the migration behavior of blacks reflected and influenced the impact of larger forces, including the impact of industrial capitalism. Black migration was indeed shaped by larger economic, social, and political changes in national and international capitalism, but black migrants were also active agents in their own movement into the industrial city. Thus, they were not merely reflectors of larger forces, as most of the contemporary scholarship suggested, but were shapers of such forces as well.

In helping us to understand the Great Migration as a dynamic historical process, the wartime and postwar studies were also hampered by their sociological approach. As suggested above, although scholars of the period connected contemporary and past patterns of black population movement, they were mainly concerned with changes in the volume, directions, and sources of black migration under the impact of World War I and its aftermath. They were not concerned with black migration as a historical phenomenon, with deep roots in southern black culture, family, and community life, nor were they interested in how this important process changed and took on new forms and meaning under the impact of World War I and the 1920s.

Finally, as in the prewar years, the treatment of black population movement during the era of the Great Migration was limited by the race relations framework. Efforts to illuminate and reform hostile patterns of black-white contact figured prominently in these studies. However, in its *Negro Migration in 1916–17*, the

Department of Labor subordinated the issue of race relations to the imperatives of national unity. The primary question was not one of how to resolve problems of black-white interactions as a means of creating a more just society, but rather one of how to resolve problems of race relations in the interest of national security. In his letter authorizing research on black migration during World War I, Secretary of Labor W. B. Wilson emphasized the national security issue.[37]

If the imperatives of national defense helped to subordinate the race relations issue, in the aftermath of World War I, race relations in the study of black migration reemerged in full force. Following the Chicago Race Riot of 1919, which resulted in the loss of thirty-eight lives, thousands of dollars worth of property damage, and over five hundred injuries, the Governor of Illinois appointed the Chicago Commission on Race Relations. The Governor charged the commission to study the underlying causes of the racial violence and to suggest remedies to prevent a recurrence. Although the *Negro in Chicago* (the commission's report, authored by Charles S. Johnson) reinforced a variety of themes in research on black migration, it also analyzed black migration as a factor in the rise of racial violence. The studies of Carter G. Woodson, Emmett Scott, Louise V. Kennedy, and Clyde V. Kiser also emphasized the role of black migration in larger efforts to improve black-white contacts.[38]

As in the cases of Du Bois, Daniels, and Wright before them, the wartime and postwar writers showed remarkable sensitivity to the impact of black migration on the nature of race contact in the industrial city. Unlike the prewar analysts, however, they treated the black migrant as a valuable asset in the interest of national security and continued economic development. Nonetheless, by framing their research around the imperatives of interracial relations, they failed to explore in sufficient depth the intraracial dimensions of the black migration experience. Such new dimensions in our understanding of the black migration would have to await a later period. Unfortunately, that later period would not be the Depression and World War II.

Black Migration Studies:
Mid-1930s to 1950s

Framed by the race relations imperative, the war and postwar studies of black migration would influence the shape of black migration research through the 1950s. However, during the Great Depression when the net migration of blacks from the South dropped by more than 50 percent, black migration studies took a different turn. Unlike the earlier race contact writers, a new generation of scholars turned increasingly toward the social anthropological caste-class approach to black urban life.[39] They curtailed their interest in black migration as a phenomenon, and thus added little to our understanding of black migration as a social process. Research on southern blacks especially neglected the migration theme. Between 1937 and 1941, for example, in a series of impressive studies on black life in southern towns, social anthropologists like John Dollard, Hortense Powdermaker, Allison Davis, Burleigh Gardner, and Mary Gardner paid little attention to the dynamics of black population movements.[40]

Studies of black life in the North also utilized social and anthropological insights. Unlike studies of southern towns, however, they paid substantial attention to the migration theme. In their study of blacks in Chicago during the 1930s and early 1940s, for example, St. Clair Drake and Horace R. Cayton built upon Charles Johnson's *The Negro in Chicago*. They illuminated the push of poor conditions in southern agriculture, the lure of higher wages in Chicago industries, the role of the northern black community (especially as reported in the *Chicago Defender*), and the role of the black family and friend networks. Like *The Negro in Chicago*, however, Drake's and Cayton's *Black Metropolis* gave insufficient attention to the migration process as it developed and changed over time. While they noted the dramatic changes during World War I and the 1920s, they ignored the continuing influx of blacks into Chicago during the Great Depression.[41]

In his comprehensive study of blacks in America during the late 1930s and early 1940s, Swedish economist Gunnar Myrdal and his associates gave significant attention to how and why black migration changed over time. *An American Dilemma: The Negro Problem and Modern Democracy* (1944) helped to crystallize an explanation for why black migration took off after 1915, continued through the 1920s, and persisted, despite high levels of unemployment, during the Depression. Because mass migration "did not get a start and become a pattern" before World War I, Myrdal suggested that black "migration potentialities" failed to gain full expression. However, a variety of factors coincided and "created a shock effect after 1915." Once set in motion, black migration continued, although its volume and particular causal factors would change over time. Thus, despite high unemployment, nearly 300,000 blacks moved out of the South during the 1930s, partly because new public assistance programs helped to mitigate the impact of declining employment in the private sector.[42]

Much like *Black Metropolis*, however, *An American Dilemma* (1944) only synthesized existing knowledge, even though in more comprehensive terms than Drake and Cayton. Moreover, while the study offered a model of interdisciplinary social science research—economics, sociology, political science, anthropology, and history—the latter was the weakest link in the chain. Myrdal used history to illuminate "present situations and trends." He also drew a sharp line between what he called the historian's interest in the "uniquely historical datum" and the social scientist's interest in "broad and general relations and main trends."[43]

Yet not all studies on the subject during the period were equally ahistorical. Nor were all studies of the period equally deficient in thinking about the black migration in new ways. In his study *The Negro Family in the United States* (1939), sociologist

E. Franklin Frazier illuminated important social and cultural dimensions of the black migration. Although briefly, he utilized the blues songs of the early twentieth century, the letters of World War I migrants, and the depression era study *Twenty Thousand Homeless Men* (1936).[44] Frazier sketched a revealing portrait of black migrants from their own perspective. In a chapter titled, "Flight from Feudal America," he emphasized the rise of the black industrial proletariat as the "most significant element in the new social structure" of black life. This development, he believed, had affected "the whole outlook on life and the values" of the black masses. "Such phrases as 'class struggle' and 'working-class solidarity,' once foreign to the ears of black workers, are the terms in which some Negroes are beginning to voice their discontent with their present status."[45]

His valuable insights notwithstanding, Frazier emphasized its negative impact, at least in the short-run. Like other race relations analysts, Frazier failed to appreciate the positive role of black family and communal networks in the migration and resettlement of blacks in cities. Building upon his earlier study of the black family in Chicago, he believed that black migrants had left their cultural moorings behind in the small towns and rural districts of the South.[46]

Despite the resurgence of black migration during World War II, the new migration failed to capture the attention of scholars as had the Great Migration of World War I. In the post–World War II years, some scholars, like Hylan Lewis in *Blackways of Kent* (1955), continued to pursue the caste and class mode of research on Afro-Americans, paying little attention to the migration theme. At the same time, the cold war undoubtedly deflected scholarly attention away from broad systemic issues, like massive black migration and its attendant impact on social relations in American society. However, by failing to analyze such important demographic and economic issues, scholars of the caste-class school of race relations helped to push black migration to the margins of scholarly concerns.[47]

Published in 1959, *The Newcomers: Negroes and Puerto Ricans in a Changing Metropolis* both reflected and encouraged the renewal of scholarly interest in black migration. In this slim volume, immigration historian Oscar Handlin briefly analyzed black migration to the New York metropolitan region from the turn of the twentieth century through World War II. *The Newcomers* added little to our overall understanding of black migration, however, for Handlin treated black migrants much as Du Bois did at the turn of the century—in pathological terms. Yet, he offered the provocative conclusion that the recent migrants "followed the general outline of the experience of earlier [white] immigrants."[48] Racial and ethnic barriers, he believed, were only temporary impediments to the full integration of the new groups into the American social order. While Handlin's study offered a useful target for the ghetto formation studies of the 1960s and 1970s, it came too late and was, at any rate, insufficient to pull black migration studies out of the doldrums during the 1950s.

The Ghetto School and Black Migration Studies:
The 1960s and 1970s

During the 1960s and 1970s, the ghetto model gained a commanding sway over historical research on blacks in cities. Seeking to document the rise of nearly all-black ghettos in American cities, historians pinpointed black migration as a critical factor. The sociological studies of the early twentieth century, they argued, overstated the significance of the Great Migration of World War I. Thus historians like Gilbert Osofsky, Allan Spear, David Katzman, and Kenneth Kusmer, all turned the clock back to the prewar years. They treated the prewar migration as the "advance guard of the Great Migration," which laid the foundations for the rapid spread of racially segregated communities in the urban North.[49]

As the ghetto studies counteracted the chronological bias of the race relations tradition, they also attacked the Handlin thesis: that blacks were the most recent of the immigrant groups. Partly for this reason, as well as the pull of the expanding Civil Rights Movement, the ghetto studies adopted a social disorganization perspective. Thus, like the race relations school, the ghetto historians failed to probe the content of southern black life, showing how the dynamics of black population movement were deeply rooted in prior patterns of rural to urban movement. In much of the ghetto literature, then, black migrants were frequently portrayed as passive objects of external forces beyond their control. By focusing primarily on patterns of urban housing and institutional segregation in northern cities, the ghetto scholars not only neglected black migration as a social process with deep southern roots, they also paid insufficient attention to the interconnection between black migration and working-class formation.[50]

Fortunately, even as the ghetto model gained increasing dominance, certain modifications in perspective gradually took shape. Historians William M. Tuttle, Elizabeth Pleck, Florette Henri, and James Borchert, all produced studies that challenged aspects of the ghetto thesis. As such, they offered a somewhat different slant on the lives of black migrants. As early as 1970, Tuttle analyzed the Chicago Riot of 1919, emphasizing the perspective of working-class participants. Five years later, in her synthesis on the subject, Florette Henri concluded that black migration represents "a tremendous feat of initiative, planning, courage, and perseverance . . . not by one or two 'exceptional individuals' but by at least five hundred thousand perfectly average southern Negroes." Focusing on poverty in late nineteenth century Boston and alley life in Washington D.C., respectively, Elizabeth Pleck and James Borchert also heightened interest in black urban life from the bottom up.[51]

Taken together, Borchert, Pleck, Henri, and Tuttle heightened the connection between black migration, working-class life, and the role of blacks in shaping their own movement. Nonetheless, by emphasizing racial violence, urban poverty, alley life, and the militant race consciousness that resulted therefrom, these scholars also reinforced the relationship between black migration and ghetto formation. In other words, the connection between black migration and working-class formation was subordinated to a different agenda. Such limitations sparked vigorous new departures in research on black urban life during the late 1970s and early 1980s. The new studies would bring forth fresh opportunities to examine the black migration in historical perspective.

The Race/Class or Proletarian Approach:
Since 1980

The most explicit challenge to the ghetto synthesis slowly emerged in a series of Ph.D. dissertations completed between 1978 and the early 1980s. Richard Walter Thomas, "From Peasant to Proletarian: The Formation and Organization of the Black Industrial Working Class in Detroit, 1915–1945" (1976); Peter Gottlieb, "Making Their Own Way: Southern Blacks' Migration to Pittsburgh, 1916–30" (1977); Dennis C. Dickerson, "Black Steelworkers in Western Pennsylvania, 1915–1950" (1978); Joe William Trotter, Jr. "The Making of an Industrial Proletariat: Black Milwaukee, 1915–1945" (1980); James R. Grossman, "A Dream Deferred: Black Migration to Chicago, 1916–1921" (1982); and Earl Lewis, "At Work and At Home: Blacks in Norfolk, Virginia, 1910–1945" (1984): these all wrestled quite explicitly with the connection between black migration and proletarianization, i.e., the rise of the black urban working class.[52]

In her groundbreaking study, *Exodusters: Black Migration to Kansas after Reconstruction* (1976), social historian Nell Irvin Painter had helped to pave the way for the new conceptualization of black population movement. She emphasized its class as well as its racial dimensions. According to Painter, the "Exodusters" who left the lower Mississippi Valley for the freedom of Kansas "were ordinary, uneducated former slaves, who one of them called 'a class of hard laboring people.' " Thus, Painter concluded that the class of these early post-Reconstruction black migrants was "practically as important as their race (although not in their eyes or in the eyes of their oppressors)."[53]

From the mid-1980s, studies employing some variant of the race/class or proletarian approach rapidly reached print: Trotter (1985); Dickerson (1986); Gottlieb (1987); Grossman (1989); Lewis (1990), and Trotter (1990).[54] Unfortunately, while Thomas, Dickerson, and Trotter (in *Black Milwaukee*) moved black workers to the center of their analyses, they were primarily interested in events within the city. Much like the ghettoization school, they paid insufficient attention to black migration as a dynamic process, deeply rooted in southern black kin, friend, and communal networks. As we will see in the following section, this was not true of

Gottlieb, Grossman, Moore, Lewis, and Trotter in his recent book on black coal miners. Neither is it true of recent studies by Elizabeth R. Bethel and Allen B. Ballard, whose work anticipates and reinforces the essays that follow in this volume.[55]

Migration Studies:
Toward a New Subfield in Black Urban History

The essays in this book address the connection between migration, proletarianization, and southern black culture at a pivotal movement in black history. They aim to facilitate our understanding of black migration as a historical process. As such, they also suggest the slow emergence of black migration studies as a subfield within black urban history. Based on book length projects, the various essays illuminate the complex interrelationship between changes in southern black rural life and subsequent patterns of community change in southern, northern, and western cities, as well as the southern Appalachian coal fields.

James Grossman begins his investigation of black migration to Chicago in the South. Unlike most studies of the black migration, Grossman documents the Great Migration as a grass roots social movement, replete with its own indigenous leadership and channels of information for decision making. "This 'dynamic of migration,' " he argues, "not only affected how migrants reacted to what they found; it also informs our understanding of those reactions." In this volume, Grossman examines the impact of southern black culture on the labor market experiences of Afro-Americans.[56]

Peter Gottlieb analyzes the southern blacks' migration to Pittsburgh as "a process of self-transformation." Through "seasonal migration and temporary industrial work within the South," he demonstrates that Afro-Americans "prepared themselves for geographic movements further afield." Along with their participation in the emerging industries of the New South, Gottlieb reconstructs the premigration status of blacks in southern agriculture, as owners, as tenants, and as farm laborers.[57] In this volume, however, he deepens our understanding of black migration to Pittsburgh by extending his analysis backward into the prewar era and forward into the Depression, World War II, and beyond.

Other essays in this book not only address conceptual limitations in research on the black migration, but fill important regional and topical gaps in our understanding of the process. Earl Lewis investigates black migration, work, and community in the upper urban South—Norfolk, Virginia between 1910 and 1945. With few exceptions, he notes, black life in Norfolk and other southern cities has been essentially ignored. Black migration to southern cities like Norfolk took a different turn than the literature suggests; the southern city represented the end of the migration line for many Afro-Americans, who found jobs, put down roots, and built families there. Black kin and friendship networks sustained linkages between Norfolk blacks and the nearby countryside, other southern cities, and the urban north.[58]

Focusing on black coal miners in southern West Virginia, Trotter reinforces the study of black migration in the southern context. Unlike the study of Norfolk blacks, however, his essay illuminates a dimension of black migration that was neither northern nor southern urban, but rather rural to industrial. Drawing upon the insights of recent scholars like Grossman, Gottlieb, and Lewis, as well as his earlier study of blacks in Milwaukee, he links the rise of the black coal mining working class to "the social imperatives of black life in the rural South, as well as the dynamics of industrial capitalism." Using their intricate network of family and friends, southern black coal miners helped to organize their own movement to the region, facilitated their own transition to the industrial labor force, and helped to transform the larger contours of Afro-American community life.[59]

In her illuminating essay on black migration to Richmond, California, during the interwar years, Shirley Ann Moore offers a close look at black population movement to a west coast city. Her essay not only highlights the small volume of black migration to the urban West before the 1940s, but reveals an important variant on the black migration theme. For black Richmondites, entry into the urban industrial work force proved to be a process more prolonged than elsewhere: it began slowly before the 1930s and accelerated during World War II, as blacks moved into the shipyards in growing numbers. Like other scholars in this volume, Moore also emphasizes the role of southern black kin and friendship networks in stimulating and organizing the black migration to Richmond.[60]

Not only are the race/class analysts bringing a different theoretical perspective to the study of black migration, they are also using a broader range of sources and different methodologies. Based upon the imaginative use of oral interviews, company records, newspapers, photo analyses, manuscript collections, and a variety of statistical accounts, recent scholars are carefully documenting the themes of black migration and working class formation. Based upon the personnel files of the A. M. Byers Company, a Pittsburgh metal manufacturer, Gottlieb offers a unique analysis of black labor turnover in one company. In his study of black migration to Chicago, Grossman provides a detailed analysis of the Chicago *Defender's* "shipping list," drawn from the records of the Military Intelligence Division of the U.S. Department of War. Based upon the extensive reports of the Universal Negro Improvement Association's *Negro World* and the black weekly *Norfolk Journal and Guide*, Earl Lewis provides fascinating profiles of Garveyites and statistical analyses of black visitation patterns.[61]

For her part, through the lens of gender, Darlene Clark Hine critiques and synthesizes the existing literature. She urges us to document the gender-specific causes of black migration as well as the class and racial ones. She notes, for example, that the movement of black men and women was often propelled by different factors. Based upon the interplay of class, race, and gender, Clark Hine also challenges us to reinterpret not just the African-American migration experience, but the larger American experience with migration.[62]

Black migration was indeed a complex phenomenon. Its comprehension requires an appreciation of the established scholarship as well as a variety of new sources and approaches. In many ways, the essays in this volume represent the culmination of a century of black urban-migration research, unfolding within the successive, but overlapping, theoretical frameworks of race relations, ghetto formation, and proletarianization. Emphasizing the dynamic role of southern black migrants in their own movement, resettlement, and subsequent experiences in the city, these studies suggest that we need to rethink a number of issues in Afro-American and American urban history. Before turning to a discussion of these issues, as we will do in the conclusion, let us now permit the essays to speak for themselves.

NOTES

1. W. E. B. Du Bois, *The Philadelphia Negro: A Social Study* (1899; reprint, New York: Schocken Books, 1967); John Daniels, *In Freedom's Birthplace: A Study of the Boston Negro* (1914; reprint, New York: Arno Press, 1969); U.S. Department of Labor, *Negro Migration in 1916–17* (1919; reprint, New York: Negro Universities Press, 1969); Carter G. Woodson, *A Century of Negro Migration* (New York: Russell and Russell, 1918); Emmett J. Scott, *Negro Migration during the War* (1920; reprint, New York: Arno Press, 1969) based in large part on research conducted by Charles S. Johnson; Thomas J. Woofter, *Negro Migration: Changes in Rural Organization and Population of the Cotton Belt* (New York: W. D. Gray, 1920); Chicago Commission on Race Relations (written by Charles S. Johnson), *The Negro in Chicago: A Study of Race Relations and a Race Riot* (1922; reprint, New York: Arno Press, 1968); Louise V. Kennedy, *The Negro Peasant Turns Cityward: Effects of Recent Migrations to Northern Cities* (New York: Columbia University Press, 1930); Edward E. Lewis, *The Mobility of the Negro* (1931; reprint, New York: AMS Press, 1968); and Clyde V. Kiser, *Sea Island to City: A Study of St. Helena Islanders in Harlem and Other Urban Centers* (1932; reprint, New York: AMS Press, 1967). The pioneering study of sociologist E. Franklin Frazier, it should be noted, drew upon the foregoing studies of black migration and reinforced the race relations paradigm; cf. E. Franklin Frazier, *The Negro Family in Chicago* (Chicago: University of Chicago Press, 1932).

2. Gilbert Osofsky, *Harlem: The Making of a Ghetto, 1890–1930*, 2d ed. (New York: Harper Torchbooks, 1971); Allan H. Spear, *Black Chicago: The Making of a Negro Ghetto, 1890–1920* (Chicago: University of Chicago Press, 1967); and Kenneth L. Kusmer, *A Ghetto Takes Shape: Black Cleveland, 1870–1930* (Urbana: University of Illinois Press, 1976); cf. David M. Katzman, *Before the Ghetto: Black Detroit in the Nineteenth Century* (Urbana: University of Illinois Press, 1972).

3. Peter Gottlieb, *Making Their Own Way: Southern Blacks' Migration to Pittsburgh, 1916–30* (Urbana: University of Illinois Press, 1987); Dennis C. Dickerson, *Out of the Crucible: Black Steelworkers in Western Pennsylvania, 1875–1980* (New York: State University of New York Press, 1986); Joe William Trotter, Jr., *Black Milwaukee: The Making of an Industrial Proletariat, 1915–45* (Urbana: University of Illinois Press, 1985); James R. Grossman, *Land of Hope: Chicago, Black Southerners, and the Great Migration* (Chicago,

University of Chicago Press, 1989); Earl Lewis, *In Their Own Interests: Race, Class, and Power in Twentieth Century Norfolk* (Berkeley: University of California Press, 1991); Richard W. Thomas, "From Peasant to Proletarian: The Formation and Organization of the Black Industrial Working Class in Detroit, 1915–1945" (Ph.D. diss., University of Michigan, 1976); and Shirley Ann Moore, "Blacks in Richmond, California, 1930–1945" (Ph.D. diss., University of California-Berkeley, 1989). For my effort to explore the broader implications of proletarianization in a different context, see Joe William Trotter Jr., *Coal Class, and Color: Blacks in Southern West Virginia, 1915–32* (Urbana: University of Illinois Press, 1990). Cf. Carole Marks, *Farewell—We're Good and Gone: The Great Black Migration* (Bloomington: Indiana University Press, 1989) and Nell Irvin Painter, *Exodusters: Black Migration to Kansas after Reconstruction* (1976; reprint, Lawrence: University of Kansas Press, 1986). Although Painter focused on rural to rural black migration following the end of Reconstruction, she pioneered in establishing a working class approach to black population movement.

4. Du Bois, *Philadelphia Negro*, p.73.

5. Ibid., p. 76.

6. W. E. B. Du Bois, "The Negroes of Farmville Virginia: A Social Study," *Bulletin of the U.S. Department of Labor* 3 (Jan. 1898).

7. Du Bois, *Philadelphia Negro*, p. 3.

8. Du Bois, *Philadelphia Negro*, pp. 58–65, 73, 76–78.

9. Ibid., pp. 80, 97–98.

10. Daniels, *In Freedom's Birthplace*, p. ix.

11. Ibid., pp. 142, 314.

12. Ibid., pp. 136–37, 325.

13. For a useful bibliography of these articles, see Osofsky, *Harlem*, pp. 205–14.

14. R. R. Wright, "Migration of Negroes to the North," *Annals of the American Academy of Political and Social Science* 27 (Jan.–Feb. 1906): 559–78.

15. Ibid., p. 574.

16. Ibid., p. 570.

17. George Edmund Haynes, "Conditions among Negroes in the Cities," *Annals of the American Academy of Political and Social Science* 49 (Sept. 1913): 105.

18. U.S. Department of Labor, *Negro Migration in 1916–17*, pp. 5–7. U.S. Secretary of Labor W. B. Wilson appointed James H. Dillard of Charlottesville, Virginia, "to organize and supervise" the inquiry. A graduate of Washington and Lee University, Dillard was also the director of the Jeanes and Slater Funds for black education in the South. Upon accepting the assignment, Dillard, in turn, engaged the assistance of others scholars to conduct the actual field work and write the preliminary reports. The researchers included R. H. Leavell, a graduate of the University of Mississippi; Thomas J. Woofter, a graduate of Georgia State University; T. H. Snavely, a graduate of Emery and Henry College and the University of Virginia; Francis D. Tyson of the University of Pittsburgh; W. T. B. Williams, a graduate of Hampton Institute and of Harvard University, a field agent of the Jeanes and Slater Funds, and the only black investigator on the team. Leavell studied conditions in Mississippi and Louisiana; Woofter, Georgia and South Carolina; Snavely, Alabama and North Carolina; Tyson, Northern conditions; and Williams served as a specialist on black affairs, without any particular region.

19. See Note 1.

20. *Negro Migration in 1916–17*, pp. 115–17; Kennedy, *The Negro Peasant Turns Cityward*, p. 23; Chicago Commission on Race Relations, *The Negro in Chicago*, pp. 79–80; Scott, *Negro Migration*, pp. 3–112; Kiser, *Sea Island to City*, pp. 85–113.

21. Kennedy, *The Negro Peasant Turns Cityward*, p. 23.

22. Kennedy, *Negro Peasant*, pp. 23–40; *Negro Migration in 1916–17*, pp. 17–19, 51–58, 75–86, 115–17; Scott, *Negro Migration*, pp. 3–112; *Negro in Chicago*, pp. 79–89; Woodson, *A Century of Negro Migration*, pp. 160, 163; Kiser, *Sea Island to City*, pp. 85–113. Though contemporary studies did not emphasize the variable impact of black migration

on different northern cities, in cities like Chicago, Cleveland, Detroit, and Milwaukee, black men had dominated the migratory stream of the prewar years; thus, the war and postwar years heightened a process in these cities that was already well underway.

23. In *Negro Migration in 1916–17*, pp. 77–85.

24. *Negro Migration in 1916–17*, pp. 16–17, 52–58, 77–86; Scott, *Negro Migration*, pp. 68, 38–48, 69; *The Negro in Chicago*, p.87; Scott, *Negro Migration*, pp. 106, 134.

25. Scott, *Negro Migration*, pp. 106, 134.

26. Kiser, *Sea Island to City*, pp. 173, 214.

27. Lewis, *Mobility of the Negro*, pp. 12–20.

28. Scott, *Negro Migration*, p. 13; Lewis, *Mobility of the Negro*, pp. 87–114; *Negro in Chicago*, pp. 80–89; Kennedy, *Negro Peasant*, pp. 30–41.

29. *Negro Migration in 1916–17*, pp. 11–12. Cf. Charles S. Johnson, "How Much Is Migration a Flight from Persecution?" *Opportunity* 1, no. 9 (Sept. 1923): 273–75.

30. Scott, *Negro Migration*, pp. 26–27, 39. See also Kennedy, *Negro Peasant*, pp. 54–55 and *Negro Migration in 1916–17*, pp. 94–95.

31. Scott, *Negro Migration*, pp. 26–27; Kennedy, *Negro Peasant*, pp. 53–54; *Negro Migration in 1916–17*, pp. 12, 100–101.

32. Kiser, *Sea Island to City*, pp. 7–13, 113, 210.

33. T. J. Woofter, *Black Yeomanry: Life on St. Helena Island* (1930; reprint, New York; Octagon Books, 1978).

34. Ibid., pp. 7–13, 18, 113, 135, 210; Kiser, *Sea Island to City*, pp. 7–13, 85–113.

35. *Negro Migration in 1916–17*, pp. 15, 112; Woodson, *Century of Negro Migration*, p. 188; *The Negro in Chicago*, p. 400; Kennedy, *Negro Peasant*, p. 10; Kiser, *Sea Island to City*, p. 27.

36. See Frazier, *The Negro Family in Chicago*; Kennedy, *Negro Peasant*, p. 182; *Negro Migration in 1916–17*, pp. 138–45.

37. *Negro Migration in 1916–17*, pp. 5–13.

38. Ibid., p. 9–10; Woodson, *Century of Negro Migration*, pp. 160–63; Scott, *Negro Migration*, introduction and foreword, p. iii; *Negro in Chicago*, p. xxiii; Kennedy, *Negro Peasant*, p. 238; Kiser, *Sea Island to City*, p. 55.

39. W. Lloyd Warner, "Introduction: Deep South—A Social Anthropological Study of Caste and Class," in Allison Davis, Burleigh B. Gardner, and Mary R. Gardner, *Deep South: A Social Anthropological Study of Caste and Class* (Chicago: University of Chicago Press, 1941), pp. x, 3–14.

40. John Dollard, *Caste and Class in a Southern Town* (1937; reprint, Garden City, NY: Doubleday Anchor Books, 1957); Hortense Powdermaker, *After Freedom: A Cultural Study of the Deep South* (New York: Viking Press, 1939); Davis, Gardner, and Gardner, *Deep South*.

41. St. Clair Drake and Horace R. Cayton, *Black Metropolis: A Study of Negro Life in a Northern City* (1945; reprint, New York: Harcourt Brace, and World, 1962), vol. 1, pp. xxiii–xl, 58.

42. Gunnar Myrdal, *An American Dilemma: The Negro Problem and Modern Democracy* (1944; reprint, New York: Pantheon Books, 1962), pp. xxv, xlix, lxxiii, lxxix, 193–97.

43. Ibid., lxxix.

44. Edwin H. Sutherland and Harvey J. Locke, *Twenty Thousand Homeless Men* (Philadelphia: J. B. Lippincott, 1936).

45. E. Franklin Frazier, *The Negro Family in the United States* (1939; reprint, Chicago: University of Chicago Press, 1969), pp. 230–31, 366; cf. Robert A. Warner, *New Haven Negroes: A Social History* (1940; reprint, New York: Arno Press, 1969), p. 159. Warner described the changing patterns of black migration from the Civil War through 1930; however, he analyzed few of the underlying causes and emphasized the negative impact of southern life on black migrants. Highly descriptive rather than analytical, Warner's study did little to stimulate historical research on the black migration.

46. Frazier, *The Negro Family in the United States*, pp. 209–44.

47. Hylan Lewis, *Blackways of Kent* (Chapel Hill: University of North Carolina Press, 1955); Abram Kardiner and Lionel Ovesey, *The Mark of Oppression: Explorations in the Personality of the American Negro* (1951; reprint, Cleveland and New York: Meridian Books, World Publishing Company, 1967), p. xvi; Gordon W. Allport, *The Nature of Prejudice* (1954; reprint, Garden City, NY: Doubleday Anchor Books, 1958), p. xii.

48. Oscar Handlin, *The Newcomers: Negroes and Puerto Ricans in a Changing Metropolis* (1959; reprint, Garden City, NY: Doubleday Anchor Books, 1962), pp. 120–21.

49. For a critique of this literature, see Trotter, ''Afro-American Urban History: a Critique of the Literature,'' in his *Black Milwaukee*, pp. 264–91. Also see note 2.

50. As I suggested in my earlier critique of this literature, however, the ghetto studies were by no means uniform. Compared to Spear and Osofsky, for example, Kusmer developed an extensive comparative framework and gave greater attention to the internal dynamics of the black community. See Trotter, ''Afro-American Urban History,'' pp. 271–75.

51. William A. Tuttle, *Race Riot: Chicago in the Red Summer of 1919* (1970; reprint, New York: Atheneum, 1984), pp. v-xi; Florette Henri, *Black Migration: Movement North, 1900–1920* (Garden City, NY: Anchor Press, 1975), pp. vii–xi, 80; Elizabeth H. Pleck, *Black Migration and Poverty: Boston, 1865–1900* (New York: Academic Press, 1979), pp. 66, 98, 166, 204; James Borchert, *Alley Life in Washington: Family, Community, Religion, and Folklife in the City, 1850–1970* (Urbana: University of Illinois Press, 1980), pp. ix–xiv, 218–41. Cf. Daniel M. Johnson and Rex R. Campbell, *Black Migration in America: A Social and Demographic History* (Durham: Duke University Press, 1981); Robert B. Grant, *The Black Man Comes to the City* (Chicago: Nelson-Hall, 1972); and Thomas C. Cox, *Blacks in Topeka, Kansas, 1865–1915: A Social History* (Baton Rouge: Louisiana State University Press, 1982). Douglas H. Daniels, *Pioneer Urbanites: A Social and Cultural History of Black San Francisco* (Philadelphia: Temple University Press, 1980), p. xvii; Daniels advances the notion of a ''travelcraft,'' closely related to the notion of kin and friendship networks, and describes the ''outlook and complex of skills that facilitated both long-distance travel and residency in the Bay Area'' (p. 59).

52. Richard Walter Thomas, ''From Peasant to Proletarian: The Formation and Organization of the Black Industrial Working Class in Detroit, 1915–1945'' (Ph.D. diss., University of Michigan, 1976); Peter Gottlieb, ''Making Their Own Way: Southern Blacks' Migration to Pittsburgh, 1916–30'' (Ph.D. diss., University of Pittsburgh, 1977); Dennis C. Dickerson, ''Black Steelworkers in Western Pennsylvania, 1915–1945'' (Ph.D. diss., Washington University, 1978); Joe William Trotter, Jr., ''The Making of an Industrial Proletariat: Black Milwaukee, 1915–1945'' (Ph.D. diss., University of Minnesota, 1980); James R. Grossman, ''A Dream Deferred: Black Migration to Chicago, 1916–1921'' (Ph.D. diss., University of California-Berkeley, 1982); and Earl Lewis, ''At Work and at Home: Blacks in Norfolk, Virginia, 1910–1945'' (Ph.D. diss., University of Minnesota, 1984).

53. Painter, *Exodusters*, p. vii.

54. To be sure, the recent studies are not Marxian in the usual sense. They do not document the decline of an independent black artisan class on the one hand, or the fall of a black yeomanry on the other. Indeed, by focusing on blacks in the early twentieth century, they could not pursue such an agenda: African-Americans were neither substantial landowners in rural America, nor substantial craftsmen in urban America. Even so, the transformation of black landless sharecroppers into an urban working class was part of the larger proletarianization of labor under the onslaught of industrial capitalism. Since the foregoing studies deal pointedly with that process, they may be usefully analyzed as research on a black proletariat. See note 3, and Elizabeth R. Bethel, *Promiseland: A Century of Life in a Negro Community* (Philadelphia: Temple University Press, 1981); Allen R. Ballard, *One More Day's Journey: The Making of Black Philadelphia* (Philadelphia: Institute for the Study of Human Issues, 1984); and Marks, *Farewell—We're Good and Gone*.

55. Bethel, *Promiseland*; Ballard, *One More Day's Journey*.

56. Grossman, *Land of Hope*, p. 6.

57. Gottlieb, *Making Their Own Way*, p. 7.

58. Lewis, *In Their Own Interests*.

59. Trotter, *Coal, Class, and Color*.

60. Moore, "Blacks in Richmond, California, 1910–1945."

61. Gottlieb, *Making Their Own Way*, pp. 232–34; Grossman, *Land of Hope*, pp. 76–77; Lewis, *In Their Own Interests*, chapters 4 and 5; Trotter, *Coal, Class, and Color*, chapters 3 and 4.

62. See below, Darlene Clark Hine, "Black Migration to the Urban Midwest: The Gender Dimension, 1915–1945."

Expectations, Economic Opportunities, and Life in the Industrial Age
Black Migration to Norfolk, Virginia, 1910–1945

Earl Lewis

There they sat, two women, one black and the other white, one a longtime resident of black Norfolk and the other a WPA interviewer. Over the course of the interview, Lucille Johnson would recall the many factors that brought her to Norfolk; detail some of the intimate aspects of her adult life, including her marriage; recount the painful story of spousal desertion; and describe the difficulties she had since experienced trying to raise five children under age thirteen. In the process of recording Lucille's story, Edith Skinner illustrated the degree to which Lucille Johnson's life and the lives of all Afro-Americans intersected with the region's political economy.[1] This intersection between expectations and economic opportunities framed the history of twentieth-century black migration.

The story of black migration has intrigued both scholars and non-academic writers for some time. Numerous studies have detailed the migration of Afro-Americans to northern and midwestern cities, especially during the period of the first Great Migration—the decade of the First World War.[2] Unfortunately, none considered those Afro-Americans who migrated to southern cities. Thus South to North migration has been confused with rural to urban migration. Since more blacks migrated to southern cities between 1900 and 1920 than to northern cities—and would continue to migrate to those cities through World War II—this oversight is quite curious. Moreover, recent scholarship has shown that many blacks who later settled in the urban North or Midwest spent some time in the urban South.[3] This chapter, therefore, seeks to help fill a significant lacuna by examining the migration of blacks to Norfolk, Virginia, between 1910 and 1945. It is concerned with the structure of black migration, the reasons for migrating, the job migrants acquired and the efforts they undertook to maintain contact with kith and kin elsewhere.

George W. Bennett stood at the threshold of adulthood when his father abandoned a comfortable position as a sawyer with an Edenton, North Carolina, lumbering company to take a new job in Norfolk, Virginia. It was wartime and the once sleepy seaport town was about to be transformed into "the primary Naval base of

TABLE 1

Increase in Black Population for Selected Cities, 1910–1930

| City | Population | | | Percent Increase | | Average Annual Increase |
	1910	1920	1930	1910–1920	1920–1930	1910–1930
Norfolk	25,039	43,392	43,942	73.3	1.3	3.77
Atlanta	51,902	62,796	90,075	21.0	43.4	3.68
Baltimore	84,749	108,322	142,106	27.8	31.2	3.38
Birmingham	52,305	70,230	99,077	34.3	41.1	4.47
Charleston	31,056	32,326	28,062	4.1	− 13.2	− .48
Houston	23,929	33,960	63,337	41.9	86.5	6.72
Jacksonville	29,293	41,520	48,196	41.7	16.1	3.23
Memphis	52,441	61,181	96,550	16.7	57.8	4.20
New Orleans	89,262	109,930	129,632	13.1	28.4	2.26
Richmond	46,733	54,041	52,988	15.6	− 1.9	.68
					Median	3.53

Source: U.S. Bureau of the Census, *Negroes in the United States, 1920–1932* (Washington, DC: Government Printing Office, 1935), p. 55.

the Atlantic Coast'' and needed laborers. Bennett, Sr., in migrating to Norfolk, took part in a national pattern of out-migration. Nationwide about 1.5 million Afro-Americans left the rural South during the war decades, more than half of whom went to southern cities.[4]

As Bennett, Sr. and others flocked into Norfolk to answer the initial demand for labor, the city's black population jumped. Between 1910 and 1920 it grew at an average rate of 7.3 percent per year. This rate fell during the next decade to .127 percent annually, when as Trotter noted, many northern cities experienced a second surge.[5] With natural increase, the gain in percentage should have been larger; thus, the decade 1920–1930 was characterized by considerable out-migration. Consequently, the period 1910–1930, despite a real increase of nearly 20,000, had an average annual increase of 3.8 percent (see table 1).

Nonetheless, when put in context, the increase in Norfolk's black population between 1910 and 1930 was quite significant. If we consider the region's twenty-five largest southern cities, the Norfolk growth rate (3.8 percent) ranked second. If we restrict our discussion to the region's ten largest cities, excluding the nation's capital, Norfolk had the most rapid war-associated population increase. Furthermore, Norfolk's growth rate exceeded the median for the ten cities (3.8 percent versus 3.5 percent), and just three cities—Houston, Memphis, and Birmingham—

had a larger annual average population increase than Norfolk.[6] The difference between Norfolk and the other cities stemmed from its inability to sustain the growth during the postwar decade.

Those who migrated to Norfolk followed migration streams along the eastern seaboard rather than the Mississippi River corridor. As a result most came from Norfolk's surrounding rural hinterland, other parts of Virginia, or North Carolina, which considerably enhanced the maintenance of contact with kith and kin. Many local migrants actually came from Norfolk County, an immense rural hinterland abutting the city's eastern edge and sprawling southward toward North Carolina. As blacks moved into the city between 1910 and 1930 the county lost population. Some of the decline is explained by Norfolk's annexation of portions of the county in 1911 and again in 1923; however, the movement of blacks to Norfolk, especially around World War I, also played a central role.[7]

If not from the immediate vicinity, newcomers typically came from other Virginia locations or from North Carolina. Through 1930, two-thirds of all blacks who settled in Norfolk claimed Virginia as their state of birth.[8] The data are not as detailed for non-Virginia immigrants. Yet earlier evidence indicates that North Carolina was the biggest supplier of nonresidents, as does a perusal of the 1910 manuscript census. Moreover, at the state level, more residents listed North Carolina as their state of birth than any other state, except Virginia.[9]

The reasons blacks migrated to Norfolk were complex and varied. Like Bennett, Sr. mentioned previously, some sought better economic opportunity; others resembled Clifton J., a Norfolk County native, who despised rural life—its pace and social milieu—and the future it promised. For others the interplay between life cycle stage and perceptions of opportunity prompted a relocation and influenced the final destination. After her father died, a youthful Lucille Johnson had few options other than to follow her stepmother. Too young to effectively care for herself, she was pushed out of Franklin, Virginia, by life circumstances. Her stepmother selected the Norfolk area because she had relatives nearby, and, presumably, a support system. Hence the pair were lured to the area by anticipated assistance and the perception of better opportunities.[10]

Assistance, expected and actual, often figured in migrants' decisions. Frequently support from family and friends initiated a process of chain migration, defined by MacDonald and MacDonald "as that movement in which prospective migrants learn of opportunities, are provided with transportation, and have initial accommodation and employment arranged by means of primary social relationships with previous migrants."[11] This process had several interlocking dimensions. As many have observed, in some cases, family and friends actually recruited kin and kith. These earlier migrants would write letters describing their wonderful new environment and encouraging others to move.[12] In other instances simple promises of assistance directed migrants. These indirect solicitations proved as important as direct overtures. Susan J., for example, left rural St. Brides, an area of black concentration in Norfolk County, only after Norfolk relatives assured her of various support. Lloyd D., in fact, remembered that Susan moved into their house for several months while she searched for work and made other living arrangements.[13]

Although many came to the city directly from the country, scores of others moved in a stepwise pattern. They simply moved from a rural place to a small town, where they stayed for a while before moving on to a larger city. This was how Maria Ruffin reached Norfolk. She moved from several small towns to Petersburg and from Petersburg to Norfolk. Oftentimes such movement signaled another dimension of the process of chain migration, since in each location the migrant typically utilized the resources of a network of family and friend contacts.[14]

If, however, we isolate one factor to explain black migration to Norfolk between 1910 and 1930, that factor would be expected economic opportunity. Obviously, labor agents, the ubiquitous threat of violence, and an open disgust with southern life fueled the movement.[15] At the same time, migration was an act of individual and collective empowerment. African-Americans constantly worked to improve their place in the region's political economy and to share the nation's bounty as full citizens. Improving their material conditions was central to this effort.

Blacks needed only look around them or to read the regionally circulated *Norfolk Journal and Guide* to learn of the expanded possibilities. In 1913, more than $3 million in marine foodstuffs left the Hampton Roads ports for national consumption. The amounts increased as the war approached as did the demand for dockworkers. By 1914, "Norfolk possessed an invested capital of $30 million in 362 manufacturing plants." In addition, the federal government spent about $14 million per year to maintain several military installations. With the war imminent, new businesses like E. I. Dupont, British-American Tobacco, Texas Oil, and Norfolk Shipbuilding and Drydock helped fill in the industrial landscape.[16] Hence, blacks saw in the war economy an opportunity to add jobs in well established areas and to make major inroads into previously excluded sectors. Occasionally they told whites of their desires. For example, when approached by a representative of Norman R. Hamilton, Collector of Customs, about using their pulpits to announce openings at the Norfolk Navy Yard, members of the Interdenominational Ministers Union responded,

> We have . . . requested your representative to bear to you our earnest wish that you use the great influence of your position to have the honorable Secretary of the Navy and others to do their utmost to breakdown every barrier . . . so that the opportunity not only for labor but for promotion and the loftiest patriotic effort may be opened to them [black workers] according to their several abilities.[17]

While expanded opportunities no doubt appealed to all, seemingly teenagers and young adults were in the best position to migrate. An examination of intercensal

TABLE 2

Black Net In-Migration By Cohort, 1910–1920

Age in 1920	Males	Females
10–14	591	747
15–19	1,124	1,220
20–24	2,096	2,048
25–34	2,580	2,282
35–44	1,396	974
45–	a	a

Source: U.S. Bureau of the Census, *Negro Population in the United States, 1790–1915* (Washington, DC: Government Printing Office, 1920), p. 205; *Fourteenth Census of the United States (1920)*, vol. 2, pp. 356–57.
[a]Differences in cohort breakdowns prevent further analysis.

net migration figures reveals that the bulk of black newcomers—males and females—were young adults between 20 and 34 years old. The youngest of this group would have been 10 in 1910 and the oldest 24. More likely, however, most were close to 17 by the time of the largest wave of in-migration between May 1917 and June 1918.[18] Regardless of their ages, most were young workers, workers with the least experience, and workers who, because of their age and experience, were most likely to be let go during periods of economic retrenchment (see table 2).

Unfortunately, many discovered that movement from the field did not always result in movement into the factory, or the enlarged opportunities they had hoped. In 1910 David Alston, who later achieved great prominence as the city's preeminent labor leader, left rural North Carolina. After two years in Richmond, where he met and married his wife of forty-seven years, Irene (Johnson) Alston, the pair moved to Norfolk. David quickly landed a job dismantling streetcar lines. His tenure was cut short by the offer of a meager 25¢ per hour from a Lamberts Point dredging company. Seeking to escape poverty wages, he changed jobs again in 1917. "I had to go to Baltimore for work then and joined the union [International Longshoremen's Association] there," he later recalled. For more than a year Alston commuted between the two Chesapeake Bay cities. Eventually he aligned his expectations with opportunities, but only after a year under fire as a member of the regional proletariat: "It was hard coming home every weekend and going back to Baltimore for work, but I was able to get a job on the Norfolk and Western coal piers in 1918 and stayed there 28 years."[19] Alston's later life catapulted him into the world of labor's aristocracy, but, in the beginning, he, like thousands of migrants, lived on the edge of the industrial order.

The labor force participation rates for 1920 and 1930 dramatize the extent to which work was available and the degree to which black men were underemployed.

Spread across the occupational spectrum, although over-represented as labors— unskilled, more so than semi-skilled or skilled—nearly nine-tenths of all working- age black males secured gainful employment in 1920. Both their clustering in unskilled laboring jobs and their labor force participation rate exceeded that of native-born white males. Blacks did have a lower participation rate, however, than foreign-born white males, but the difference stems from dissimilar age structures. Ninety-four percent of all foreign-born males were over age 20 as compared to 81 percent of black males. Consequently, more black households came to depend on the earnings of teenage sons, preponderantly errand boys and bootblacks.[20]

Economic recessions both at the beginning and the end of the next decade ad- versely affected the labor force participation rate of black males, although not the class structure of the black community. More than 85 percent of working-age black males labored as unskilled or semi-skilled workers in 1920. By 1930, however, the labor force participation rate had declined to 80.3 percent, reflecting a net loss of nearly 3,000 jobs. At the same time whites added more than 4,500 jobs, thereby negating the once noticeable racial differentials. As this decline in opportunity increased during the 1930s, some black males would leave the city.[21]

Moreover, because of the region's dual or segmented labor market, characterized by certain jobs that became the exclusive province of blacks and others of whites, most black males worked at non-industrial jobs and ones with black majorities. Most were low paying, which required a disproportionate number of their wives and children to work for wages. Many of these were waterfront jobs. In fact, in 1920, transportation or communication jobs constituted the largest occupational grouping. Over half of the workers in these jobs joined J. C. Skinner along the docks as stevedores or longshoremen. Others, like Charlie Johnson, found em- ployment as fishermen or in the ancillary trades like oyster shucking.[22]

To suggest that most black males worked at non-industrial pursuits did not mean no blacks found factory work. Nearly 30 percent of all black males worked in manufacturing or mechanical industries in 1920; however, almost half (44 percent) were laborers (see table 3). Arguably, many more may have been laborers. Most skilled workers labored for one of the military installations as a census of residents at Truxton—a showcase all-black community built for black Navy Yard employees by the United States Housing Corporation (USHC)—indicates. Like E. B. Wil- liams, driller, and Henry Jones, pipefitter's helper, one-quarter of the Yard's blacks labored as skilled workers or their helpers. Others worked in non-industrial factory settings like bakeries. Edward Weller, who moved to Norfolk in 1922, was one such individual. After a series of odd jobs, he became a baker's helper, a job he kept for more than fifteen years.[23]

The general configuration of the laboring population remained the same through 1930, although, after World War I, many black males became expendable (see table 4). The largest losses came in manufacturing and transportation jobs, areas that had spawned the movement from field to factory. They suffered additional losses

TABLE 3

Occupation by Race, Norfolk, 1920, Males

Occupation	Native White	Foreign-Born	Black
Agriculture, Forestry and animal husbandry	118 (.5)	11 (.3)	173 (1.0)
Extraction of Minerals	24 (.1)	1 (.0)	14 (.1)
Manufacturing and Mechanical	8,302 (36.6)	1,338 (32.2)	5,101 (30.5)
Transportation	3,182 (14.0)	805 (19.4)	5,308 (31.7)
Trade	4,575 (20.1)	1,129 (27.2)	1,668 (10.0)
Public Service	1,153 (5.1)	84 (2.0)	1,531 (9.2)
Professional Services	1,427 (6.3)	157 (3.8)	241 (1.4)
Domestic and Personal Service	655 (2.9)	490 (11.8)	2,446 (14.6)
Clerical	3,279 (14.4)	141 (3.4)	238 (1.4)
Total	22,715 (100.0)	4,156 (100.0)	16,720 (100.0)

Source: *Fourteenth Census of the United States (1920)*, vol. 4, pp. 1183–84.

TABLE 4

Occupation by Race, Norfolk, 1930, Males

Occupation	Native White	Foreign Born	Black
Agriculture	169 (.6)	13 (.6)	308 (2.2)
Forestry and Fishing	62 (.2)	—	50 (.4)
Manufacturing and Mechanical	7,995 (29.1)	575 (23.6)	4,482 (32.8)
Extraction of Minerals	10	—	14 (.1)
Transportation and Communication	2,923 (10.6)	251 (11.2)	3,969 (29.1)
Trade	5,665 (20.6)	833 (37.1)	1,664 (12.2)
Public Service	5,292 (19.3)	136 (6.1)	503 (3.0)
Professional Service	1,642 (6.0)	130 (5.8)	410 (3.0)
Domestic and Personal Service	628 (2.3)	221 (9.8)	2,163 (15.8)
Clerical	3,096 (11.3)	86 (3.8)	98 (.7)
Total	27,482 (100.0)	2,245 (100.0)	13,661 (100.0)

Source: *Fifteenth Census of the United States (1930)*, vol. 4, pp. 1673–74.

TABLE 5

Occupation by Race, Norfolk, 1920, Females

Occupation	Native White	Foreign Born	Black
Agriculture, Forestry and animal husbandry	3	—	26 (.3)
Extraction of Minerals	—	—	1
Manufacturing and Mechanical Industries	740 (13.2)	42 (11.7)	1,013 (11.7)
Transportation	166 (3.0)	3 (.8)	29 (.3)
Trade	885 (15.8)	128 (35.6)	123 (1.4)
Professional Services	788 (12.1)	43 (12.0)	296 (3.4)
Domestic and Personal Service	680 (12.1)	74 (20.6)	7,094 (81.9)
Public Service	18 (.3)	—	22 (.2)
Clerical	2,320 (41.4)	69 (19.2)	61 (.7)
Total	5,600 (100.0)	359 (100.0)	8,665 (100.0)

Source: *Fourteenth Census of the United States (1920)*, vol. 4, pp. 1184–85.

in public service, clerical and to some extent personal service jobs. Simultaneously, they added more agricultural and professional jobs.

High labor force participation rates by black men cloaked the sobering realization that most black households were overwhelmingly dependent upon the productive capabilities of black women. As a result, black women had a labor force participation rate nearly twice that of native white women and almost three times that of foreign-born white women. Such differences illustrate the structural nature of employment. Black female labor was crucial because, relative to whites, blacks were underemployed, despite what they may have hoped when they migrated. Moreover, few black women could expect to rectify the disparities, since the majority worked as domestic or personal servants (80 percent), a labor intensive, low paying job.[24]

Ironically, black women claimed over half of the city's manufacturing jobs. Unfortunately this did little to ease the larger underemployment problem. Most worked in industries which paid by the piece. The largest group worked as dressmakers in a non-factory setting (253 out of 1013). The clear majority in a factory setting in 1920 worked as tobacco stemmers at the American Cigar Company. Others worked for one of the smaller clothing companies like Mar-Hof or Chesapeake Knitting Mills. The former produced "cotton, linen [and] woolen, middy blouses and skirts," whereas the latter manufactured "union-suits, drawers and shirts."[25]

Although they had fewer occupational options than black males, a larger proportion of black women secured professional jobs (see table 5). Typically, occu-

TABLE 6

Occupation by Race, Norfolk, 1930, Females

Occupation	Native White	Foreign Born	Black
Agriculture	1	1 (.4)	191 (2.0)
Manufacturing and Mechanical Industries	859 (12.4)	38 (13.2)	1,276 (13.4)
Transportation and Communication	201 (2.9)	3 (1.1)	11 (.1)
Trade	1,241 (18.0)	103 (36.1)	110 (1.2)
Public Service	9 (.1)	—	6 (.1)
Professional Services	1,373 (19.9)	38 (13.3)	428 (4.5)
Domestic and Personal Services	818 (11.8)	57 (20.0)	7,482 (78.3)
Clerical	2,405 (34.8)	45 (15.8)	55 (.6)
Total	6,907 (100.0)	285 (100.0)	9,559 (100.0)

Source: *Fifteenth Census of the United States (1930)*, vol. 4, pp. 1673–74.

pational mobility, and thus class mobility, hinged on the ability to obtain one of the coveted teaching jobs. Of the 296 female black professionals in 1920, 71.6 percent were teachers. Life as a teacher was a tenuous existence, however, because, as quickly as attained, mobility could be erased. Because of local laws, when Mrs. Ruth V. married in the 1920s, she had to abandon her teaching position. She later became a beautician to bring in the needed money.[26] Almost all others were nurses, musicians or music teachers.

Employment opportunities changed very little for black women between 1920 and 1930. Heading into the Depression, eight out of ten continued to work as either domestic or personal servants. They did gain an additional 1,000 jobs, 200 of which were in manufacturing or mechanical trades (see table 6). Yet the acquisition of these jobs failed to offset the overall decline caused by the loss of 2,500 jobs for black males. Thus the new material reality would lead to other migratory decisions as the recession of the late 1920s became the Depression of the 1930s.

All too often the story of black migration has simply been the story of movement from country to city. For this reason, earlier scholars emphasized the disruptive aspects of migration. They depicted an isolated, atomized urban dweller, wrenched from family and friends. Of course such arguments ignored the adaptive abilities of Afro-American families. These arguments also ignored the importance of visiting and its function as an adaptive strategy.[27]

Although scholars have tended to minimize the importance of visiting, it has not gone unnoted. In his classic *Harlem: The Making of a Negro Ghetto*, Gilbert Osofsky observed:

It was common practice for migrants who lived within a day's journey of their former homes, to shuttle back and forth for regular visits. If European immigrants found the Atlantic no great barrier to such journeys . . . the Negro migrant was even less restricted by distance and cost. Practically every issue of the *New York Age* carried some report of such movement.[28]

The *Age* was not the only newspaper that carried such details. All of its contemporaries also chronicled the travel habits of Afro-Americans. Yet until recently, no scholar has submitted those accounts to a systematic analysis.[29]

Visiting's importance to black Norfolkians was captured weekly in the *Norfolk Journal and Guide*, which recorded the traveling habits of both residents and nonresidents. A typical citation listed the name of the persons coming to or leaving the city, the individuals they visited, the duration of the trip, the traveling party's size, and the type of family unit. The following example was common:

Mr. Lonnie Jones, Norfolk, visited his parents, the Rev. and Mrs. Jones in Durham, North Carolina . . . [30]

This example tells a considerable amount about visiting, interpersonal contact and Afro-American culture. We know Lonnie Jones lived in Norfolk and that, presumably, he was single. We also know he visited his parents and, thus, was a child returning to his family of origin. And we know that he traveled alone, although we cannot tell with absolute certainty how long he stayed. Moreover, the prevalence of such citations suggests that Afro-Americans attached a cultural and social importance to the visit, which they publicly acknowledged each week.

Thus visiting was one strategy adopted by Afro-Americans to counter the potentially deleterious effects of extra-local residence. Through visits black Americans were able to mend taxed family relations, rekindle old friendships and maintain primary social relationships, and still move from field to factory. Virginia C.'s parents began the regular return to the countryside not long after they moved to Norfolk. They continued the practice with their children, who regularly went to see family and friends in Norfolk County. Virginia C. noted that her parents saw this as an adaptation, a way of maintaining important ties to kith and kin without having to return to the country permanently. Likewise, those who lived elsewhere returned to Norfolk. In February 1921 Mrs. Blanche Lewis arrived from Boston to care for her sick uncle, Montgomery Hamilton.[31]

A systematic analysis of sampled visiting columns in the *Norfolk Journal and Guide* for the years September 1916–October 1917, 1921 and 1925 reveals a distinct pattern to the visits.[32] Nearly two-thirds of the primary visitors in the 840 cases were women, even though as many travelers left the city as entered (51.2 percent versus 48.8 percent). Furthermore, similar to Sarah Wills, three-quarters described their trip as a social visit, which enhanced the opportunity for contact with friends

TABLE 7

Reason for Trip

Reason	Number	Percent
Visit	631	77.4
Death	53	6.5
Convention	38	4.7
Business	34	4.2
Personal	33	4.1
Illness	19	2.3
Move	6	.7
Revival (Church)	1	.1
Total	815	100.0

and relatives. Surprisingly, given what others have noted, few traveled to attend a funeral or to sit at the bedside of a sick loved one.[33] Fewer yet attended a conference, traveled for business reasons, or planned a permanent move (see table 7).

Meanwhile, efforts to maintain contact through visits required the establishment of a visiting protocol, since it was impossible to visit everyone. A primary concern, of course, was cost. A family of four paid $25 to travel to New York from Norfolk by ship, which was more than a fertilizer worker or oyster shucker earned in a week, and therefore it was not always practical or affordable for an entire family to travel together. W. H. Morris traveled alone when he went to visit nieces, nephews, and cousins in Philadelphia, as did 62 percent of those sampled.[34]

As part of the protocol, certain family members and friends were selected for visits more than others. In the 600 cases where we have complete data, 42.5 percent indicated they visited first-order kin, that is, past or present members of the family of procreation or orientation (see table 8). The immediate family obviously remained an important reference despite residential separation. This was not as true of second-order kin like grandparents, grandchildren, uncles, aunts, cousins or in-laws. Just over 16 percent listed them as the persons visited. Even fewer persons called on individuals of unspecified relations. The remainder, about 30.5 percent, traveled to see friends. Clearly, as blood ties became more distant, contact became less important; as it did, friends replaced family members as important social relations.

Although most traveled alone, group travel highlights the little discussed patriarchal and patrilineal make-up of the black household. Most who traveled in a group did so with one other person (75.7 percent of known cases). In addition, few of these groups were nuclear families (4.8 percent). Obviously family members traveled together, but such groups contained a parent and one or more children

TABLE 8

Categories of Persons Visited by Migrants

Category	Number	Percent
First-Order Kin[a]	265	42.5
Second-Order Kin[b]	100	16.1
Unspecified Relations	68	10.9
Friends	190	30.5
Total	623	100.0

[a]First-order kin consists of those who were members of either the family of origin, like parents, siblings, or the family of orientation created by marriage.
[b]Second-order kin is comprised of aunts, uncles, nephews, nieces, in-laws, step-relations, and grandparents.

(30.4 percent). In about one-fifth of the known cases a husband and wife traveled together. When they did, they visited the husband's relative in 87.1 percent of the cases. Yet, where we have evidence of a nuclear family, fathers were listed as the primary visitors in 80 percent of the cases. This would suggest that women were considered part of their husbands' lines and thus had to visit his relatives or friends, but husbands were not viewed as necessarily part of their wives' lines. Moreover, the patterns reveal the degree to which women were the primary kinkeepers, since they traveled in all social settings—alone, with children, with husbands, and with intact families.[35]

Of course it is impossible to construct an emotional index for visits, but we can map their importance. Such a mapping underscores the enduring importance and multi-layered character of "home." In the Afro-American cultural vernacular home was always more than the house in which one lived. Home was the household and the community; home was a shared culture and a shared culture of expectations; home was the community of origin and the community of residence; home was a state of mind and the link between the past, the present, and the future.

Kith and kin were predisposed to travel considerable distance to reaffirm ties and in many cases search for home. Some came from as far away as Illinois, Michigan, and Canada, while black Norfolkians visited family and friends in Hawaii, California, and Arkansas.[36] The range of these visits as well as the overall pattern of visits suggest a relatively complex social network and reveal a lot about the migratory experiences of Afro-Americans during the First World War.

In 1925 George Gilmore rushed to Norfolk to be at the bedside of his critically ill brother, Joseph. He represented the many who came to Norfolk for manifold reasons. And like George who arrived from Montclair, New Jersey, non-local visitors came from a number of cities and towns along the eastern seaboard. In fact, excluding Norfolk's immediate vicinity, visitors came from thirty-eight north-ern communities, thirty-two North Carolina communities, twenty-one Virginia towns and cities, and eleven other southern locales.[37]

Mrs. George Walker's three-week visit with cousins in New York City, in con-trast, represented the counterflow. Black Norfolkians visited ninety communities outside of the immediate area. Where they visited suggests the community of origin of many residents. They went to twenty-nine communities in North Carolina, twenty-seven northern communities, twenty-three towns and cities in other parts of Virginia, ten southern cities and towns, and Honolulu.[38]

Visitors, in addition, both went to and came from large and small places. Roughly 38 percent of the communities visited had fewer than 2,500 residents and, by most standards, were rural. Within Virginia, 24.2 percent of the visitors went to non-urban places. In North Carolina, where no city exceeded 75,000 in 1920, most either went to or came from a small town or rural setting. In actuality, less than 10 percent came from or visited a North Carolina community with more than 50,000 residents. The pattern reversed itself in the North where most blacks came from or visited individuals from large urban places (84.1 percent went to towns with populations larger than 75,000). Surprisingly, fewer than 5 percent went to or came from rural northern communities, although 20.9 percent of black New Englanders and 25.4 percent of blacks living in mid-Atlantic states lived in such places (see table 9). This again highlights the importance that chain migration played in the history of black movement from field to factory.

The visits also underscore the adaptive abilities of Afro-American families. In a time period when few had telephones and many could not read well, if at all, the visit counterbalanced the effects of spatial separation. That black Norfolkians employed the visit so effectively is important; that similar accounts are found in numerous newspapers suggests a more universal strategy or adaptation to problems of residential dislocation. Such responses played an important role in the movement from field to factory, since they demonstrate the continued importance of family, friends, and home.

The Great Depression produced another migratory response. The economic op-portunities that lured many into the city during the preceding two decades began to rapidly disappear. As early as the Spring of 1928, a wide cross section of Norfolk blacks convened an Unemployment Conference. The conferees were upset because black unemployment had already reached critical levels. Estimates indicated that many had been reduced to part-time work, while others could not find work at all. The placement rate for black women had dropped to 5 percent per month. As conditions deteriorated, many foresaw the creation of a new class of unemployed. The conferees lamented:

> Those who are suffering are not the indolent and shiftless who would readily patronize a public soup kitchen or beg a public dole in order to buy life ne-

TABLE 9

Size and Region of the Country of the Communities of Origins of Those Who Traveled to or from Norfolk by the Number of Persons

Size	Region										
	Norfolk		Va. Other		N. Carolina		North		South		Other	
	No.	%	No.	%	No.	%	No.	%	No.	%	No.	%
Less than 2,500	40	8.5	15	24.2	27	37.5	7	4.3	—	—	1	33.3
2,500–4,999	1	.2	5	8.1	3	4.2	1	.6	1	9.1	—	—
5,000–9,999	12	2.5	1	1.6	17	23.6	—	—	2	18.2	—	—
10,000–19,999	—	—	5	8.1	6	8.3	5	3.0	1	9.1	—	—
20,000–29,999	—	—	4	6.4	10	13.9	4	2.4	—	—	—	—
30,000–39,999	6	1.3	7	11.3	2	2.8	4	2.4	2	18.2	—	—
40,000–49,999	—	—	—	—	7	9.7	—	—	—	—	—	—
50,000–74,999	130	27.5	3	4.8	—	—	5	3.0	2	18.2	—	—
75,000	283	60.0	22	35.5	—	—	138	84.1	2	18.2	2	66.7
Total	472		62		72		164		11		3	

cessities. The real sufferers are the self-respecting men and women of families who hitherto have been regular in their payments for rents, groceries, fuel, furniture and clothes, but who are being slowly but surely forced into insolvency and poverty.[39]

Conditions did worsen, but the migratory response was quite complex.

The first phase of the response dates from the 1920s. Black Norfolk was hard hit by two recessions, one coming early (1921) in the decade and another coming late (1928). It is impossible to determine with any precision which caused the large out-migration between 1920 and 1930, but the shift in population closely followed a decline in job opportunities. Black males lost more than 3,000 jobs between the dates; they also lost 2,297 to migration. The largest loss occurred among those just coming of age in 1920, 20–24 year olds. No doubt they experienced the greatest difficulty holding onto jobs in the first half of the decade and finding jobs in the

TABLE 10

Net Migration Among Blacks By Cohort, 1920–30 and 1930–40

Age Group	Decade			
	1920–30		1930–40	
	Male	*Female*	*Male*	*Female*
10–14	37	120	96	268
15–19	250	387	242	165
20–24	455	688	416	288
25–29	27	304	400	324
30–34	− 684	− 272	130	156
35–39	− 620	− 432	182	95
40–44	− 307	− 104	148	− 9
45–49	− 422	− 220	− 111	− 60
50–54	− 587	− 86	− 218	− 145
55–59	− 229	− 69	− 266	− 165
60–64	− 140	− 41	− 47	− 90
65–69	− 50	− 10	− 76	− 94
70–74	− 16	1	− 18	− 37
75 +	7	17	− 7	− 21
Total	− 2281	289	870	675

Source: *Fourteenth Census of the United States (1920)*, vol. 2, pp. 356–57; *Fifteenth Census of the United States (1930)*, vol. 3, part 2, p. 1156; *Sixteenth Census of the United States (1940)*, vol. 2, part 7, p. 194.

second half of the decade. If net out-migration is an adequate measure, then those 25–29 years old fared no better. They too migrated in great numbers (see table 10). In fact, young males were twice as likely to migrate as older males, ones with family obligations and longer job tenures.

Opportunities actually increased for black women during the decade but, ostensibly, not for young women. Like their male counterparts, black women age 20–29 left Norfolk in great numbers during the 1920s (see table 10). Thus although the number of domestic service and factory jobs increased during the decade, the expansion was not large enough to handle the correspondent need for female employment caused by the contraction of the male labor market. As a result, both young men and women migrated to larger urban places like Philadelphia, Washington and Pittsburgh.

Surprisingly, fewer saw out-migration as a viable option during the 1930s. Rather, more males and females moved to the city than left (see table 10) even though many black Norfolkians suffered greatly during the Depression. They constituted most of the relief recipients, were discriminated against by local officials, and lacked the political clout to alter conditions. Yet, for some it was a question of relative advantages. Compared to Gary, New York City, or Pittsburgh, Norfolk was a good place.[40] Moreover, the structure of the labor market and the character of the local economy offered some an economic niche.

John Chase represented such a person. Just prior to the beginning of the Depression, Chase, a longtime Norfolk native, moved to Baltimore to work on the docks. He believed his new job as a longshoreman promised a more secure and remunerative future than life as an independent fisherman. Chase's timing was poor, however. He soon returned to Norfolk and the tenuous security of his old profession. From the middle of April through the end of November he fished to support himself and his wife. The days were long, averaging twelve to thirteen hours. After catching his haul, he had the added task of selling the catch. Six days a week, weather permitting, his voice could be heard above the rumble of the city, advertising the day's fare.[41] Chase returned to Norfolk for the same reason he migrated: the costs of staying put outweighed the benefits derived from moving. In this instance, a return to Norfolk enabled him to escape the prison of abject poverty.

Others weighed the costs of staying put and moved. Lucille Johnson's husband of eleven years abandoned her and their children because he could no longer support them. As Lucille told Edith Skinner, "He said I done showed him up a fore de white folks and shamed him" and left. Apparently others left as well, according to the 1940 internal migration census. Between 1935 and 1940, 2,403 nonwhites entered the city and 3,362 left. Interestingly, the majority of the non-persisters were women rather than men (660 versus 299). Why they left is not readily known. Perhaps the differences stem from the standardization of relief efforts, which made migration a less precarious venture. Possibly, the pattern reflects gender differences in the structure of the family welfare system, that is parents were more willing to take in adult daughters than adult sons, so daughters returned to their community of origin as the Depression deepened. And it is possible the data are flawed, given what we know about census collection during the Depression.[42]

Inasmuch as it is impossible to reconcile the differences, it may be useful to pursue a related question: where were the migrants headed? Here again we see clear gender differences. Many nonwhite males (99 percent of whom were black) moved to cities with populations in excess of 100,000. A quarter, however, moved to nonfarm, rural areas. Indeed, as a group, males returned to the countryside at a rate almost equal to their movement to the city (46.9 percent as compared to 53.2 percent). This was particularly true of in-state migrants, 69.9 percent of whom returned to the country (see tables 11–13). Women too moved to the country, but to a lesser degree than males. Nearly two-thirds (62.5 percent) of the women migrated to large cities. Thus, if they were returning to communities of origin, then we had a previously unnoted pattern of reverse migration: black women went from large cities to smaller cities in search of opportunities during the late 1920s and early 1930s.

TABLE 11

**Net Population Change of Residency for Black Males Who Lived
in Norfolk in 1935, But Not in 1940**

Residence in 1940	Type of Place							
	Large Cities		Other Urban		Rural Non Farm		Rural Farm	
	No.	%	No.	%	No.	%	No.	%
New England	14	53.8	11	42.3	1	3.8	0	0
Mid-Atlantic	280	77.3	63	17.4	14	3.9	5	1.4
E. North Central	14	56.0	9	36.0	2	8.0	0	0.0
W. North Central	1	330	2	67.0	0	0.0	0	0.0
South Atlantic	239	19.8	220	18.2	440	36.4	311	25.7
E. South Central	6	66.7	1	11.1	2	22.2	0	—
W. South Central	3	50.0	2	33.3	1	16.7	0	—
Mountain	—	—	—	—	—	—	—	—
Pacific	17	70.8	3	12.5	4	16.7	0	—
Total	574	34.5	311	18.7	464	27.9	316	19.0

Source: *Sixteenth United States Census (1940)*, pp. 315, 338, 361, and 384.

The pattern of black migration changed again as the country entered World War II. For a second time large numbers moved from field to factory. Only this time, however, a new migration stream was born. In addition to the east coast and Mississippi Valley streams that took blacks from the southeast to the northeast and from Mississippi and Tennessee to Chicago and Detroit, respectively, blacks moved West. Hundreds left Louisiana, Arkansas, and Texas to settle in California. At the same time, scores moved from rural places to southern cities like Birmingham, Atlanta, and Norfolk.[43] In the process the renewed call for labor arrested the Depression-induced return to the countryside.

The Norfolk area was a particularly attractive place. Blessed with a complex array of military installations, shipbuilding facilities, harbors, and railroad terminals, it became a prime defense center. With its war-related transformation came a call for defense workers. In a short time the population increased dramatically. As recently as 1940, the city housed 144,332 residents, a third of whom were black; by November 1941 the count had reached 194,000.[44] Both the military and civilian populations jumped again after the general declaration of war a month later.

Meanwhile, Afro-Americans reluctantly answered the summons. Gunnar Myrdal estimated that through the fall of 1941 blacks accounted for just 14 percent of the new arrivals.[45] The reasons for this hesitancy were many: first, the Army discour-

TABLE 12

Net Population Change of Residency for Black Females Who Lived in Norfolk in 1935, But Not in 1940

Residence in 1940	Type of Place							
	Large Cities		Other Urban		Rural Non Farm		Rural Farm	
	No.	%	No.	%	No.	%	No.	%
New England	22	48.9	12	26.7	9	20.0	2	4.4
Mid-Atlantic	485	77.3	93	14.8	46	7.3	3	.5
E. North Central	8	61.5	5	38.5	0	—	0	—
W. North Central	0	—	1	100.0	0	—	0	—
South Atlantic	223	21.2	234	22.2	383	36.4	213	20.2
E. South Central	1	20.0	3	60.0	0	—	1	20.0
W. South Central	—	—	0	—	4	100.0	0	—
Mountain	0	—	1	100.0	0	—	0	—
Pacific	10	55.6	7	38.9	1	5.6	0	—
Total	749	42.4	356	20.1	443	25.1	219	12.4

Source: *Sixteenth United States Census, (1940)*, pp. 407, 430, 453, and 476.

aged black enlistment, which kept many black servicemen and their dependents from moving to the area; second, a retarded housing market, characterized by outdated structures, deterred more; third, reports of racial discrimination in hiring turned others away, especially since Norfolk was not the only center along the east coast; and fourth, the structure of the labor market must have been a factor. Unemployment among black Norfolkians hovered around 10 percent in 1940, although it dipped later. Local residents, consequently, filled many available positions, which decreased opportunities for prospective immigrants.

The flow of black migrants increased some time after 1942, although it is impossible to obtain a precise count. Instead, we can outline the change by examining net in-migration between 1940 and 1950. Norfolk's black population grew by 36.9 percent during the war decade or approximately 17,000. Most of the new arrivals were young adults under the age of 35, although the migratory pool was never constant. Contemporary accounts, for example, described most early migrants as unattached young men; however, the large numbers in the 10–14 and 15–19 cohorts suggests that this changed after 1943 (see table 14). Seemingly, with improvements in living conditions, migrants either brought or sent for families.

New migrants would face many hardships in the early years. With the sudden increase in population and associated pressures on city resources, inflation spiralled. As a result, many working class blacks had a difficult time making ends meet. As

TABLE 13

Intra-State Migration between 1935 and 1940 among Former Residents of Norfolk

	Males	
Residence 1940	*No.*	*%*
	Males	
Richmond	76	10.4
Other Urban	144	19.7
Rural Non-Farm	300	41.0
Rural-Farm	211	28.9
Total	731	100
	Females	
Richmond	37	6.6
Other Urban	164	29.5
Rural Non-Farm	209	37.6
Rural Farm	146	26.3
Total	556	100

Source: *Sixteenth United States Census (1940)*, pp. 361 and 453.

one black female tenement dweller complained, her 25¢ per week raise ''[had] been more than offset in the increase in just a few foodstuffs'' let alone what she paid in rent. Others found housing accommodations lacking or insufficient.[46] But foremost, black migrants had to hurdle the barriers to occupational advancement.

Most came to take advantage of new opportunities, particularly better paying factory jcbs, but, even after President Roosevelt bowed to black pressure and signed Executive Order 8802, which supposedly ended discrimination in all defense hiring, Afro-Americans experienced considerable discrimination. Oftentimes the perpetrator was a governmental agency like the Navy Yard, Naval Base, or Munitions Depot, but private contractors also discriminated. Women encountered greater impediments than men, especially when they tried to enter the industrial proletariat. The problem became so acute that federal investigator Lionel Florant was prompted to write,

> It is in time of crisis that the mores break down and new forms of adjustment arise. During World War I, the status of the Negro in American life was considerably enhanced by his economic, political and consequent social gains. Thus far there has not been much evidence of a change in social status as far as Norfolk Negroes are concerned.

TABLE 14

Black Net In-Migration by Cohort, 1940–50[a]

Age in 1950	Male	Female
10–14	436	513
15–19	442	437
20–24	1,333	654
25–29	1,354	1,060
30–34	1,125	946
35–39	672	663
40–44	411	239
45–49	167	191
50–54	136	31
55–59	58	− 25
60–64	34	13
65–69	− 25	− 71
70–74	− 34	− 5
75 +	− 24	−[b]
Total	6,085	4,646

Source: *Sixteenth Census of the United States (1940)*, vol. 2, part 7, p. 265; *Seventeenth Census of the United States (1950)*, vol. 2, part 46, p. 55.

[a]The total is slightly inflated because the 1950 Census lumped blacks with all other non-whites. Blacks, however, comprised 99.0 percent of the population.

[b]Total less than 1 percent.

Florant continued,

> Despite the numerous requests and the great demand for training courses for Negroes, relatively little attention has been paid to the Negro labor market as a current and future reservoir of workers for skill and semi-skilled tasks.[47]

This time, however, black Norfolkians exhibited a greater determination to win permanent improvements. Many used the Committee on Fair Employment Practices (FEPC) to secure semi-skilled and skilled positions. In addition, all black workers were encouraged to ally with similarly situated white workers to advance the overall cause of labor. Perhaps as crucial was the subtle difference in perspective that grew out of the war experience. For the first time, blacks publicly acknowledged that home sphere (the household and the community) development hinged on workplace advancement. Although it was not easy to realize improvements in both areas, the change signaled a new strategy. From now on the movement into factory jobs became a community-wide concern. And according to a 1943 survey, the new orientation produced tangible results: of 17,000 in defense jobs, 11.8 percent held skilled positions, 41.2 obtained semi-skilled jobs, and 47 percent worked as un-skilled laborers. Importantly, many would retain these jobs after the war and through the country's entrance into a post-industrial age.[48]

Conclusion

The history of black migration is complex, varying as it did by region, gender, age, and, presumably, class. The story of black migration to Norfolk between 1910 and 1945 highlights the nature of the complexity. Through 1945 three periods of migration from field to factory occurred. During each, individual choices became tied to larger forces, particularly perceived and realized economic opportunities. Movement to the city failed to produce the family dislocation so many early urban sociologists feared. Rather, Afro-Americans adapted to the new conditions by writing letters and visiting. When conditions worsened during the Depression, they moved again. Some migrated to larger cities, no doubt in search of better oppor-tunities, while others abandoned the dream of entry into the industrial proletariat. The abandonment did not last long, however. After a slow start, many migrated to Norfolk to work at the many defense industries. World War II signaled the birth of a new chapter in the history of black migration. For the first time Norfolk blacks, newcomers and oldtimers, tied home sphere development to workplace advance-ment. This time they struggled to make sure that the movement from field to factory was a permanent one. It would be for some, but by the late 1950s, a new employment opportunity structure was in place.[49] As a result, the last chapter of twentieth century black migration is still being written. Like its predecessors, it is a story about the link between expectations, economic opportunities, and life in the in-dustrial age.

NOTES

    Portions of this article have appeared in Earl Lewis, *In Their Own Interests: Race, Class, and Power in Twentieth Century Norfolk* (Berkeley: University of California Press, 1991). Reprinted by permission of University of California Press, and the *Journal of Family History*. Reprinted by permission of JAI Press.

    1. Lucille Johnson, interview, 20 January 1939, Virginia Writer's Project (VWP 58–71) (Virginia State Library).

    2. The migration literature is voluminous. A sample of those works include Emmett J. Scott, *Negro Migration during the War* (New York: Oxford University Press, 1920); Charles S. Johnson, "How Much Is Migration a Flight from Persecution?" *Opportunity* 1, no. 9 (September 1923): 272–75; Louise V. Kennedy, *The Negro Peasant Turns Cityward: Effects of Recent Migrations to Northern Cities* (New York: Columbia University Press, 1930); H.

G. Hamilton, "The Negro Leaves the South," *Demography* 1 (1964): 273–95; and Karl and Alma Taueber, "Changing Characteristics of Negro Migration," *American Journal of Sociology* 70 (1964): 429–41. Some of the recent works include Florette Henri, *Black Migration* (Garden City, NY: Anchor Books, 1976); Neil Fligstein, *Going North: Migration of Blacks and Whites from the South 1900–1950* (New York: Academic Press, 1981); the recently published Peter Gottlieb, *Making Their Own Way: Southern Blacks' Migration to Pittsburgh, 1916–1930* (Urbana: University of Illinois Press, 1987); and James R. Grossman, *Land of Hope: Chicago, Black Southerners, and the Great Migration* (Chicago: University of Chicago Press, 1989). Other recent works treated nineteenth-century black migration. See, for example, Nell Irvin Painter, *Exodusters: Black Migration to Kansas after Reconstruction* (New York: W. W. Norton, 1976), and Elizabeth H. Pleck, *Black Migration and Poverty: Boston 1865–1900* (New York: Academic Press, 1979).

3. John Bodnar, Roger Simon, and Michael P. Weber, *Lives of Their Own: Blacks, Italians and Poles in Pittsburgh, 1900–1960* (Urbana: University of Illinois Press, 1982), pp. 32–36.

4. George W. Bennett, *Life Behind the Wall of My Self-Made Fate* (self-published, June 1964), pp. 28–29, 48–49; Blaine Brownell, *The Urban Ethos in the South, 1920–1930* (Baton Rouge: Louisiana University Press, 1975), p. 7.

5. Joe William Trotter, Jr., *Black Milwaukee: The Making of an Industrial Proletariat, 1915–45* (Urbana: University of Illinois Press, 1985), p. 45.

6. U.S. Department of Commerce, *Negroes in the United States, 1920–1932* (Washington: Government Printing Office, 1935), pp. 53–55; also see table 1.

7. For a discussion of migration streams, see Fligstein, *Going North*, p. 66 and chapter 6. For a discussion of Norfolk County population shifts, see Earl Lewis, "At Work and At Home: Blacks in Norfolk, Virginia, 1910–1945" (Ph.D. diss., University of Minnesota, 1984), pp. 68–69.

8. *Thirteenth Census of the United States (1910)*, vol. 3, p. 951; *Fourteenth Census of the United States (1920)*, vol. 3, p. 1069; *Fifteenth Census of the United States, (1930)*, vol. 3, part 2, p. 157.

9. *Fourteenth Census of the United States (1920)*, vol. 3, p. 665; *Fifteenth Census of the United States (1930)*, vol. 2, p. 203.

10. Bennett, *Life Behind the Veil of My Self-Made Fate*, pp. 48–49. Virginia C., conversation, 23 September 1984; earlier conversations with the deceased, Clifton J.; interview with Lucille Johnson, 20 January 1939.

11. John S. MacDonald and Leatrice D. MacDonald, "Chain Migration, Ethnic Neighborhood Formation and Social Networks," *Milbank Memorial Fund* 42, (1964): 82.

12. Bodnar, Simon, and Weber, *Lives of Their Own*, pp. 31–33; Grossman, *Land of Hope*, especially pp. 89–91.

13. Lloyd D., conversation, 9 March 1983.

14. Maria Ruffin, interview, 23 December 1938, Virginia Writers' Project (VWP 58–71) (Virginia State Library).

15. There is considerable disagreement among scholars over the importance of labor agents, violence, or the social milieu as factors fueling black migration. For a sense of the debate, see Carole Marks, *Farewell—We're Good and Gone: The Great Black Migration* (Bloomington; Indiana University Press, 1989) and Grossman, *Land of Hope*.

16. See *Norfolk, Virginia: The Sunrise City By The Sea* (The [Norfolk] Industrial Commission, 1914), pp. 7–19; Arthur Kyle Davis, "Norfolk City in War Time: A Community History," in *Virginia Communities in War Time* (Richmond: Virginia War Commission History, 1925), pp. 295, 322–27; Paul Nasca, "Norfolk in the First World War" (M.A. thesis, Old Dominion University, 1979), pp. 29, 51 and 60.

17. *Norfolk Journal and Guide*, 17 April 1917.

18. The procedure for determining net migration is described in Everett S. Lee, *Studies of Population Redistribution and Economic Growth, Net Intercensal Migration, 1870–1940*

(Philadelphia: Philosophical Society, 1953). The rapid increase in the city's population caused considerable alarm in Washington. See *Black Workers in the Era of the Great Migration* (reel 24, frame 26) for a discussion of the impact on local housing.

19. *Ledger Star*, 8 November 1974; *The Virginian-Pilot*, 9 November 1974.

20. Lewis, "At Work and At Home," pp. 72–74. Also see the *Twenty-fifth–Thirty-Third Annual Reports of the Department of Labor and Industry of the State of Virginia*, 25–33 (Richmond).

21. Lewis, "At Work and At Home," pp. 72–74, 78–80.

22. Gavin Wright, *Old South, New South* (New York: Basic Books, 1986), especially chapter 6. Federal Mediation and Conciliation Service, File 33/661, National Archives (R.G. 280); Skinner is identified as President of the all-black longshoremen union. Charlie Johnson, interview, 24 February 1939, Virginia Writers' Project.

23. United States Housing Corporation, *Truxton Household Census*, National Archives (R.G. 3). Edward Weller, interview, 24 February 1939, Virginia Writers' Project.

24. Lewis, "At Work and At Home," pp. 76–82.

25. Hellen Bryan to Mary Anderson, Women's Bureau Bulletin, No. 10, Surveys (December 1919), National Archives (R.G. 86); a somewhat similar pattern is outlined in Jacqueline Jones, *Labor of Love, Labor of Sorrow* (New York: Basic Books, 1985), chapters 4 and 5.

26. Ruth V., conversation reported by Rudolph Lewis, 29 May 1984.

27. Robert Park, "Human Migration and the Marginal Man," *American Journal of Sociology* 33 (May 1928): 888–93, and E. Franklin Frazier, *The Negro Family in the United States* (Chicago: The University of Chicago Press, 1939, reprinted 1973). For a fuller discussion of Afro-American visiting patterns, see Earl Lewis, "Afro-American Adaptive Strategies," *Journal of Family History* 12, no. 4 (Winter 1987): 407–20.

28. Gilbert Osofsky, *Harlem: The Making of a Negro Ghetto, 1890–1930* (New York: Harper and Row, 1963), p. 30.

29. Excluding my own study, the only one to consider the visiting columns in newspapers has been Jane M. Pederson, "The Country Visitor: Pattern of Hospitality in Rural Wisconsin, 1880–1925," *Agricultural History* 58 (July 1984): 347–64. She fails, however, to make full use of the columns. Others have examined Afro-American adaptive strategies, however; see, for example, Carol Stack, *All Our Kin* (New York: Harper and Row, 1974).

30. *Norfolk Journal and Guide*, 26 March 1921.

31. Virginia C., conversation, 7 June 1985. *Norfolk Journal and Guide*, 26 February 1921.

32. For a description of the sampling procedure, see Lewis, "Afro-American Adaptive Strategies." These three years were chosen for two reasons: first, I wanted to cover the period of intense migration, as well as the years which followed, when the pattern of visiting should have become entrenched; and second, after 1925, the black middle class became over-represented in the columns. This had not been the case previously.

33. *Norfolk Journal and Guide*, 13 August 1921. James Borchert, *Alley Life in Washington* (Urbana: University of Illinois Press, 1980), p. 84.

34. Henri, *Black Migration*, pp. 66, 68 and *Annual Report of the Offices, Boards and Institutions of the Commonwealth of Virginia, Report of the Labor Commission*, 1920, pp. 32, 37; *Norfolk Journal and Guide*, 26 March 1921.

35. Kinkeeper is a neologism. A similar phrase is used to convey the important role played by women in the family; Tamara Hareven, *Family Time and Industrial Time* (Cambridge: Cambridge University Press, 1982), pp. 105–106.

36. For a map of the visiting travel fields as well as detailed tables of the visiting, see Lewis, "At Work and At Home," pp. 223–32.

37. *Norfolk Journal and Guide*, 5 September 1925.

38. *Norfolk Journal and Guide*, 7 November 1925.

39. *Norfolk Journal and Guide*, 10 March 1928.

40. See Lewis, "At Work and At Home," chapter 6. Also see Harvard Sitkoff, *A New Deal for Blacks* (New York: Oxford University Press, 1978), p. 37.

41. "The Fisherman's Wife, Laura Chase," interview, 17 February 1939, Virginia Writers' Project. Such moves were quite common. For many years, black males moved away for extended periods as both the seasons and jobs changed; see Pleck, *Black Migration and Poverty*, chapter 5.

42. Johnson, 20 January 1939. All of the Unemployment Censuses undercounted, particularly the 1937 census, as later supplements revealed.

43. See Fligstein, *Going North*, for a general discussion of the changes. Edward F. Haas, "The Southern Metropolis, 1940–1976," in *The City in Southern History*, Blaine Brownell and David Goldfield, eds. (Port Washington, NY: Kennikat Press, 1977), chapter 6.

44. *Population Study Report No. 2. Population in Flux in the Hampton Roads Area: A Study of Population Trends in the Hampton Roads Area, 1890–1942* (Richmond, VA: Virginia State Planning Board, September 1942), pp. 7–17.

45. Gunnar Myrdal, *An American Dilemma* (New York: Harper and Row Publishers, rept. 1962). vol. 1, p. 1031.

46. *Norfolk Journal and Guide*, 18 October 1941. *Monthly Labor Review* 54 (1942): 834.

47. Lionel C. Florant, "The Impact of the War on the Norfolk Negro Community," 26 May 1942, pp. 8–9. Recreation Division, National Archives (R.G. 215, box 6).

48. See Earl Lewis, *In Their Own Interests: Race, Class, and Power in Twentieth Century Norfolk* (Berkeley: University of California Press, 1991), chapter 7, for a full delineation of the shifts in the Norfolk labor market during the war years, and the efforts undertaken by local blacks to realize long-lasting improvements in employment.

49. See "A Tale of Three Cities," in Theodore Hershberg, ed., *Philadelphia: Work, Space, Family and the Group Experience in the 19th Century* (New York: Oxford University Press, 1981), pp. 461–91 for a discussion of employment opportunity structures in the industrial age.

Race, Class, and Industrial Change
Black Migration to Southern West Virginia, 1915–1932

Joe William Trotter, Jr.

The Great Migration of blacks to northern, southern, and, to some extent, western cities is receiving increasing scholarly attention. Large numbers of blacks, however, moved to the southern Appalachian coalfields of Kentucky, Tennessee, Virginia, and especially West Virginia. Based on the growing employment of blacks in the bituminous coal industry, for example, the African-American population in the central Appalachian plateau increased by nearly 200 percent between 1900 and 1930, from less than 40,000 to over 108,000.[1]

Black migration to southern Appalachia was neither rural to urban nor rural to rural, but rather rural to rural-industrial. Thus, a focus on black migration to this region should deepen our understanding of black population movements during the late nineteenth and early twentieth centuries. For black migration to southern West Virginia, as elsewhere, was deeply rooted in the social imperatives of black life in the rural South, as well as the dynamics of industrial capitalism. This essay examines the origins of the migrants, factors precipitating their movement, and their growing employment in the coal industry. It also suggests how southern blacks helped to organize their own movement and transformation into a new class of industrial workers.

Black migration to southern West Virginia accelerated during the pre–World War I era, as the Mountain State underwent a dramatic industrial transformation. The entire state produced only 5 million tons of coal in 1887, but coal production in southern West Virginia alone increased to nearly 40 million tons in 1910, about 70 percent of the state's total output. As coal companies increased production, the region's population increased from an estimated 80,000 in 1880 to nearly 300,000 in 1910 (see table 1).[2] Like industrialization in other southern states, bituminous coal mining helped to transform the region's largely subsistence economy into a dependent industrial economy, with growing links to national and international markets.[3]

While northern industries largely excluded blacks, coal companies recruited "native whites," European immigrants, and blacks in growing numbers. The black

TABLE 1

Population of Southern West Virginia by Race and Ethnicity, 1880–1910[a]

Ethnic Group	1880		1890		1900		1910	
	No.	%	No.	%	No.	%	No.	%
Black	4,794	6.0	11,114	9.2	19,670	11.1	40,503	13.5
Foreign-Born Whites	1,375	1.7	2,662	2.2	2,776	1.5	18,061	6.0
American-Born Whites/Foreign-Born Parentage	N/A	—	3,889	3.2	5,470	3.1	8,978	2.9
American-Born Whites/American Born-Parentage[b]	74,615	92.3	102,806	85.4	147,857	84.3	232,276	77.6
Other	—		—		—		32	
Total[c]	80,784	100.0	120,471	100.0	175,773	100.0	299,850	100.0

Source: U.S. Bureau of the Census. *Eleventh Census of the United States (1890)*, p. 435; *Thirteenth Census of the U.S. (1910)*, vol. 3, pp. 1032–41.
[a]Includes nine counties: McDowell, Mercer, Mingo, Logan, Fayette, Kanawha, Raleigh, Boone, and Wyoming.
[b]For 1880 (only) includes all American-born whites.
[c]Includes a small number of other non-whites in 1900 (only).

population increased from 4,800 in 1880 to over 40,000 in 1910. Contributing over 40 percent of the state's black population in 1910, rural Virginia was the major source of black population growth and labor recruitment. Other contributing states included the surrounding Upper South and border states of North Carolina, Kentucky, Tennessee, and Maryland, supplemented by the nearby northern industrial states of Ohio and Pennsylvania. The Deep South states of South Carolina, Georgia, and Alabama also sent small numbers, bringing the proportion of blacks born elsewhere to over 50 percent.[4] With six percent of the total in 1880, by 1910 the black population had reached nearly 14 percent, more than twice the percentage of immigrants, mainly from South, Central, and Eastern Europe.

Black migration to southern West Virginia, however, built on antebellum roots. In 1850, over 3,000 slaves resided in Kanawha county, Virginia, making up the majority of the county's coal mining labor force. Although the number of blacks in Kanawha county dropped during the Civil War (as West Virginia seceded from Virginia), in the postwar years their numbers slowly increased. Booker T. Washington was among the ex-slaves who migrated into the coal fields and worked in the mines. During the Civil War, Washington Furguson escaped from slavery and followed Union soldiers into the Kanawha Valley. After the Civil War, he sent for his wife Jane and her children, including the young Booker T., "who made the trip overland in a wagon, there being no railroad connection as yet with old Virginia." Booker T. Washington later described his tenure in the mines as an unpleasant experience. "Work in the coal mines I always dreaded. . . . There was always the danger of being blown to pieces by a premature explosion of powder, or of being crushed by falling slate. Accidents from one or the other of these causes were frequently occurring and this kept me in constant fear."[5]

Although blacks had entered the region in the antebellum and Reconstruction eras, it was not until the railroad expansion of the 1890s and early 1900s that their numbers dramatically increased, giving rise to a new industrial proletariat. Black workers helped to lay track for every major rail line in the region. In his assessment of black labor on the Chesapeake and Ohio (which produced the black folk hero John Henry), sociologist James T. Laing concluded that "this important road was largely built by Negro laborers from Virginia." Upon completion of the Chesapeake and Ohio in 1873, many blacks remained behind "to work in the newly opened coal mines of the New River district." The ex-slave James Henry Woodson from nearby Virginia eventually took a job on the labor crew of the Chesapeake and Ohio Railway shops, and thus paved the way for his young son Carter G. Woodson's brief stint in the mines of the Kanawha-New River field. The young Woodson later moved out of coal mining, earned a Ph.D. degree from Harvard University, and founded the Association for the Study of Negro Life and History.[6]

In 1892, blacks played "fully as large a part" in the building of the Norfolk and Western Railroad as they did in constructing the Chesapeake and Ohio. As in the case of the Chesapeake and Ohio, following the completion of the Norfolk and

Western, many black railroad men "remained to work in the coal fields" of the Pocahontas Division. Black labor on the Virginian Railroad and the subsequent opening of mines in the Winding Gulf field followed a similar pattern. "When the Winding Gulf Field . . . opened up through the building of the Virginian Railroad in 1909 the Negro again played the part of pioneer."[7] While a few individuals like Carter G. Woodson and Booker T. Washington eventually moved out of coal mining, gained substantial education, and became part of the national black elite, most black migrants finished out their careers as part of the expanding black industrial proletariat. Under the impact of World War I, working class black kin and friendship networks would intensify, bringing a new generation of Southern black workers into the coal industry.[8]

Spurred by the labor demands of World War I, the black population increased by nearly 50 percent, from just over 40,000 in 1910 to nearly 60,000 in 1920. The percentage of West Virginia blacks living in the southern counties increased from 63 to nearly 70 percent. At the same time, the black coal mining proletariat increased from 11,000 in 1915 to over 15,000 during the war years, rising from 20 to nearly 25 percent of the labor force, as immigrants declined from 31 to 19 percent (see tables 2 and 3). Led by Virginia with over 34 percent in 1920, blacks from the Upper South states accounted for 56 percent of the state's black total.

Black migration to southern West Virginia during World War I was part of the first wave of the Great Migration of blacks northward out of the South. As elsewhere, the majority were young men between the primary working ages of 20 and 44, though the sex ratio evened out over time (as did the white ratio). Nonetheless, a substantial imbalance continued through the war years, at 125 males to every 100 females in 1920. One contemporary observer argued that the Mountain State not only received the earliest, but also the "best" of the migrants. "We got the vanguard . . . those who came voluntarily and were not encouraged to leave on account of strained relations or the strain of living." In reality, however, the majority of blacks entered West Virginia precisely because of the "strain of living" and often "strained relations" in other parts of the South.[9]

In the Upper South and border states, black farmers abandoned the land in growing numbers. During World War I, John Hayes moved his family from rural North Carolina to McDowell County, his daughter tersely recalled, "because he got tired of farming." For similar reasons, in 1917, John Henry Phillips moved his family from a small farm in Floyd County, Virginia, to Pageton, McDowell County. During World War I, Salem Wooten's family owned a farm in Henry county, Virginia near Martinsville. The family raised wheat, corn, some livestock, and especially tobacco for the market.[10]

Tobacco farming, Wooten recalled, was "back-breaking labor." "Tobacco is a delicate crop and it's a lot of hard work. . . . If you did that all day, it was very tiresome." With thirteen boys and five girls in the family, the Wootens managed to make ends meet during the war and early postwar years. The young men,

TABLE 2

Population of Southern West Virginia by Race and Ethnicity, 1910–1930[a]

Ethnic Group	1910			1920			1930		
	Number	% of Total	% of Regional Group's State Total	Number	% of Total	% of Regional Group's State Total	Number	% of Total	% of Regional Group's State Total
Black	40,503	13.5	63.1	58,819	13.5	68.1	79,007	13.2	68.7
Foreign-Born Whites	18,061	6.0	31.6	18,388	4.1	29.6	15,472	2.6	30.0
American-Born Whites/ Foreign-Born or Mixed Parentage	8,978	2.9	15.5	18,346	4.1	22.2	23,584	4.0	23.3
American-Born Whites/ American-Born Parentage	232,276	77.6	22.2	342,960	78.3	27.8	473,699	80.1	32.4
Other	32		24.8	41		33.8	194	–	51.3
Total	299,850	100.0	24.5	438,504	100.0	29.9	591,956	100.0	34.2

Source: U.S. Bureau of the Census. *Thirteenth Census of the United States (1910)*, vol. 3, pp. 1032–41; *Fourteenth Census of the U.S. (1920)*, vol. 3, pp. 1105–1109; *Fifteenth Census of the United States (1930)*, vol. 3, part 2, pp. 1268–77.

[a]Includes nine counties: McDowell, Mercer, Mingo, Logan, Fayette, Kanawha, Raleigh, Boone, and Wyoming.

TABLE 3

Coal Mining Labor Force of Southern West Virginia by Race and Ethnicity, 1915–1930[a]

Ethnic Group	1915		1917		1919		1925		1929	
	Number	%	Number	%	Number	%	Number	%	Number	%
Black	11,035	20.0	16,572	26.2	15,180	24.7	20,272	27.2	19,648	26.7
Foreign-Born Whites	17,192	31.0	12,095	19.1	12,105	19.7	10,338	13.8	8,819	11.9
American-Born Whites	27,080	48.9	34,497	54.6	34,214	55.5	43,811	58.8	45,151	61.2
Other or Unknown	69	0.1	111	0.1	76	0.1	191	0.2	17	—
Total	55,376	100.0	63,275	100.0	61,575	100.0	74,612	100.0	73,635	100.0

Source: West Virginia Department of Mines, *Annual Reports* (Charleston, West Virginia: 1915–1929).
[a]Includes nine counties: McDowell, Mercer, Mingo, Logan, Fayette, Kanawha, Raleigh, Boone, and Wyoming.

however, "wanted to get away from the farm." The elderly Wooten fought in vain to keep his sons on the land. Shortly after his discharge from the army in 1918, the oldest son migrated to southern West Virginia, setting in motion a process that would eventually bring seven of his younger brothers into the coalfields.[11]

With the labor demands of the bituminous coal industry intersecting with the boll weevil and destructive storms on southern farms, hundreds of black share-croppers and farm laborers from the Deep South also migrated to southern West Virginia. The Deep South states of Alabama, Georgia, South Carolina, and Mississippi sent increasing numbers of black migrants to southern West Virginia. Indeed, among all contributing states, the Deep South state of Alabama was third, making up over 6 percent of West Virginia blacks in 1920.

Under the deteriorating agricultural conditions in the Deep South, some white landowners eased their tenacious grip on black farm laborers and helped to stimulate out-migration. In a revealing letter to the U.S. Department of Justice, Alexander D. Pitts, U.S. Attorney for the Southern District of Alabama, explained: "There has been no corn [and little cotton] made and this country only raises cotton and corn, you can readily see that the negroes have nothing to eat. The planters are not able to feed them and they are emigrating."[12]

Black miners averaged $3.20 to $5.00, and even more, per 8–hour day, compared to a maximum of $2.50 per 9-hour day for southern industrial workers. Black southern farm laborers made even less, as little as 75¢ to $1.00 per day. It is no wonder, as one migrant recalled, some blacks moved to southern West Virginia, when "they heard that money was growing on trees."[13]

In 1916, Thornton Wright's family moved from a sharecropping experience in Montgomery, Alabama, to the coal mining community of Accoville, Logan County. At the same time, a Union Springs, Alabama, migrant wrote from Holden, Logan County, "I make $80 to $90 per mo. with ease and wish you all much success. Hello to all the people of my home town. I am saving my money and spending some of it." Writing in a detailed letter to his friend, another Alabama migrant wrote back from Omar, Logan County, "You can make 1 dollar heaire quicker than you can 20 ct theaire in Alla."[14]

Important social, cultural, and political factors reinforced the attractiveness of West Virginia as a target of black migrants. Racial lynchings were fewer; education opportunities were greater; and voting was not restricted by race as elsewhere in the South. In his letter back home, one migrant, W. L. McMillan, enclosed a flyer announcing a political rally, bearing the bold captions, "Republican Speaking— Mr. Colored Man Come Out And Bring Your Friends to Hear." "Now listen," McMillan concluded, "I will vote for the president on the 11 of this mont Collered man tick[e]t stands just as good as white man heare." Although it frequently overstated the case, during the 1920s, the Bureau of Negro Welfare and Statistics (BNWS), a State agency, repeatedly emphasized the political and social attractions of West Virginia.[15]

Though most blacks came to West Virginia from agricultural backgrounds, many had already made a substantial break with the land. As opportunities in southern agriculture steadily declined, rural blacks increasingly moved into southern non-farm industries, especially lumber, coal, and railroad work before coming to West Virginia. Before bringing his family to Pageton, McDowell County, John Henry Phillips had alternated between work in a local saw mill and farm labor. Salem Wooton recalled that one of his brothers worked in a furniture factory in Martinsville, Virginia, before migrating to southern West Virginia. Before migrating to Coalwood, McDowell County, Pink Henderson and his father were coal miners in the Birmingham district of Alabama. Alabama coal operators were infamous for the highly unjust contract labor and convict lease systems of employment. Taken together, these systems placed miners—mainly blacks—at a severe disadvantage, protected management, and helped to drive numerous Alabama miners to West Virginia. Commenting on the low wages in Alabama mines, Henderson stated: "That's why we came to West Virginia. They wasn't paying nothing [in Alabama]. They was paying more here in West Virginia mines than they was down there."[16] Since they entered the mines from industrial or semi-industrial backgrounds, black men like the Hendersons, Phillips, and Wooten experienced a less radical change than farm laborers did.

In addition to the economic conditions from which they came, the recruitment and advertising campaigns of coal companies provided important stimuli to the black migration. In the spring of 1916, the United States Coal and Coke Company, a subsidiary of the U.S. Steel Corporation, advertised for workers at Gary, McDowell County: "Wanted at once / 1000 Miners and Coke Drawers / 11 mines and 2000 coke ovens working Six Days Per Week / Five Percent Increase in Wages / Effective May 8, 1916." At the height of World War I, such advertising intensified. In the summer of 1917, the King and Tidewater Coal and Coke Company at Vivian, McDowell County frantically announced: "10 Automobiles Free / Men Wanted: miners and Day Men Money without limit to be made with Ten Automobiles given away free."[17]

Professional labor recruiters for the coal companies also encouraged southern blacks to move to the coal fields. During World War I, E. T. McCarty, located in the Jefferson County Bank Building, Birmingham, Alabama, recruited black coal miners for major southern West Virginia coal producers. His clients included the New River Coal Company and the New River and Pocahontas Coal Corporation. In Bessemer, Alabama, the renowned Jones and Maddox Employment Agency also served a variety of coal companies in the region. These agents carefully calculated their messages, skillfully aiming to uproot blacks from their tenuous foothold in the southern economy: "Do you want to go North where the laboring man shares the profits with the boss? Are you satisfied with your condition? Are you satisfied with your pay envelope? Are you making enough wages [to] take care of you in the times of distress? If you are not satisfied we want you to come to see us."[18]

Coal companies also enlisted the support of middle class black leaders. Especially important was the local black weekly—the *McDowell Times*—which circulated in West Virginia and nearby Virginia. During World War I, the *McDowell Times* editorially proclaimed: "Let millions of Negroes leave the South, it will make conditions better for those who remain." In lengthy articles, the *Times* celebrated the movement of blacks into the various coal camps like those of Glen White, Raleigh County. "The old saying that 'All roads lead to Rome' surely has its modern analogy . . . 'All railroads seem to lead to Glen White' for every train drops its quota of colored folks who are anxious to make their homes in the most beautiful spot in the mining district of West Virginia." The *Times* columnist, Ralph W. White, stated simply: "To one and all of them we say WELCOME."[19]

Despite the optimistic portrayals of the *McDowell Times*, a substantial degree of private and public coercion underlay the recruitment of black labor. Operators often advanced the migrants transportation fees, housing, and credit at the company store. Using privately employed Baldwin-Felts detectives, some coal operators were notorious for their violent control of black workers. One black miner recalled, "I can show you scars on my head which were put in there by the Baldwin-Felts men in 1917. There was four of them jumped me until they thought me dead, but I didn't die. They kicked two or three ribs loose—two or three of them—on Cabin Creek."[20]

The operators' autonomy over company-owned land was strengthened in 1917 when the West Virginia legislature enacted a law to "prevent idleness and vagrancy . . . during the war and for six months thereafter." "All able bodied men between 18 and 60 years of age, regardless of color, class or income must toil thirty-five hours each week to support themselves and their dependents."[21] Failure to work as prescribed could result in arrests and sentences to work for the county or city for six months. Neutral in its class and racial provisions, however, the law received the enthusiastic endorsement of middle class black leaders, like T. Edward Hill who approvingly exclaimed: "So the boys who 'toil not' in McDowell County have 30 days to make up their minds [to work in the mines or on public road crews]. . . . Don't crowd boys."[22]

Moreover, West Virginia had passed a prohibition law in 1914, and some of the prohibition arrests, convictions, and sentences to hard labor on county road projects were scarcely veiled efforts to discipline and exploit the black labor force. Even the local black weekly soon decried the arrest of what it condescendingly called "a lot of ignorant men and depriving their families of support for months and in some cases years." According to the State Commissioner of Prohibition, southern West Virginia had the highest incidence of arrests, convictions, and sentences to hard labor on county road projects.[23]

Although some black miners felt the impact of public and private coercion, most migrants chose southern West Virginia voluntarily, using their network of kin and friends to get there. After arriving, they often urged their southern kin and friends to join them. Acute contemporary observers understood the process. In his investigation of the great migration, the U.S. attorney for the Southern District of Alabama reported that at least 10 percent of those who had left had returned, but half of the returnees had come back for relatives and friends. "It is the returned negroes who carry others off."[24]

Coal companies soon recognized the recruitment potential of black kin and friendship networks, and hired black miners to recruit among relatives and friends. During World War I, the Rum Creek Collieries Company hired Scotty Todd as a labor recruiter. On one trip back to Alabama, the company gave Todd enough money to bring fifty men to West Virginia. Several relatives and friends returned to the state with Scotty Todd, including his younger brother Roy. At Hollow Creek, McDowell County, the company added a second and then a third shift. When one newcomer asked why, the superintendent's reply, although highly paternalistic, revealed the familial pattern of black migration: "If you stop bringing all your uncles and . . . aunts and cousins up here we wouldn't have to do that. We got to make somewhere for them to work. . . . They can't all work on day shift. They can't all work on evening shift."[25]

As suggested above, coal mining was an overwhelmingly male occupation, with few opportunities for black women outside the home. Yet, black women played a crucial role in the migration process. Before migrating to southern West Virginia during the war years, Catherine Phillips married John Henry who worked in a nearby sawmill in rural western Virginia. Catherine raised crops for home consumption, performed regular household chores, and gave birth to at least three of the couple's eight children. In 1917, she took care of the family by herself for several months, while John Henry traveled to southern West Virginia, worked in the coal mines, and finally returned for her and the children.[26]

Nannie Bolling, more than a decade before she moved with her family to southern West Virginia, married Sam Beasley in rural North Carolina. Sam eventually travelled to Gary, McDowell County, and worked in the mines for several pay periods, leaving Nannie to take care of the couple's four children until he returned for them. In a family group, including her husband, four children, and one grandparent, Vallier Henderson travelled from Jefferson County, Alabama, to McDowell County during World War I. The Hendersons traveled with a party of three other Alabama families, along with their household furnishings, and the trip took nearly seven days by rail. Upon reaching McDowell County, the families made a time-consuming and arduous horse and wagon trip into the mountains of Coalwood.[27] Black women—desiring to hold their families together, escape rural poverty, and gain greater control over their destinies—played a key role in the migration to southern West Virginia.[28]

Involving a web of legal entanglements and debts, some blacks found it more difficult than others to escape southern sharecropping arrangements. In such cases, their kin and friends served them well. Notwithstanding deteriorating conditions in the southern economy, southern landowners and businessmen often resisted the black migration. They feared a permanent loss of their low-wage labor pool. Thus, for many black migrants, white resistance necessitated a great deal of forethought, planning, and even secrecy. In his effort to ascertain the character and extent of black migration from Mississippi, Jasper Boykins, a U.S. Deputy Marshall, reported: "It is very difficult to get the names and addresses of any of the negroes going away. It seems that this movement is being conducted very quietly." [29] Another investigator likewise observed: "I, myself, went to see the families of several negroes who have left and they are loath to tell where these people have gone. Of course, I did not tell them what I want to know. . . . they are secretive by nature." [30] Black migrants were by no means "secretive by nature," but many of them were secretive by design, and for solid reasons. The coercive elements of southern sharecropping would die hard.

Yet, not all black migrants to southern West Virginia received the blessings of their kin. In deciding to leave their southern homes, some young men moved despite the opposition of their fathers who sought to keep them on the land. Scotty Todd and his brother moved to West Virginia when their father rejected their effort to bargain: they had requested a car in exchange for staying on the farm. [31] Salem Wooten's father also fought a losing battle to keep his sons on the land. The oldest son "slipped away" and his brother later vividly recalled the occasion: "My father sent him over in the field to do some work. . . . And he packed his clothes, what few he had, and slipped them over there at the edge of the field and worked a little bit, well something like a half an hour in the field. Then he went to the cherry tree, ate all the cherries he could eat. Then he came down the tree and got his little suit case and he had to cross Smith River to get what we called the Norfolk and Western Railroad Train . . . into Roanoke [VA] from there into West Virginia. . . . He had money enough. . . . He came to McDowell County." [32] Such family tensions undoubtedly punctuated the lives of numerous blacks as they made their way into the coalfields during the war and early postwar years.

Whereas the vigorous recruitment of black workers characterized the war years, in the economic downturn of the early 1920s, black miners suffered rising unemployment. The Bureau of Negro Welfare and Statistics reported that the two years from July 1, 1921, to June 30, 1923, "were the most unsettled and dullest in the coal industry of this state for many years." Numerous black miners like John henry Phillips moved to farms in Virginia and North Carolina, until work in West Virginia was "more plentiful and wages higher." At the same time, other black miners left the state for Pennsylvania and other northern industrial centers. [33]

More important, as the United Mine Workers of America accelerated its organizing activities in the aftermath of World War I, coal companies intensified their efforts to retain a solid cadre of black labor. As early as June 1920, the Williamson Coal Operators Association addressed a full page advertisement to black workers: the statement emphasized "the discrimination practiced against their race in the unionized fields," where the United Mine Workers held contracts with the operators of the northern Appalachian mines. Logan County coal operators developed a pamphlet for black workers that exaggerated the virtues of coal mining in the area. "You are now living in the best coal field in the country, working six days a week in perfect harmony and on the seventh day resting, where there are churches and schools furnished by the coal company, while in the so-called Union fields, churches and schools are not furnished. . . . You are getting better pay than any other field and better coal."[34]

During the early postwar years, the Bureau of Negro Welfare and Statistics reinforced the operators' lively campaigns to keep black workers. Under its black director, T. Edward Hill, an attorney and business manager of the *McDowell Times*, the bureau often served the labor needs of the bituminous coal industry. In 1921–22, for example, the bureau proudly proclaimed credit for deterring over 100 black men from joining the violent "Armed March" of miners on Logan and Mingo counties. Equally important, the bureau recognized the cyclical swings of the coal industry. When work was "irregular and wages reached a certain minimum," the bureau observed that hundreds of black miners moved to nearby southern farms until work resumed at higher wages. In an effort to help stabilize the black labor force, the BNWS advocated the permanent resettlement of southern blacks on available West Virginia farm land.[35]

As the coal industry recovered between roughly 1923 and 1928, black migration to the region also resumed. The black population in southern West Virginia increased from close to 60,000 in 1920 to nearly 80,000 in 1930. By 1925, the black coal mining labor force had increased to an estimated 20,300, about 27 percent of the labor force as immigrants continued to decline to less than 14 percent. When black workers left the area during the economic downturn and coal strikes of the early postwar years, other blacks, some serving as strike-breakers, had slowly filled their places. It was during this period that the Deep South states of Alabama, Georgia, and South Carolina dramatically increased their numbers. Alabama moved up from third to second place in the number of West Virginia blacks born elsewhere. Blacks born in Alabama now made up nearly 10 percent of the number born in other states. Unlike the black migration to the industrial North, however, the Upper South and border states of Virginia, North Carolina, Tennessee, and Kentucky continued to dominate the migration stream to West Virginia.[36]

Established black kin and friendship networks played a key role in stimulating the new cycle of black migration into the coal fields. Born in Leesville, Virginia, Sidney Lee visited relatives in the region for several months off and on, before moving to Omar, Logan County in 1926. Beginning at age 15, Lee had alternated between work on the Virginian Railroad and farm labor, before taking his first permanent job loading coal in southern West Virginia. Lester Phillips (son of John Henry and Catherine Phillips) returned to southern West Virginia to work in the mines shortly after his sister married a Pageton, McDowell County, man during the late 1920s. Salem Wooten's oldest brother, after migrating to southern West Virginia from Virginia in the early postwar years, assisted seven of his younger brothers to enter the coal fields, most arriving during the mid-to-late 1920s. The youngest, Salem Wooten, was the last to arrive. He migrated during the early 1930s. According to Elizabeth Broadnax, she and her mother moved from North Carolina to Capels, McDowell County, during the 1920s because her brother lived and worked there.[37]

The growing importance of black kin and friendship networks was also reflected in the rising number of West Virginia-born black miners. In increasing numbers southern-born fathers taught their West Virginia-born sons how to mine coal. This process gained momentum during the 1920s. In 1923, the Virginia-born miner, James B. Harris took his 15-year old son into the mines at Giatto, Mercer County. The young Charles T. Harris entered coal mining from a coal mining family, he later recalled, "as a career." "I never even thought about it. Just coal mining was all I knew. My father was a coal miner." Three years later, with his father and cousin, Preston Turner loaded his first ton of coal at the Winding Gulf Colliery Company. Under the shadow of the impending Depression, Lawrence Boling entered the mines of Madison, Boone County, in 1930. While Gus Boling had hoped to educate his son, he now relented and carried the young man into the mines. Lawrence Boling later recalled: "My dad and I talked it over. . . . Things were tough in the mines. . . . I seen I didn't have a chance to go to college even if I finished high school. So I decided at that point that I wanted to work in the mines and would be helping him too. I went in with him. . . . He was responsible for me for a certain length of time."[38]

During the 1920s, like most of their white counterparts, Afro-Americans entered the mines primarily as unskilled coal loaders. They worked mainly in underground positions, called "inside labor," as opposed to outside or surface works. In 1922 and again in 1927, the BNWS reported that more than 90 percent of black miners worked as manual coal loaders or as common day laborers. The percentage of black laborers declined during the Great Depression. Yet, according to Laing's survey of twenty coal-mining operations, over 75 percent of black miners continued to work in such positions in 1932.[39]

Coal loading was the most common, difficult, and hazardous job in the mine. Yet, blacks often preferred it because it paid more than other manual labor jobs and "provided the least supervision with the greatest amount of personal freedom in work hours." As one black miner recalled, coal loaders could make more money because they were paid by the ton, and could increase their wages by increasing their output.[40] On the other hand, while the average wage-rates for coal loading were indeed higher than most outside jobs, inside work was subject to greater seasonal fluctuations and greater health hazards than outside positions.

Although coal loading was classified as unskilled work, it did require care and skill. For the novice especially, the apparently simple act of loading coal into a waiting train car could not be taken for granted. Watt Teal's father taught him techniques for preserving his health as well as his life. As an important component of his informal apprenticeship, Watt Teal learned how to carefully pace his work. Indeed, he concluded, "There is a little art to it. . . . After all you could load it the wrong way and get broke down and you couldn't do business. . . . So [at first] you get so much on the shovel and start off and get used to it and then you can gradually pick up more on the shovel."[41]

Coal loading involved much more than merely pacing the work, though. It took over an hour of preparation before the miner could lift his first shovel of coal. The miner deployed an impressive repertoire of skills: the techniques of dynamiting coal, including knowledge of various gases and the principles of ventilation; the establishment of roof supports to prevent dangerous cave-ins; and the persistent canvassing of mines for potential hazards. Referring to the training he received from his brother, Salem Wooten recalled: "The first thing he taught me was . . . my safety, how to set props and posts. Wood posts were set up to keep the slate and rocks from caving in on you . . . safety first."[42]

Wooten's brother also taught him techniques for blasting coal: how to drill holes with an auger and place several sticks of dynamite in them properly, how to judge atmospheric conditions and be acutely sensitive, not only to his own safety, but to the safety of fellow workers as well. Salem Wooten also learned the miner's distinctive vocabulary of terms like "bug dust," particles of coal remaining after machines undercut the coal; "kettlebottom," a huge fossilized rock, responsible for numerous injuries and even deaths, when it dislodged from the roof of mines; and the frequently shouted "Fire! Fire in the Hole!" warning fellow workers of an impending dynamite blast.[43]

Coal loading was not the only job that blacks entered. In small numbers, they worked in skilled positions as machine operators, brakemen, and motormen. In its 1921–22 report, the Bureau of Negro Welfare and Statistics proudly announced its success, although modest, in placing "three machine men, two motormen . . . [as well as] 57 coal loaders and company men." Labor advertisements sometimes specified the broad range of jobs available to Afro-Americans: "Coal Miners, Coke Oven Men, Day Laborers, Contract Men and Helpers, Motormen, Track Layers, Machine Runners, Mule Drivers, Power Plant Men, and other good jobs to offer around the mines." According to state-wide data, the number of black motormen and machine men (or mechanics) increased nearly 150 percent, from 218 in 1921 to 536 in 1927. Although their numbers declined thereafter, some blacks retained their foothold in skilled positions through the 1920s. Among these, machine-running was the most lucrative. Between 1926 and 1929, for example, Roy Todd and his brothers worked as machine operators at the Island Creek Coal Company, at Holden, Logan County. On this job, Roy Todd recalled, he made enough money to buy a new car; bank $100 monthly; pay his regular expenses and still have "money left over."[44]

However skillful black loaders may have become, coal loading took its toll on the health of black men. Some men literally broke themselves down loading coal. Pink Henderson painfully recalled: "My daddy got so he couldn't load coal. He tried to get company work [light labor, often on the outside] but the doctor turned him down, because he couldn't do nothing. He done broke his self down. . . . My brothers done the same thing. They used to be the heavy loaders." Moreover, all coal loaders, black and white, careful and careless, were subject to the inherent dangers of coal mining: black lung, then commonly called "miners' asthma," the slow killer of miners caused by the constant inhalation of coal dust; explosions, the most publicized and dramatic cause of miners' deaths; and slate falls, the largest and most consistent killer of miners. All miners and their families had to learn to live with the fear of death, although few fully succeeded. As one black miner and his wife recalled, reminiscent of Booker T. Washington's experience in the early prewar years: "That fear is always there. That fear was there all the time, because . . . you may see [each other] in the morning and never [see each other] any more in the flesh."[45]

As Afro-Americans abandoned southern life and labor for work in the coal fields, the foregoing evidence suggests that their rural and semirural work culture gradually gave way to the imperatives of industrial capitalism. New skills, work habits, and occupational hazards moved increasingly to the fore, gradually supplanting their older rural work patterns and rhythms of "alternating periods of light and intensive labor." Indeed, with the dramatic expansion of their numbers during World War I and the 1920s, black miners increasingly experienced southern West Virginia as a permanent place to live and labor.[46]

The working lives of black women also underwent change in southern West Virginia, but it was less dramatic for them than it was for black men. Along with their regular domestic tasks, working-class black women nearly universally tended gardens. Although the men and boys cleared and broke the ground, women and children planted, cultivated, harvested, and canned the produce: corn, beans, cabbage, collard and turnip greens, supplemented by a few hogs, chickens, and sometimes a cow.[47] Gardening not only nourished the bodies of black men, women, and children, it also symbolized links with their rural past. The pattern soon became deeply entrenched in the economic and cultural traditions of the region. Not yet 11 years old, while confined to a local hospital bed, a young black female penned her first verse, illuminating the role of black women in the life of the coal fields:

> When I get [to be] an old lady,
> I tell you what I'll do,
> I'll patch my apron, make my dress
> And hoe the garden too.[48]

Although Afro-American coal mining families gained a significant foothold in the bituminous coal industry, not all blacks who entered the coal fields were equally committed to coal mining life. Some of the men were indeed gamblers, pimps, and bootleggers. Middle-class black leaders attacked these men as "Jonahs" and "kid-glove dudes," who moved into the coal fields, exploited the miners, and, often, moved on.[49] Like European immigrants, other black men used coal mining as a means of making money to buy land and farms in other parts of the South. On the eve of World War I, for example, Ike Mitchell came to West Virginia from South Carolina. After two years, he had saved $2,000 in cash from his job in the Kanawha-New River coal field. During the early war years, he took his money, returned his family to South Carolina, bought land, and began raising cotton for the market. In its 1921–22 report, the Bureau of Negro Welfare and Statistics noted that, some black miners continued to work, sacrifice, and save in order "to buy a farm 'down home,' pay the indebtedness upon one already purchased or, after getting a 'little money ahead,' return to the old home." Again in 1923–24, the bureau reported that several hundred blacks in the mines of McDowell, Mercer, and Mingo Counties either owned farms in Virginia and North Carolina themselves or had relatives who owned farms there. In order to curtail the temporary and often seasonal pattern of black migration and work in the mines, the BNWS accelerated its campaign for the permanent resettlement of blacks on available West Virginia farm land.[50]

If some black workers entered the region on a temporary and often seasonal basis, shifting back and forth between southern farms and mine labor, it was the up and down swings of the business cycle that kept most black miners on the move. Although there was an early postwar economic depression in the coal economy, as noted above, it was the onslaught of the Great Depression that revealed in sharp relief the precarious footing of the black coal mining proletariat. In December 1930, the black columnist S. R. Anderson of Bluefield reported that "more hunger and need" existed among Bluefield's black population "than is generally known. It is going to be intensified during the hard months of January and February."[51] In the economic downturn that followed, their numbers dropped from 19,600 in 1929 to 18,500 in 1931, though fluctuating only slightly between 26 and 27 percent of the labor force. Heretofore the BNWS had advocated black farm ownership as a mode of labor recruitment for the coal industry; it now advocated farming as a primary solution to permanent unemployment for a growing number of black miners.[52]

As unemployment increased during the late 1920s and early '30s, the advice of the Bureau of Negro Welfare and Statistics notwithstanding, intra-regional movement accelerated. Unlike the earlier downturn, when many black miners moved to nearby southern farms and to northern industrial centers, most now struggled to maintain their foothold in the coal mining region. Their desperation is vividly recorded in the "Hawk's Nest Tragedy" of Fayette County. In 1930, the Union Carbide Corporation commissioned the construction firm of Rinehart and Dennis of Charlottesville, Virginia, to dig the Hawk's Nest Tunnel, in order to channel water from the New River to its hydroelectric plant near the Gauley Bridge. As local historian Mark Rowh has noted: "Construction of the tunnel would mean hundreds of jobs, and many saw it as a godsend. Unfortunately, it would prove the opposite."[53]

Requiring extensive drilling through nearly four miles of deadly silica rock, in some areas approaching 100 percent, the project had claimed the lives of an estimated 500 men by its completion in 1935. Afro-Americans were disproportionately hired on the project and they were the chief victims. They made up 65 percent of the labor force and 75 percent of the inside tunnel crew. Official company reports invariably underestimated the number of casualties on the project. Even so, company reports highlight the disproportionate black deaths among the work crews. According to P. H. Faulconer, president of Rinehart and Dennis, for example, "In the 30 months from the start of driving to the end of 1932, a total of 65 deaths of all workmen, both outside and inside the tunnel occurred, six whites and fifty-nine colored." Although the firm was aware of a safer, wet-drilling method, it elected to use the more efficient, but lethal dry-drilling process, allowing workers to use water "only when state inspectors were expected at the scene."[54] The Depression was not only a period of extensive unemployment, as the Hawk's Nest calamity demonstrates, it was also a time of excessive labor exploitation.

If unemployment pressed some men into the lethal Hawk's Nest Tunnel, it also required substantial contributions from black women. While he worked on a variety of temporary jobs during the early Depression years, Pink Henderson recalled that his wife "canned a lot of stuff," kept two or three hogs, raised chickens, and made clothing for the family. In 1930, the U.S. Census Bureau reported that 57.6 percent of black families in West Virginia were comprised of 3 persons or less, compared to 37.5 percent for immigrants and 40.8 percent for American born whites; but the actual difference in household size was offset by the larger number of boarders in black families. During the late 1920s and early 1930s, for example, Mary Davis not only enabled her own family to survive hard times, she also aided the families of unemployed coal miners at her boarding house restaurant. "We were pretty fortunate," her son later recalled, "and helped a lot of people."[55]

Black migrants and their families were inextricably involved in the larger proletarianization process. Their experiences were shaped by the dynamics of class, race, and region. Yet, southern West Virginia between World War I and the Great Depression offered a unique setting for the development of black life. Blacks in the Mountain State faced fewer incidents of mob violence, less labor exploitation, and, since they retained the franchise, fewer constraints on their civil rights than their southernmost kinsmen. In 1918, for example, not one, but three black men, one a coal miner, were elected to the state legislature from southern West Virginia.[56]

Compared to the urban North, however, blacks in the coalfields confronted a legal system of racial segregation. They also faced greater injustice before the law and a more hostile social environment, including a lynching atmosphere, when they allegedly violated segregationist norms. Although lynchings virtually disappeared from the coalfields during the 1920s, in 1919, a white mob lynched two black coal miners at Chapmanville, Logan County. Lynching sentiment remained just below the surface throughout the period. The State retained its statute against interracial marriage, and whites threatened to lynch any black man accused of raping a white woman.[57]

Despite important contrasts, based on the peculiar interplay of class and race in the southern mountains, migration to southern West Virginia was an experience that black miners shared with black and white workers in different regional, national, and international settings. Their socioeconomic footing remained volatile, as reflected in the significant economic contributions of black women, work in the deadly Hawk's Nest Tunnel, and substantial geographic mobility throughout the period. Yet, through their southern kin and friendship networks, black coal miners played a crucial role in organizing their own migration to the region. They facilitated their own entrance into the industrial labor force, and to a substantial degree shaped their own experience under the onset of industrial capitalism.

NOTES

Portions of this article have appeared in Joe William Trotter, Jr., *Coal, Class, and Color: Blacks in Southern West Virginia, 1915–32* (Urbana: University of Illinois Press, 1990). Reprinted by permission of University of Illinois Press.

1. Ronald L. Lewis, "Migration of Southern Blacks to the Central Appalachian Coalfields: The Transition from Peasant to Proletarian," *Journal of Southern History* 55, no. 1 (Feb. 1989): 77–102; Robert P. Stuckert, "Black Populations of the Southern Appalachian Mountains," *Phylon* 48, no. 2 (Summer 1987): 141–51.

2. Ronald D Eller, *Miners, Millhands, and Mountaineers: Industrialization of the Appalachian South, 1880–1930* (Knoxville, TN: University of Tennessee Press, 1982), pp. 128–40; David A. Corbin, *Life, Work, and Rebellion in the Coal Fields: The Southern West Virginia Coal Miners, 1880–1922* (Urbana: University of Illinois Press, 1981), pp. 1–7; Darold T. Barnum, *The Negro in the Bituminous Coal Industry* (Philadelphia: University of Pennsylvania Press, 1970), pp. 1–24; Sterling D. Spero and Abram L. Harris, *The Black Worker: The Negro and the Labor Movement* (1931; reprint, New York: Atheneum, 1968), pp. 206–45; Ronald L. Lewis, *Black Coal Miners in America: Race, Class, and Community Conflict, 1770–1980* (Lexington, KY: University Press of Kentucky, 1987), chapter 7; West Virginia Department of Mines, *Annual Reports* (Charleston, WV: 1909, 1910).

3. John A. Williams, *West Virginia and the Captains of Industry* (Morgantown, WV: West Virginia University, 1976), pp. 109–29; Charles Kenneth Sullivan, "Coal Men and Coal Towns: Development of the Smokeless Coalfields of Southern West Virginia, 1873–1923" (Ph.D. diss., University of Pittsburgh, 1979); Otis K. Rice, *West Virginia: A History* (Lexington, KY: University Press of Kentucky, 1985), pp. 184–204; Corbin, *Life, Work, and Rebellion*, pp. 3–4; Eller, *Miners, Millhands, and Mountaineers*, pp. 132–40, 165–68; Randall G. Lawrence, "Appalachian Metamorphosis: Industrializing Society on the Central Appalachian Plateau, 1860–1913" (Ph.D. diss., Duke University, 1983), pp. 28–42, 64–81.

4. Corbin, *Life, Work, and Rebellion*, pp. 8, 43–52; Eller, *Miners, Millhands, and Mountaineers*, pp. 129, 165–75; Barnum, *The Negro in the Bituminous Coal Mining Industry*,

pp. 1–24; Lawrence, "Appalachian Metamorphosis," pp. 224–28; Price V. Fishback, "Employment Conditions of Blacks in the Coal Industry, 1900–1930" (Ph.D. diss., University of Washington, 1983), pp. 44–51; Lewis, *Black Coal Miners in America*, ch. 7; Kenneth R. Bailey, "A Judicious Mixture: Negroes and Immigrants in the West Virginia Mines, 1880–1917," *West Virginia History* 34 (1973): 141–61. On the exclusion of blacks from northern industries, see William H. Harris, *The Harder We Run: Black Workers Since the Civil War* (New York: Oxford University Press, 1982), pp. 29–50; Philip S. Foner, *Organized Labor and the Black Worker, 1619–1973* (New York: International Publishers, 1974), pp. 64–135; Spero and Harris, *The Black Worker*, pp. 53–115; U.S. Bureau of the Census, *The Negro Population in the United States, 1790–1915* (1918; reprint, New York: Arno Press 1968), p.85; U.S. Bureau of the Census, *Negroes in the United States, 1920–1932* (1935; reprint, New York: Arno Press 1966), p. 45; *Fourteenth Census of the U.S. (1920)*, vol. 2, pp. 636–40.

5. Booker T. Washington, *Up From Slavery* (1901; reprint, New York: Bantam Books, 1967), pp. 26–28; R. G. Hubbard, et al. (Malden Homecoming Committee), to Booker T. Washington, 29 May 1913, in B. T. W. Tuskegee Records, Lecture File, boxes 811 and 816, Booker T. Washington Papers (Library of Congress); Louis R. Harlan, *Booker T. Washington: The Making of a Black Leader* (New York: Oxford University Press, 1972), pp. 28–29.

6. James T. Laing, "The Negro Miner in West Virginia" (Ph.D. diss., Ohio State University, 1933), pp. 64–69; J. M. Callahan, *Semi-Centennial History of West Virginia* (Charleston, WV, 1913), also quoted in Laing, p. 64; A. A. Taylor, *The Negro in the Reconstruction of Virginia* (Washington, DC: Associated Publishers, 1926), also quoted in Laing, pp. 64–65.

7. Laing, "Negro Miner," pp. 64–69; Callahan, *Semi-Centennial History of West Virginia*, also quoted in Laing, p. 64; Taylor, *The Negro in the Reconstruction of Virginia*, also quoted in Laing, pp. 64–65.

8. Corbin, *Life, Work, and Rebellion*, pp. 64–65; Lewis, *Black Coal Miners in America*, chapter 7; and Joe William Trotter, Jr., *Coal, Class, and Color: Blacks in Southern West Virginia, 1915–32* (Urbana: University of Illinois Press, 1990), chapter 3.

9. Ralph W. White, "Another Lesson from the East St. Louis Lynching," *McDowell Times*, 20 July 1917; Carter G. Woodson, *A Century of Negro Migration* (1918; reprint New York: AMS Press, 1970), pp. 147–66.

10. Lester Phillips and Ellen Phillips, interviews, 20 July 1983; Salem Wooten, interview, 25 July 1983; see also Reginald Millner, "Conversations with the Ole Man: The Life and Times of a Black Appalachian Coal Miner," *Goldenseal* 5 (Jan.–Mar. 1979): 58–64; Tim R. Massey, "I Didn't Think I'd Live to See 1950: Looking Back with Columbus Avery," *Goldenseal* 8 (Spring, 1982): 32–40; Eller, *Miners, Millhands, and Mountaineers*, pp. 153–98; Corbin, *Life, Work, and Rebellion*, chapters 7, 8, and 9; Fishback, "Employment Conditions," pp. 72–82, 116–20.

11. Wooten, 25 July 1983.

12. Robert N. Bell, U.S. Attorney, Northern District of Alabama, to U.S. Attorney General, 25 Oct. 1916; and Alexander D. Pitts, U.S. Attorney, Southern District of Alabama, to Samuel J. Graham, U.S. Assistant Attorney General, 27 Oct. 1916, both in Department of Justice, Record Group No. 60, Straight Numerical File No. 182363 (Washington, DC, National Archives). Thelma O. Trotter, conversation, 1 Aug. 1983; Solomon Woodson, conversation, 9 Nov. 1985.

13. Florette Henri, *Black Migration: Movement North, 1900–1920* (Garden City: Anchor Press Doubleday, 1975), pp. 132–73; Laing, "The Negro Miner," chapter 4; Eller, *Miners, Millhands, and Mountaineers*, pp. 168–72; Corbin, *Life, Work, and Rebellion*, pp. 61–63; Roy Todd, interview, 18 July 1983.

14. Thornton Wright, interview, 27 July 1983; W. L. McMillan, Omar, WV, to R. L. Thornton, Three Notch, AL, 2 Nov. 1916, Department of Justice, Record Group No. 60, Straight Numerical File no. 182363; "Migration Study, Negro Migrants, Letters Fr. (Type-

script), 1916–18,'' in National Urban League Papers Series 6, Box 86 (Washington, DC, Library of Congress).

15. McMillan to Thornton, 2 Nov. 1916; West Virginia Bureau of Negro Welfare and Statistics (WVBNWS), *Biennial Reports* (Charleston, WV), 1921–22, p. 5, and 1925–26, p. 8.

16. Phillips and Phillips, 20 July 1983; Pink Henderson, interview, 15 July 1983; Wooten, 25 July 1983; Lewis, *Black Coal Miners in America*, chapters 3 and 4; McMillan to Thornton, 2 Nov. 1916; "From Alabama: Colored Miners Anxious for Organization,'' *United Mine Workers Journal (UMWJ)*, 1 June 1916; Rev. T. H. Seals, "Life in Alabama,'' *UMWJ*, 15 Sept. 1924; and "The Horrors of Convict Mines of Alabama,'' *UMWJ*, 19 Aug. 1915. Bell to U.S. Attorney, 25 Oct. 1916; Pitts to Graham, 27 Oct. 1916; "Memorandum: Willie Parker'' (recorded by Edwin Ball, General Manager, Tennessee Coal, Iron, and Railroad Company) and "Statement of Tom Jones,'' all of the preceding in Department of Justice, Record Group No. 60, Straight Numerical File No. 182363.

17. "Wanted at Once . . . ,'' 12 May 1916 and "10 Automobiles Free . . . ,'' 25 May 1917, both in *McDowell Times*; "Safety First,'' "Go North,'' "Wanted,'' and "Employment Office,'' in U.S. Department of Labor, Box 2 folder 13/25, Record Group No. 174 (Washington, DC, National Archives).

18. Bell to U.S. Attorney General, 25 Oct. 1916; Pitts to Graham, 27 Oct. 1916; "Labor Agents Succeed in Inducing Negroes to Leave Southern Farms,'' *Atlanta Constitution*; "Memorandum: Willie Parker''; "Statement of Tom Jones''; "Early Surveys . . . Migration Study, Birmingham Summary,'' National Urban League Papers, Series 6, box 89 (Washington, DC, Library of Congress); "Safety First''; "Go North''; "Wanted''; and "Employment Office.''

19. "The Exodus,'' 18 Aug. 1916; "Southern Exodus in Plain Figures,'' 1 Dec. 1916, both in *McDowell Times*; Ralph W. White, "Another Lesson . . . ,'' 20 July 1917; "Colored Folks Enjoying Universal Industrial and Social Advancement . . . ,'' 28 July 1917, in *McDowell Times*.

20. *Conditions in the Coal Fields of Pennsylvania, West Virginia, and Ohio* (Washington, DC: Government Printing Office, 1928); for excerpts of the committee hearings, see *UMWJ*, 1 Mar. 1928; "Testimony of J. H. Reed,'' in *West Virginia Coal Fields* (Washington, DC: Government Printing Office, 1921), pp. 479–82.

21. "Idlers between Ages of Eighteen and Sixty Will Be Forced to Work,'' *McDowell Recorder*, 25 May 1917; T. Edward Hill, "Loafers and Jonahs,'' *McDowell Times*, 25 May 1917; "Dig Coal or Dig Trenches Is the Word to the Miner,'' *Raleigh Register*, 12 July 1917.

22. Hill, "Loafers and Jonahs.''

23. "Educate All the People,'' 16 April 1915; "To Whom It May Concern,'' 29 Jan. 1915; "Good People of McDowell County Outraged,'' 17 May 1918, all in *McDowell Times*; State Commissioner of Prohibition, *Fourth Biennial Report* (Charleston, WV), 1921–22.

24. Wooten, 25 July 1983; Pitts to Graham, 27 Oct. 1916.

25. Todd, 18 July 1983; Watt B. Teal, interview, 27 July 1983; Laing, "The Negro Miner,'' chapter 4.

26. Phillips and Phillips, 20 July 1983; Campbell, 19 July 1983; Bell to U.S. Attorney General, 25 Oct. 1916; Pitts to Graham, 27 Oct. 1916; WVBNWS *Biennial Report*, 1923–24, pp. 22–23; "Adams' Russel,'' 14 July 1916 and "Gannaway-Patterson,'' 22 Dec. 1916, both in *McDowell Times*; *The New River Company Employees Magazine* 2, no. 3 (9 Nov. 1924): 9–10.

27. William M. Beasley, interview, 26 July 1983; Henderson, 15 July 1983; Thomas D. Samford, U.S. Attorney, Middle District of Alabama, to U.S. Attorney General, 2 Nov. 1916, and Samford to U.S. Attorney General, 21 Oct. 1916, in Department of Justice Record Group, No. 60, Straight Numerical File No. 182363.

28. Wright, 27 July 1983.

29. Jasper Boykins to U.S. Attorney General, 16 Oct. 1916, Department of Justice, Record

Group No. 60, Straight Numerical File No. 182363. For a discussion of coercive elements in southern agriculture, see Jay R. Mandle, *The Roots of Black Poverty: The Southern Plantation Economy after the Civil War* (Durham, NC: Duke University Press, 1978).

30. Pitts to Graham, 27 Oct. 1916.

31. Todd, 18 July 1983.

32. Wooten, 28 July 1983.

33. WVBNWS, *Biennial Reports*, 1921–22, pp. 57–58, and 1927–28, pp. 17–19; Phillips and Phillips, 20 July 1983; Laing, "The Negro Miners in West Virginia," *Social Forces* 14 (1936): 416–22; Laing, "The Negro Miner," chapter 5.

34. "Discrimination Against the Negro," *Bluefield Daily Telegraph*, 20 June 1920; "Negro Tricked into Logan County . . . ," *UMWJ*, 15 June 1921, includes extensive excerpts of the operator's pamphlet to black workers.

35. WVBNWS, *Biennial Reports*, especially the reports for 1921–22, pp. 38–41, and 1923–24, pp. 29–35.

36. WVBNWS, *Biennial Reports*, 1923–24, pp. 39–45; Children's Bureau, U.S. Department of Labor, *The Welfare of Children in Bituminous Coal Mining Communities in West Virginia* (Washington, DC: Government Printing Office, 1923), p. 5; U.S. Bureau of the Census, *The Negro Population in the United States, 1790–1915*, p. 85; *Negroes in the United States, 1920–32*, p. 45; *Fourteenth Census of the U.S.*, vol. 2, pp. 636–40.

37. Sidney Lee, interview, 19 July 1983; Phillips and Phillips, 20 July 1983; Wooten, 25 July 1983; R. Lawrence (interview with Eliza Broadnax), " 'Make a Way Out of Nothing': One Black Woman's Trip from North Carolina to the McDowell County Coalfields," *Goldenseal* 5, no. 4 (Oct.–Dec. 1979): 27–31.

38. North Dickerson, interview, 28 July 1983; Charles T. Harris, interview, 18 July 1983; Preston Turner, interview, 26 July 1983; Lawrence Boling, interview, 18 July 1983.

39. WVBNWS, *Biennial Report*, 1921–22, pp. 57–58, and 1927–28, pp. 17–19; Laing, "The Negro Miner," p. 195.

40. Laing, "The Negro Miners in West Virginia," pp. 416–22; Laing, "The Negro Miner," chapter 5; Dickerson, 28 July 1983.

41. Teal, 27 July 1983; Laing, "The Negro Miner," chapter 5. For general insight into the miner's work, see Carter G. Goodrich, *The Miner's Freedom* (1925, reprint, New York: Arno Press, 1971), and Keith Dix, *Work Relations in the Coal Industry: The Handloading Era, 1880–1930* (Morgantown, WV: West Virginia University, Institute for Labor Studies, 1977), chapters 1 and 2.

42. Wooten, interview, 25 July 1983; Harris, interview, 18 July 1983; Leonard Davis, interview, 28 July 1983.

43. Wooten, 25 July 1983. While some scholarly accounts refer to the particles left by the undercutting machine as "buck dust," black miners used the term "bug dust." Indeed, the nickname of one black miner was "Bug Dust." See Laing, "The Negro Miner," p. 171; Dix, *What's a Coal Miner to Do?: The Mechanization of Coal Mining and Its Impact on Coal Miners* (Pittsburgh: University of Pittsburgh Press, 1988), chapter 1; and Goodrich, *The Miner's Freedom*, p. xx.

44. WVBNWS, *Biennial Report*, 1921–22, pp. 58–59, and 1927–28, pp. 17–19; "Safety First"; "Go North"; "Wanted"; "Employment Office"; "Wanted Sullivan Machine Men," *Logan Banner*, 8 June 1923; Todd, interview, 18 July 1983; Beasley, interview, 26 July 1983. See also Dix, *Work Relations* chapter 1; Laing, "The Negro Miner," pp. 264–65; Fishback, "Employment Conditions," chapter 6; and Dix, *Work Relations in the Coal Industry*, chapter 1.

45. Henderson, interview, 15 July 1983; Fishback, "Employment Conditions," pp. 182–229; Eller, *Miners, Millhands, and Mountaineers*, pp. 178–82; Walter Moorman and Margaret Moorman, interview, 14 July 1983. For recurring reports of black casualties, see "Six Miners Killed in Explosion at Carswell," *Bluefield Daily Telegraph*, 19 July 1919; "Gary (Among the Colored People)," 11 Dec. 1923, 2 Jan. 1924; "Compensation for Six Injured Miners," 10 Dec. 1923; "Russel Dodson Killed Monday by Slate Fall," 14 July 1925;

"Walter McNeil Hurt in Mine," 22 July 1925, all in the *Welch Daily News*; "Negro Miner Is Killed at Thorpe," 12 June 1929; "Colored Miner Killed Friday in Slate Fall," 5 Mar. 1930; "McDowell County Continues Out in front in Mine Fatalities," 24 July 1929; "Negro Miner Electrocuted in Tidewater Mines," 9 Oct. 1929; "Hemphill Colored Miner Killed in Mining Accident," 8 Jan. 1930, all in *McDowell Recorder*.

46. For a discussion of these processes in the urban-industrial context, see Peter Gottlieb, *Making Their Own Way: Southern Blacks' Migration to Pittsburgh, 1916–30* (Urbana: University of Illinois Press, 1987); James R. Grossman, *The Land of Hope: Chicago, Black Southerners, and the Great Migration* (Chicago: University of Chicago Press, 1989); Earl Lewis, *In Their Own Interests: Race, Class, and Power in Twentieth Century Norfolk* (Berkeley: University of California Press, 1991); and Joe William Trotter, Jr., *Black Milwaukee: The Making of an Industrial Proletariat, 1915–45* (Urbana: University of Illinois Press, 1985).

47. Boling, 18 July 1983; Campbell, 19 July 1983; Beasley, 26 July 1983; and Harris, 18 July 1983; "Annual Garden Inspection at Gary Plants," 17 July 1925, and 23 July 1925; "Annual Inspection of Yards and Gardens: Consolidation Coal Company," 27 July 1925, all in *Welch Daily News*; Agricultural Extension Service, *Annual Reports* (Morgantown, WV), 1921–32, especially "Negro Work" and "Extension Work with Negroes"; "The Annual Garden and Yard Context Complete Success," *The New River Company Employees Magazine* 3, no. 1 (Sept. 1925): 3–4 and 2, no. 2 (Oct. 1924): 8–9; "55 Individual Awards Made Today in Yard and Garden Contests," *McDowell Recorder*, 31 July 1929.

48. The Peters Sisters, *War Poems* (Beckley, WV: n.p., 1919), p. 7.

49. See note 21 above, especially Hill, "Loafers and Jonahs."

50. "How a Coal Miner Can Save Money," *McDowell Times*, 19 Feb. 1915; Laing, "The Negro Miner," chapters 3 and 4. Also see "Local Items," *McDowell Times*, 26 Mar. 1915; WVBNWS, *Biennial Report*, 1921–22, pp. 5–11, 38–41, and 1923–24, pp. 8–10, 39–45; "Kimball (Colored News)," *Welch Daily News*, 28 Jan. 1924; "Among Our Colored," *The New River Company Employees Magazine*, various issues, 1924–30; "Agricultural Extension Work in Mining Towns," Agricultural Extension Service, *Annual Reports*, 1921–26.

51. S. R. Anderson, "News of the Colored People," *Bluefield Daily Telegraph*, 28 Dec. 1930; WVBNWS, *Biennial Reports*, 1929–32, pp. 12–14.

52. WVBNWS, *Biennial Reports*, 1929–32, pp. 4–7; Laing, "The Negro Miner," pp. 254, 503–504.

53. Martin Cherniack, *The Hawk's Nest Incident: America's Worst Industrial Disaster* (New Haven: Yale University Press, 1986), pp. 18–19, 89–91; Mark Rowh, "The Hawk's Nest Tragedy: Fifty Years Later," *Goldenseal* 7, no. 1 (1981): 31–32.

54. Cherniack, *The Hawk's Nest Incident*, pp. 18–19, 90–91; Rowh, "The Hawk's Nest Tragedy," pp. 31–32.

55. Henderson, 15 July 1983; Davis, 28 July 1983; *Fifteenth Census of the United States (1930)*, vol. 6, p. 1428.

56. Trotter, *Coal, Class, and Color*, especially chapter 9. Cf. George C. Wright, *Life Behind a Veil: Blacks in Louisville, Kentucky* (Baton Rouge: Louisiana State University Press, 1985). Wright adopts the notion of "polite racism," in order to highlight the nature of race relations in that border city compared to further south.

57. Trotter, *Coal, Class, and Color*, particularly chapter 5.

Rethinking the Great Migration
A Perspective from Pittsburgh

Peter Gottlieb

The noted historian Carter G. Woodson probably was the first to place African-Americans' mass movement from the South to northern cities during World War I in historical perspective. In 1918, he observed that "the migration of the blacks from the Southern States . . . is nothing new." Having surveyed the preceding hundred years of black history, he published *A Century of Negro Migration* at the very height of the wartime migration to show "how the Negroes in the United States have struggled under adverse circumstances to flee from bondage and oppression in quest of a land offering asylum to the oppressed and opportunity to the unfortunate."[1] His theme naturally fitted an epoch that bridged slavery and freedom, in which migrations included forced transplanting, colonization, and voluntary movements.

Though we occupy a very different position from Woodson's in relationship to the Great Migration of 1916–1930, the 1990s offer a vantage point as good in many ways for gaining perspective on that episode of geographic movement. In fact, we can survey another century of black migration in order to place the 1916–1930 era in context. From the 1870s to the 1970s, African-Americans traveled out of the southern hinterland to make a place for themselves in the emerging urban, industrial society of the United States. It was Woodson's contribution to point to the long precedent for the Great Migration; we can start to locate that population shift within the overarching transformation of African-American life which began after Emancipation.

This essay is a contribution to the historical assessment of black migration from the end of Reconstruction to the Civil Rights struggle. In particular, though, it is an attempt to place the Great Migration from 1916 to 1930 in the context of blacks' northward movement from the 1870s to the 1970s. Drawing on the example of migration to Pittsburgh, Pennsylvania, and its surrounding industrial region (Allegheny County), it examines the dynamics of blacks' movement to northern cities as a way of understanding both the underlying conditions from which migration sprang as well as the distinctive character of the Great Migration.

Recent studies of African-American migration have demonstrated the migrants' creative role in their geographic movement. Unlike earlier investigations that primarily concerned the exterior facets of migration—the causes, destinations, numbers of migrants, and living conditions in origin and destination areas—the newer studies focus on the experience of geographic movement. Rather than explore only why and where southerners moved, this literature also reconstructs how they moved. It looks at the structures of group life and the values, attitudes, perceptions, and status that migrants brought to their movement. This view moves the forces that produce migration into the background and places the migrants themselves closer to the center of the geographic movement. Here the picture is not one of economic, political, or social conditions shuttling rural peoples from country to city. The emerging portrayal of African-American migration shows men and women responding to these conditions on the basis of deep-rooted social practices and customs, developing a pattern of movement which reflected both the general causes of migration and their own social organization and aspirations.[2]

Approached in this way, African-Americans' voluntary migration springs from an interplay between socioeconomic structures and the migrants' community and culture. Migrants draw in particular ways on various resources to contend with inducements stemming from socioeconomic structures. The way in which African-Americans engage their resources with the pressures on them to move creates a migration dynamic—the motive force behind their movement. From the end of the Civil War to the 1960s, the structures of southern agricultural backwardness, African-Americans' lack of land, capital, and occupational skills, and racial segregation and discrimination conditioned geographic mobility. But particular inducements to migration changed over time, as did the material and cultural resources that African-Americans deployed in different ways to make their journeys. Thus the dynamic of northward migration shifted from one period to another, marking distinct phases in the 100-year flow of African-Americans out of their native region.

We can begin to explore the dynamics of northward migration by reviewing the genesis of blacks' World War I movement to Pittsburgh, examining factors in both the South and the North that contributed to the particular energy of that migration. Then we can look at the episodes of migration that preceded and followed the World War I movement. For the purposes of this essay, periods of geographic movement before and after the Great Migration will be grouped respectively and discussed as the pre-migration and post-migration phases. Combining several different migration episodes in this way obscures some of the important differences among them but highlights the dynamics in each period of time.

We usually describe the Great Migration in terms of several characteristics that distinguished the movement during World War I and the 1920s. First, there was a rapid growth in the northward migration streams when hundreds of thousands of southern blacks began journeys to eastern and midwestern cities. Behind this sudden increase in the number of migrants were material and social forces that simultaneously encouraged blacks to leave their rural homes and attracted them to the northern destinations. Finally, two results of the wartime migration have seemed most salient: the entry of black migrants to industrial jobs previously closed to them; and the élan of the migrants themselves, which reflected an awareness of a new historical period beginning and their power to enter it on advantageous terms.

Viewed from Pittsburgh, the Great Migration displayed most of these aspects. Black newcomers from the South began flooding into the city and its surrounding industrial district a little after the onset of the general northward movement during World War I. From 1916 to 1919, the Pittsburgh area's workshops, mines, transportation facilities, construction crews, hotels, and private homes badly needed employees to replace men going into the army and women shifting to new and better-paying jobs. The European conflict disrupted the flow of foreign-born workers to Pittsburgh on which the city's employers depended for their labor force and even drew some of Pittsburgh's immigrant workers into the armies of their native countries. The arriving southern blacks wanted the vacant jobs and the wages they paid that were two or three times higher than daily earnings in the South. As news of job openings and comparatively high wages spread through southern communities, African-Americans expressed an eagerness to reach Pittsburgh and to learn more about conditions there. "I have a very large family and would like very much to come north if I could get a good job for all of my folks . . . ", wrote one man from Georgia in 1922. Another prospective migrant stated, " . . . if I can get [an] inside Job for the winter I will get rady [sic] and come in short."[3]

Beneath this tableau of enthusiastic northward movement, powerful inducements to migration were at work. Primary among these was demand for African-American labor. Its source and its impact on male and female workers differed according to northern city or industry, but labor demand influenced most aspects of migrants' journeys and subsequent experiences. The male newcomers in wartime Pittsburgh were wanted for jobs both where they had customarily been employed, and, more noticeably, where few had been hired before—in the large, integrated steel mills and in some of the foundries, machine shops, and electrical equipment factories. Several large employers who had never before hired African-Americans enrolled hundreds after 1915, including Oliver Iron and Steel, Pittsburgh Forge and Iron, Duquesne Steel Foundry, and Mackintosh-Hemphill. The explosive growth during World War I in the number of black laborers in such Pittsburgh workplaces was an indicator of the demand for their services. By 1920, black iron and steel laborers alone had increased nearly 500% over the number in the Pittsburgh area in 1910.[4]

While male migrants could enter jobs in heavy industry, construction, and transportation, female migrants in Pittsburgh during the war had a much smaller range of job possibilities. The women could occasionally find temporary places in the packing and shipping rooms of department stores and in a few industrial plants, but they most often were limited to the same occupations they had had before the war: cooking, cleaning, and washing in private homes. Black men had a definite advantage over black women, both in terms of their expanding work opportunities and in the wage differential between their new jobs and their old ones.[5]

Labor demand in rural and urban areas of the South also shaped the dynamic of the Great Migration. Though rural African-Americans faced natural disasters and threats to cash crop harvests, as a group they were not losing their place on the land. It is true that flooding of homes and crop lands in 1916 at least temporarily uprooted families in certain localities of Alabama.[6] More significant was the destruction of cotton crops by boll weevils that had become a fact of agricultural life since the turn of the century. Dwindling cotton harvests in many areas did make life precarious for thousands of African-American cultivators, particularly in South Carolina and the Georgia Piedmont during the early 1920s.[7] Some landowners and tenants, however, had learned how to use pesticides on weevils or how to grow other crops until the infestation passed, and rising prices for the smaller total harvest sometimes yielded higher incomes for successful farmers.[8] This was especially the case during World War I, when demand for American cotton rose sharply. Despite weevils and natural disasters, agricultural incomes in the South increased during the War and postwar years, bringing a measure of prosperity to rural African-Americans as well. This reflected only a trickle from the net gains of the wartime cotton boom, yet reports from farming districts in 1917–19 refer to African-American cotton growers purchasing their first cars, buying new clothes for their families, and refurbishing homes and farm equipment.[9]

There were widening avenues to employment in southern urban areas too, where African-Americans had moved in search of work for many years. The war economy generated new jobs in industries throughout the South. Coal and iron ore mining, dockside labor, railroad and trolley line construction, and the lumber and turpentine industries all had openings in this period for male laborers. Building and maintaining military installations in the South provided additional jobs.[10] African-Americans had filled these occupations in the past, moving seasonally from farms to industrial sites to earn extra income before returning to their rural homes. The annual cycle of cotton cultivation, from ground breaking to harvest, included rest periods when men customarily looked for day labor and women tried to find domestic work in white households.[11] Other African-Americans had shifted permanently from agriculture to wage labor, filling the unskilled jobs in extractive industries, construction, transportation, and domestic service throughout the South.[12] Long experience in moving to jobs within their native region gave southern blacks added traction as they began moving toward new job openings during the war.

African-Americans' outlook on this escalating labor demand framed their responses to wartime conditions. Through life-long racial oppression in the South, they regarded work opportunities in the North in a different light from those closer to home. Codes of racial conduct and status had been tightly constricting their lives

since the 1880s. Whites had barred access to adequate education, skilled occupations, and the franchise. Segregation and discrimination were often most strictly
enforced in the southern towns and cities where African-Americans went in search
of wage labor.[13] The most prosperous black landowners and town merchants sometimes attracted whites' resentment and reprisals for lifting their living standards
above sanctioned levels.[14] Whites' growing sensitivity to any kind of encroachment
on their status, real or imagined, frequently broke out in violence against African-
Americans.[15] Middle-aged men and women saw their lives blighted in this atmosphere, but the rising generation of African-Americans, born in the late 1880s or
early 1890s and approaching adulthood around 1916, felt especially restless at the
prospect of coming of age in such an incubus.[16]

African-Americans' quick departures from the South after 1915 under such
popular slogans as "Crossing Over Jordan" and "Going to the Promised Land"
was one expression of their engagement with the inducements to northward movement, but the dynamic of the Great Migration arose more directly from other
sources. The welling migration streams were fed by myriad kinship and community
networks that channeled individuals and small groups toward specific destinations,
northern employers, urban residential districts, and even particular boarding houses
and private homes. Families carefully rearranged their members' commitments to
allow one or more to go on northern scouting expeditions while the others remained
at home to cultivate a cash crop or earn wages for the household in nearby towns
and work sites. Favorable news about job openings and housing from the dispatched
explorers attracted other family members to the North. Though this particular
deployment of kinship resources was more feasible for the minority of landowning
African-American families, it was similar to strategies that many urban and rural
families used.[17]

Community relationships among southerners supported migration in much the
same way. Neighbors, friends and workmates passed information and offered assistance to each other. Clubs, churches, and fraternal lodges sponsored migration
of their members as well. Personal connections for information and help were
preferred to impersonal contacts, but hundreds of letters of inquiry from migrants
to public agencies, social welfare organizations, newspaper editors, and employers
demonstrated African-Americans' efforts to seek information from a variety of
sources.[18]

The kinship and community resources that migrants drew on for their initial
journeys to the North also supported return trips to the South that were a prominent
feature of the Great Migration in Pittsburgh. In some families, relatives had settled
in southern towns and cities; in others, they had retained farms against all odds.
More important, the persistence of labor-intensive tenant farming and daywork in
cotton cultivation through the 1920s protected the foundations of rural African-
American communities. These conditions made it possible for northern migrants

to return to their relatives, to birthplaces, to family homes, and to native communities during the Great Migration.

Aside from sheer homesickness or loneliness, there were a variety of reasons for return journeys: illness, injury, loss of work, whites' hostility (especially in crises like strikes and race riots), and family and community celebrations. Walter H. and Laura L. each left Pittsburgh to fulfill obligations to family members who had remained in Virginia. Harrison G. and Charner C. returned to Georgia and South Carolina, respectively, to marry women from their home communities. Trips such as these were temporary returns to the South, but in the aggregate they helped to maintain migrants' links to their origin communities. Visits "down home" for some southerners in Pittsburgh became a regular part of the calendar, scheduled to coincide with the Christmas holidays or the lay-by period in cotton cultivation, when rural blacks held church revivals, barbecues, and homecoming celebrations for former residents.[19] Members of migrants' families reunited in northern cities as well, but southern communities and southern branches of migrants' kinship groups played a crucial nurturing role in the northward movement.

Social structures in Pittsburgh contributed in a number of ways to the constant circulation of migrants between their origin and destination areas. First, southerners found, at best, cramped space in the city for building their northern homes. The unskilled, casual labor to which most of them were confined resulted in frequent layoffs and periods of unemployment. For male migrants in Pittsburgh, the stagnation of the steel industry after the mid-1920s heightened this general lack of job security. Though women's domestic service jobs exposed them to labor market fluctuations somewhat less than men's industrial work did, the low wages paid to all African-Americans were insufficient for supporting homes, even when two adults in a household held jobs.[20]

Second, racial discrimination and whites' resistance to black progress generally withered the hopes for prosperity, equality, and justice that some migrants had cherished. Mortgage lenders and real estate companies prevented them from buying or renting houses outside the deteriorating housing districts, forcing severe overcrowding. Housing conditions in Pittsburgh were worse than some southerners had seen in their home towns. "I never lived in such houses in my life. We had four rooms in my home," fumed a woman from Georgia as she prepared to leave her one-room apartment and return south.[21] Hospitals, police, courts, welfare agencies, and most other public service providers treated African-Americans as inferiors. In Pittsburgh, the Hill District, where most of the city's blacks lived, was subjected to sweeps by police whenever officials detected a public concern over crime.[22]

Finally, migrants in Pittsburgh got little constructive help from long-term residents of their own urban communities as they tried to assimilate to the North. Arriving in a city whose relatively small African-American community before 1916 derived largely from Virginia, whose black work force included a significant proportion of skilled men, the World War I southern migrants stirred as much alarm as any group of greenhorn newcomers to industrial America ever had. The men and women from Low Country Georgia and South Carolina, quickly distinguished by their speech and other mannerisms, were branded "Geechies" and disregarded by their Pittsburgh brethren and by other migrants alike.[23] Alabama, North Carolina, and Tennessee migrants similarly betrayed their scant education and common labor backgrounds.[24] Some black churches and settlement houses, like the Urban League of Pittsburgh, extended practical assistance, but often with a condescending attitude toward the new arrivals' backgrounds. The migrants found many community institutions that mirrored the scorn of northern-born blacks toward them.[25] Tensions that arose from growing differences of class and culture within the African-American population were not overcome by the rising awareness of a common racial identity, actively promoted by the Pittsburgh *Courier* and by some prominent figures in the community.

Whatever the adverse circumstances that forced migrants to return South during or just after World War I, changing conditions allowed them to move north again and resume their former occupations. Southerners departed from Pittsburgh in droves in 1920–21 when the postwar boom collapsed, causing widespread unemployment. Two-fifths of the entire black population of Allegheny County left the region in that interval.[26] Federal restrictions on foreign immigration, a sharp upswing in the business cycle, and the steel industry's addition of a third shift to accommodate the new eight–hour day in continuous operations elicited a new northward surge in 1922–23.[27] Some of the migrants in this period had clearly awaited the return of prosperity. As labor demand accelerated, they wrote to Pittsburgh contacts to find out if the city's industries would hire them again. "i worked in the Diamond & Corbin iron works & several mills. i boarded in 12 ward on 30th St.," were the bona fides offered by one former resident. Another man inquired about job possibilities in Pittsburgh, though his heart was clearly set on a destination further west. " . . . I prefer Ohio, as I worked at the Firestone Rubber factory and won much fame."[28] Just as the survival of African-American rural communities in the South during the 1920s provided a sheltering base for Pittsburgh migrants, recurring demand for black labor in northern industry helped to make the Great Migration more a circulation of population than a one-way passage.

Evidence from Pittsburgh suggests that the dynamic of the Great Migration arose from conditions in the North and South that strongly induced African-Americans to move, but left them wide options and resources to do so. They met these conditions by rapidly mobilizing family and community relations, converting them to conduits of information and material support for migration. Equally significant, southern blacks quickly adapted their prior experiences in intra-regional migration and wage labor to the northward movement. The result was an initial, intense burst of out-migration followed by an energetic flow of population between north and south.

This dynamic, however, was also evanescent. It grew out of an international crisis and lasted only as long as southern blacks had a wide range of choices as well as time, income, and group resources to maximize their chances for successful movement. Before the Great Migration, inducements to move north were comparatively weak, and relatively few men and women left the South. After the migration, and especially from World War II until the 1960s, changes in southern agriculture and land tenure systems forced blacks to take refuge in urban areas, whether or not they could find employment there. Though these periods of migration preceding and following the 1916–30 era also profoundly influenced the development of African-American communities, their dynamics grew from trends that were very different from those of the Great Migration.

The dynamic of migration in the late nineteenth and early twentieth centuries probably involved southern urban social structures more than conditions in rural areas. Industrialization and racial barriers undercut blacks' livelihoods in southern cities. Labor unions in the building trades, on railroads, and in the developing metalworking industries prohibited blacks from joining or agitated to remove them from their trades. The rapidly expanding textile industry limited its work force mainly to white men and women, allowing blacks to take only the most menial non-production jobs. At the same time, segregation in urban public transportation and facilities increasingly set blacks apart in an inferior status. The widening consensus on race relations stifled careers of educated and professional southern blacks as well.[29]

To judge from the prewar migrants' areas of origin and the locus of demand for black labor in Pittsburgh, such trends in the comparatively urbanized Upper South contributed to northward movement before 1916. From the 1880s until World War I, Virginia was by far the leading state of birth for Pittsburgh blacks. Border states like Maryland and West Virginia also ranked high as birthplaces. States of birth below North Carolina were rare. This region of the South gave black men and women the most chances to gain experience in city work and living. It also had ready communication and transportation links to the urban North. Like the newcomers to Pittsburgh, migrants to Boston and New York in these years who traveled from the Tidewater region of Virginia and Maryland were often southern urban workers hoping to earn more money and enjoy greater personal security.[30]

For migrants from the Upper South, proximity to Pittsburgh and experience in urban employment afforded access to the small percentage of jobs open to African-Americans in the Steel City before World War I. Depending primarily on foreign-born whites for their labor force, Pittsburgh employers hired southern blacks only in a narrow range of jobs. Black women could work in private homes, hotels, restaurants, and train stations as cooks, laundresses, and maids. Because of their concentration in the domestic service field, female migrants to Pittsburgh before 1916 were overwhelmingly menial workers. Southern men could work in a wider spectrum of occupations and skill classifications, but, with the notable exception of a few iron mills that hired southern black men exclusively for certain tasks, black men were wanted only on the periphery of Pittsburgh's manufacturing complex. They were employed as construction laborers, freight haulers, and teamsters. A significant part entered domestic and personal service jobs as well, usually as janitors or porters.[31]

The status of prewar Pittsburgh's black iron workers offers clues to the nature of the migration dynamic in this period. Certain Pittsburgh mills recruited these experienced men from Virginia and Maryland. They came in small numbers beginning in the 1870s and 1880s, undoubtedly bringing with them links of kinship and comradeship to the black wage-earners of their origin communities. A cadre of highly skilled puddlers and rollers developed from this relatively small group.[32] The emergence of this black labor aristocracy produced an important feature of men's occupational status before the Great Migration: its resemblance to that of the entire male work force in skill level distribution. Nearly the same proportions of black men held skilled and semi-skilled jobs as did Pittsburgh's male workers as a group.[33] The nature of labor demand at this time gave comparatively good work opportunities to a select cohort of migrants.

Compared to the Great Migration, however, black women workers and their journeys to Pittsburgh were more important in the prewar dyanmic of northward movement. Indirect evidence suggests that single black women were common among Pittsburgh migrants in this period, as they were in other northern cities as well. It was during these years that homes for single black women were established in the city. Such institutions were intended to protect and support newcomers and strangers who were often employed as servants and domestic workers.[34] Although the city was a magnet primarily for men looking for jobs in metal manufacturing or mining, the number of black males and females in 1910 was evenly balanced.

The development of the agricultural South did not contribute heavily to black migration before World War I. Some Pittsburgh migrants in these years undoubtedly came from Tidewater farms, but few hailed from the major tobacco and cotton areas. Plagued by capital scarcity, low productivity, soil erosion, and boll weevils, these regions still absorbed the labor of most rural southern blacks. Their educators and leaders insisted that agriculture in the South held out the best chances for blacks' improvement. Whether following this advice or pursuing the best local opportunities available to them, black farmers achieved their highest rate of land-ownership before World War I.[35]

But neither tenants, landless laborers, nor proprietors worked solely on the same acreage for long periods; incomes from the soil were meagre even in the best years. Black cotton-growers frequently moved short distances from one plot of ground to the next and from farms to industrial jobs. Some also moved longer distances to the new cotton lands of Texas, Oklahoma, and Arkansas, or to the expanding urban frontier in Florida. This constant shifting of rural blacks indicated that their efforts to raise living standards remained within their native region and were not yet oriented to northern cities.[36]

In the post-migration era, quite different migration dynamics supplanted those of earlier years. The volume of northward movement far exceeded the levels reached from 1916 to 1930 and was sustained for nearly 20 years.[37] Framed by persisting racial oppression and lagging southern economic development, the 1945–70 period of black migration was hardly a buoyant redistribution of population around new frontiers of economic opportunity. As demand for black labor oscillated sharply in northern and west coast cities, large landowners fundamentally transformed southern agriculture at tenant farmers' and farm laborers' expense. Black out-migration from the region became a recourse, rather than a strategy, for individual and group betterment—almost a movement of resignation and despair.

Beginning in the 1930s, growing numbers of southern blacks were literally evicted from rural areas. Generally, southern agriculture changed from a labor- to a capital-intensive enterprise and sharply reduced the requirement for a resident rural labor force. Even before the adoption of tractor plows, cultivators, sprayers and harvesters in the South, efforts to stabilize farm prices in the 1930s through crop reduction put black tenant farmers and laborers off the land. In contrast to earlier periods of time, the number of rural blacks whose ties to the land were being severed far exceeded the jobs that southern urban and industrial growth could provide. Particularly in the 1930s, few of the displaced could find alternative employment in the shrunken labor markets. The small number of southern blacks moving to Pittsburgh in the late 1930s came mainly in search of shelter, though some newcomers in the 1930s got on relief rolls or obtained public works and Civilian Conservation Corps jobs.[38]

The alternatives for southern rural blacks after the 1930s shrank drastically, leaving them few choices for survival. Except for brief periods during the 1940s and 1950s, they were as much refugees as migrants. World War II production jobs briefly revived a significant migration of southern blacks to Pittsburgh, though far greater numbers went to Los Angeles, Chicago, and Detroit. A portion of this cohort probably was seizing the opportunity to escape the non-mechanized field labor that had become their lot after the mid-1930s. Thus the men and women arriving in the city in the 1940s had no long-term prospects of remaining on cotton farms. The quickening pace of agricultural mechanization after World War II— especially the introduction of motor driven harvesters—forced more southern blacks to commit themselves to urban lives. It also gradually erased the rural black communities themselves, making migrants of this period uprooted in a sense that earlier migrants had not been.[39]

The changes in cotton growing fixed northward migration in the life cycles of southern blacks for twenty–five years after World War II. Bus tickets for New York, Philadelphia, Cleveland, Detroit, Chicago, or Los Angeles became customary graduation presents for southern black high school students—their passes to the next stage of their lives. Teen-agers and young adults were prominent in the Great Migration, too, but their departures differed sharply from those of their post-World War II counterparts. The earlier migrants had assertively flung off parental authority and responsibilities to their family homes when they set out for Pittsburgh. Departing with hopes and visions for their future, they staked their claims to the expanding labor market.[40] By the 1950s and 1960s, northward journeys were no longer breaks with routine and custom, but necessary transfers to regions with higher family incomes and—in some respects—better treatment for blacks.

There were steady, well-paying manufacturing jobs for some of the post-World War II migrants, but comparatively few in Pittsburgh, where heavy industry enjoyed only a brief prosperity in the later 1940s and 1950s. Two other sectors of the labor market grew steadily more important for male newcomers: non-manufacturing industries such as construction and transportation; and clerical and sales jobs. While black men in traditional factory work declined proportionally, more black women were gaining such work. Since women were also finding opportunities in offices, stores, and in non-manufacturing industries during the 1940s and 1950s, their occupational horizons seemed to be widening just as black men's were closing in.[41]

Despite this promising trend for female black migrants, Pittsburgh's importance as a destination for southern travellers declined after 1945. By the late 1950s, the northward streams of migration detoured around the city. In 1960, only 3.4 percent of Pittsburgh's black population whose 1955 residence was known had moved to Pittsburgh in the preceding five years. Three-fifths of this increment in turn came from the South.[42] Though it had once been a beacon for southern migrants, the city clearly failed to attract newcomers after World War II, presaging the decline in northward migration everywhere which took place in the 1970s.[43]

For 100 years following the Civil War, migration was fundamental to redefining African-Americans' place in the nation's economy and body politic. Their movement out of the South was inseparably connected to their transition in status from a semi-free work force—bound to the land and to certain types of work by law and custom—to a free wage-labor population. It was also inextricably connected to the formulation of African-American citizenship, with all the implications that that held for growing participation in vital areas of national life. As a population of wage laborers struggling for economic and political rights, blacks consciously organized for migration to advance their collective interests. The way they marshalled personal, family, and community resources to plan and conduct geographic movement shaped and reshaped the dynamics of migration.

In retrospect, the Great Migration was the first era when broad reaches of the southern black population joined the northward movement. This was not a democratization in terms of the social status of the migrants: most of the movers before World War I resembled those of the Great Migration in being manual workers and farmers *cum* wage hands. It was, however, a popular mobilization for geographic movement and the potential advantages that living in the industrial north could bring. Southern blacks from diverse backgrounds, but conspicuously men and women from rural areas and small towns, hurtled through the opening which international conflict and national crisis had punched in the barriers that formerly limited their movement. The unskilled work which employers offered them and the historically unprecedented demand for their labor throughout the nation allowed black migrants a broader scope for bringing their kinship, neighborhood, workplace, and associational assets to bear on this project of self-transformation.

Though southern blacks' movement to Pittsburgh from the 1870s to the 1970s differed in some ways from the migration to other northern cities, we can still recognize the Great Migration in the city by its distinguishing characteristics. When we have further studies of black migration—both community-based and general investigations—we will be able to describe confidently how and why movement to Pittsburgh varied from that process in other places. As important as this additional research will be for our understanding of southern blacks' migration, it may well strengthen the reputation of the 1916–1930 period. For whether we place it in context or appraise it on its own terms, the Great Migration remains a singular convergence of agricultural and industrial trends that empowered southern blacks and made their entries to urban centers during that era truly remarkable.

NOTES

1. Carter G. Woodson, *A Century of Negro Migration* (New York: Russell and Russell, 1918), pp. i, 1.

2. James R. Grossman, *Land of Hope: Chicago, Black Southerners, and the Great Migration* (Chicago: University of Chicago Press, 1989); Peter Gottlieb, *Making Their Own Way: Southern Blacks' Migration to Pittsburgh, 1916–1930* (Urbana: University of Illinois Press, 1987); Joe William Trotter, Jr., *Black Milwaukee: The Making of an Industrial Proletariat, 1915–1945* (Urbana: University of Illinois Press, 1985); James Borchert, *Alley Life in Washington: Family, Community, Religion, and Folklife in the City, 1850–1970* (Urbana: University of Illinois Press, 1980); Elizabeth Pleck, *Black Migration and Poverty: Boston, 1865–1900* (New York: Academic Press, 1979).

3. J. W. Mitchell to John T. Clark, 12 Dec. 1922; Willis Chatman to John T. Clark, 21 Jan. 1923, John T. Clark Papers, Carter G. Woodson Collection (Washington, DC, Library of Congress); Abraham Epstein, *The Negro Migrant in Pittsburgh* (1918; reprint, New York: Arno Press, 1969).

4. Ira De A. Reid, "The Negro in the Major Industries and Building Trades of Pittsburgh" (M. A. thesis, University of Pittsburgh, 1915), pp. 10, 10A; *Thirteenth Census of the United States (1910)*, vol. 4, pp. 590–91; *Fourteenth Census of the United States (1920)*, vol. 4, pp. 1197–98.

5. *Thirteenth Census of the United States (1910)*, vol. 4, pp. 590–91; *Fourteenth Census of the United States (1920)*, vol. 4, pp. 1197–1200; Ira De A. Reid, *Social Conditions in the Hill District of Pittsburgh* (Pittsburgh: General Committee on the Hill Survey, 1930), pp. 55–57.

6. Emmett J. Scott, *Negro Migration during the War* (New York: Oxford University

Press, 1920), p. 14; U.S. Department of Labor, Division of Negro Economics, *Negro Migration in 1916–17* (Washington, DC: Government Printing Office, 1919), p. 60.

7. T. J. Woofter, Jr., "Negro on a Strike," *Social Forces* 2 (November 1973): 84–86; Pittsburgh *Courier*, 30 June 1923, p. 2; 7 July 1923, p. 2; 3 Nov. 1923, p. 4.

8. Robert Higgs, "The Boll Weevil, the Cotton Economy, and Black Migration," *Agricultural History* 51 (April 1976): 343–49; Pete Daniel, *Breaking the Land: The Transformation of Cotton, Tobacco, and Rice Cultures since 1880* (Urbana: University of Illinois Press, 1985), pp. 7–20.

9. Francis Long, "The Negroes of Clarke County, Georgia during the Great War," *Bulletin of the University of Georgia* 19/*Phelps-Stokes Fellowship Studies* 5 (1919): 36–37, 52; Theodore Rosengarten, *All God's Dangers: The Life of Nate Shaw* (New York, Knopf, 1974), pp. 248–51.

10. Charles Wesley, *Negro Labor in the United States, 1850–1925* (New York: Russell & Russell, 1927), pp. 248–52; Paul B. Worthman and James R. Green, "Black Workers in the New South, 1865–1915," in *Key Issues in the Afro-American Experience*, ed. Nathan I. Huggins, Martin Kilson, and Daniel M. Fox (New York: Harcourt, Brace, Jovanovich, 1971), vol. 2, pp. 52–53.

11. Rupert B. Vance, *Human Factors in Cotton Culture* (Chapel Hill: University of North Carolina Press, 1929), p. 152; Charles S. Johnson, *The Shadow of the Plantation* (Chicago: University of Chicago Press, 1934), p. 117; Benjamin J. Free, *Seasonal Employment in Agriculture* (Washington, DC: Works Progress Administration, 1938), pp. 21, 23.

12. C. Vann Woodward, *Origins of the New South* (Baton Rouge: Louisiana State University Press, 1951), pp. 360–61; Worthman and Green, "Black Workers in the New South 1865–1915," pp. 52–53.

13. Carole Marks, *Farewell—We're Good and Gone: The Great Black Migration* (Bloomington: Indiana University Press, 1989), pp. 60–67.

14. Allison Davis, Burleigh B. Gardner, and Mary R. Gardner, *Deep South: A Social Anthropological Study of Caste and Class* (Chicago: University of Chicago Press, 1941), pp. 329–31; Roger Ransom and Richard Sutch, *One Kind of Freedom: The Economic Consequences of Freedom* (Cambridge: Cambridge University Press, 1977), pp. 85–87; Rosengarten, *All God's Dangers*, pp. 305–30.

15. Joel Williamson, *The Crucible of Race: Black-White Relations in the American South since Emancipation* (New York: Oxford University Press, 1984), pp. 459–64.

16. Gottlieb, *Making Their Own Way,* pp. 26–28.

17. Grossman, *Land of Hope*, pp. 105–107; Gottlieb, *Making Their Own Way*, pp. 47–52; Elizabeth R. Bethel, *Promiseland: A Century of Life in a Negro Community* (Philadelphia: Temple University Press, 1981), pp. 171–94.

18. Emmett J. Scott, ed., "Letters of Negro Migrants of 1916–18," *Journal of Negro History* (1919): 319–30; John T. Clark, "The Migrant in Pittsburgh," *Opportunity* 1 (1923): 303.

19. Oral history interviews conducted by Peter Gottlieb: Walter H., 25 Oct. 1973 and 30 Oct. 1973; Laura L., 23 Nov. 1973; Charner C., 21 Feb. 1976, Archives of Industrial Society (Hillman Library, University of Pittsburgh); Harrison G., 23 Aug. 1974, Bureau of Archives and History (Pennsylvania Historical and Museum Commission); Home Economics Worker's report, December 1919, Urban League of Pittsburgh Papers, Archives of Industrial Society (Hillman Library, University of Pittsburgh).

20. John T. Clark, "Industrial Problems in Cities, Pittsburgh," *Opportunity* 4 (Feb. 1926): 69.

21. Epstein, *Negro Migrant in Pittsburgh*, p. 18.

22. M. R. Goldman, "The Hill District of Pittsburgh as I Knew It," *Western Pennsylvania Historical Magazine* 51 (July 1968): 289–90; Gottlieb, *Making Their Own Way*, pp. 135–39.

23. Joseph M., interview, 16 Nov. 1973, Archives of Industrial Society (Hillman Library, University of Pittsburgh).

24. Harrison G., interview, 23 Aug. 1974; Gilbert M., interview, 9 Apr. 1976, Bureau of Archives and History (Pennsylvania Historical and Museum Commission); Matthew J., interview, 28 May 1976, Archives of Industrial Society (Hillman Library, University of Pittsburgh).

25. John T. Clark to James Byrd, 30 January 1923, Clark Papers, Carter Woodson Collection, Library of Congress; Nancy J. Weiss, *The National Urban League, 1910–1940* (New York: Oxford University Press, 1974), pp. 117, 119; Grossman, *Land of Hope*, pp. 142–54.

26. Reid, "The Negro in the Major Industries and Building Trades of Pittsburgh," p. 8.

27. "Negro Labor for the Steel Mills," *World's Work* 46 (July 1923): 243–44.

28. Letters to John T. Clark in the Clark papers, Carter Woodson Collection, Library of Congress: Frank W. Bowman, 16 Jan. 1923; Joe Sanders, 29 Jan. 1923; Samuel Moore, 30 Jan. 1923; James Purdy, 9 Feb. 1923; Cicero Whitehead, 2 Mar. 1923; Horace Rollins, 5 Mar. 1923; J. R. Hill, 3 Mar. 1923; quotations are from Rollins and Hill.

29. Marks, *Farewell—We're Good and Gone*, pp. 60–66; Jacquelyn D. Hall, James Leloudis, Robert Korstad, Mary Murphy, LuAnn Jones, Christopher B. Daly, *Like a Family. The Making of a Southern Cotton Mill World* (Chapel Hill: University of North Carolina Press, 1987), pp. 66–67; William Harris, *The Harder We Run: Black Workers since the Civil War* (New York: Oxford University Press, 1982), pp. 36–39.

30. Kellor, "Assisted Emigration from the South: The Women," in *The Negro in the Cities of the North* (New York: Charity Organization Society, 1905), pp. 11–14; W. E. B. Dubois, *The Philadelphia Negro* (1899; reprint, New York: Schocken Books, 1967), pp. 53–55; Elizabeth H. Pleck, *Black Migration and Poverty: Boston, 1865–1900* (New York: Academic Press, 1979), pp. 45–61; Helen Tucker, "The Negroes of Pittsburgh," in *Wage-Earning Pittsburgh, the Pittsburgh Survey*, ed. Paul U. Kellogg (New York: Survey Associates, 1914), p. 427.

31. Helen Tucker, "The Negroes of Pittsburgh," pp. 431, 433.

32. R. R. Wright, Jr., "One Hundred Negro Workers," in Kellogg, ed., *Wage-Earning Pittsburgh*, p. 99.

33. *Thirteenth Census of the United States (1910)*, vol. 4, pp. 590–91.

34. R. R. Wright, Jr., *The Negro in Pennsylvania* (Philadelphia: AME Book Concern, 1912), p. 181.

35. U.S. Census Bureau, *Negroes in the United States, 1920–32* (Washington, DC, Government Printing Office, 1935), pp. 577–78; Carter G. Woodson, *The Rural Negro* (1930; reprint, New York: Russell and Russell, 1964), pp. 26–28.

36. Neil Fligstein, *Going North: Migration of Blacks and Whites from the South, 1900–1950* (New York: Academic Press, 1981), pp. 122–23; Woodson, *A Century of Negro Migration*, pp. 126–46; Vance, *Human Factors*, p. 152; Clyde V. Kiser, *Sea Island to City: A Study of St. Helena Islanders in Harlem and Other Urban Centers* (1932; reprint, New York: AMS Press, 1967), pp. 149–50.

37. George Groh, *The Black Migration: The Journey to Urban America* (New York: Weybright and Talley, 1972), p. 48.

38. Pete Daniel, *Breaking the Land: The Transformation of Cotton, Tobacco, and Rice Cultures since 1880* (Urbana: University of Illinois Press, 1985). pp. 79–109, 168–83; Gilbert Fite, *Cotton Fields No More: Southern Agriculture, 1865–1980* (Lexington: University Press of Kentucky, 1984), pp. 139–206; James H. Street, *The New Revolution in the Cotton Economy: Mechanization and Its Consequences* (Chapel Hill: University of North Carolina Press, 1957), pp. 41–64, 107–91.

39. Daniel, *Breaking the Land*, pp. 181–83; Ben H. Bagdikian, "The Black Immigrants," *Saturday Evening Post*, 15 July 1967, pp. 25–29, 64–68.

40. Dwayne Walls, *The Chickenbone Special* (New York: Harcourt, Brace, Jovanovich, 1971), pp. 82–85; Groh, *The Black Migration*, pp. 193–94; Gottlieb, *Making Their Own Way*, pp. 26–28; Grossman, *Land of Hope*, p. 110.

41. *Seventeenth Census of the United States (1950)*, vol. 2, part 38, pp.. 397–99; *Eighteenth Census of the United States (1960)*, vol. 1, part 40, pp. 752–54.

42. *Sixteenth Census of the United States (1940). Internal Migration, 1930–40: Color & Sex of Migrants* (Washington, DC: Government Printing Office, 1943), p. 26; *Eighteenth Census of the United States (1960)*, vol. 1, pp. 425, 561.

43. *New York Times*, National Edition, January 10, 1990, p. A21.

The White Man's Union
The Great Migration and the Resonance of Race and Class in Chicago, 1916–1922

James R. Grossman

On July 6, 1919, members of Amalgamated Meat Cutters and Butcher Workmen of North America, Local 651, gathered at the local's State Street office for a parade and rally. Two miles away, in the shadows of the Chicago stockyards, another group of packinghouse unionists prepared to march to the same mass meeting. The two groups—one black, the other white—had intended to merge and walk the final ten blocks together, but police officials warned that racial tensions were too high to risk a joint march. Threatened with revocation of their permit, union leaders agreed to abandon plans to have white and black unionists demonstrate their brotherhood by parading along State Street through the heart of black Chicago. The Chicago Federation of Labor persuasively argued later that the packers had pressured the police into this ruling, and it is not unlikely that black political leaders had a hand in the decision as well. Reluctantly the Stockyards Labor Council segregated its parades despite its hope that the demonstration and rally would "interest the colored workers at the yards in the benefits of organization."[1]

After approximately 2,000 union members converged on a playground at the western edge of what was known as the "Black Belt," three blacks and four whites addressed the throng. "It does me good," roared Jack Johnstone, Secretary of the Stockyards Labor Council, "to see such a checkerboard crowd. . . . You are all standing shoulder to shoulder as men, regardless of whether your face is white or black." Other speakers, however, knew that self-congratulation for interracial solidarity was premature. John Kikulski, addressing his countrymen in Polish, urged them to abandon their prejudices and cooperate with their black co-workers. Charles Ford, a black organizer, reminded both groups that fighting with each other could result only in perpetual battle and mutual degradation. And while his very presence implied support for the union, T. Arnold Hill of the Chicago Urban League also warned that, "if he and his colleagues were expected to advise the colored workers to join the union, they expected the union men themselves to be fair toward [black] workers."[2]

This episode suggests many of the obstacles plaguing the Stockyards Labor Council's attempts to organize black workers during and immediately after World War I. Union leaders recognized that they had to dissolve suspicions separating black and white workers. Furthermore, they had to convince Chicago's black leadership of their sincerity and their strength. With thousands of black and white workers parading together through the ghetto, organizers hoped that this demonstration would show black Chicagoans how unions could be vehicles for racial harmony. At the same time, white marchers would recognize that black workers could be organized, that there was black community support for the union, and that they should therefore cease regarding blacks as a "scab race." But the same racial hostility that the union sought to overcome gave the packers an opening which they used to cripple the rally's effectiveness.

Moreover, some black leaders played their usual ambiguous role, fearing the consequences of the march at a time when racial tensions had made a riot seem not only possible, but imminent. Black politicians probably cooperated with packinghouse officials to influence police officials. The city's major black newspaper ignored the event. The Urban League representative who spoke at the rally refrained from either attacking the packers or explicitly endorsing the union; he balanced his support for the principle of unionization with a reference to past discrimination. Finally, a turnout that compared unfavorably with most Stockyards Labor Council rallies suggests that organizers had neither attracted as many blacks as they hoped, nor convinced white members of the demonstration's importance. But the march and rally did take place; black and white workers did mingle; an influential black leader did aid the union by agreeing to speak; and the union was able to showcase two black organizers. The Stockyards Labor Council had succeeded in making unionization a meaningful proposition to many black workers, and was continuing to present its case to thousands of others.[3]

Eventually the Stockyards Labor Council lost its battle to organize the packinghouses, partly because it failed to attract sufficient support among black workers, especially the recent migrants from the South. Although many blacks joined, most had dropped out by 1921, when a disastrous strike finally crippled the five-year organizing drive. Union leaders lamented that the migrants were ignorant about unionism and had been difficult to reach because Chicago's black leadership had adamantly and effectively opposed unionization. But the issue was more complicated. Many of Chicago's black leaders vacillated, waiting to see which side was a more valuable ally to the race. As for the black newcomers to Chicago, their presumed lack of understanding of union principles was less important than their history, their ideas about industrial society, and their perceptions of the dynamics of social relations. To most union men, the issue clearly turned on class issues.

But to blacks, both migrants and community leaders, race was the central concept: unionism had to prove its efficacy as a solution to an essentially racial problem.

Between 1916 and 1920, approximately 60,000 black southerners migrated to Chicago.[4] Most of those who found jobs in Chicago industries soon faced an important decision—whether or not to join a union and participate in a strike. Most chose to cross the picket lines. They did so for a variety of reasons: union racism; anti-union leadership within the black community; unfamiliarity with trade unionism; and intimidation by employers. The interaction and impact of these factors turned on the experiences and goals migrants brought with them to Chicago. A focus on the organizing campaign in the stockyards—which employed more black migrants than any other Chicago industry—suggests that the migrants ultimately rejected union appeals because they analyzed the situation in racial more than class terms; this analysis was a logical extension of both their migration experience and the liberal world view embodied in the meaning of the Great Migration.

Until World War I, most black southerners on the move had relocated within their home counties or sought agricultural opportunities in Florida, the Mississippi Delta, Kansas, Arkansas, or Oklahoma. Most found that landownership—and the independence it promised—remained elusive. A minority of black southerners abandoned the dream of yeoman autonomy altogether and headed for southern cities. Most of these individuals were women, as the urban South offered few jobs to black men. Nor were opportunities available in northern cities, where industrialists shared prevailing stereotypes of blacks as incapable of regular and efficient work at a machine. As long as they had a seemingly unlimited supply of white immigrants, these employers hired blacks only when they needed strikebreakers, and even then only on a temporary basis.

Previously unimaginable opportunities for blacks suddenly opened when World War I shut off immigration, dramatically stimulated production orders, and, eventually, drew upon the work force through the military draft. By 1916, northern industrialists, impelled by visions of spectacular profits, began what one industry journal referred to as "an experiment" and opened factory gates to black workers.[5] Between 1916 and 1919, approximately one-half million black southerners moved to northern cities, and twice as many followed during the 1920's. Known as the "Great Migration," this exodus was the first mass migration of black southerners to the North. They fled the South not only for higher wages, education, or relief from racial oppression, but also to cast off the burdens of a social and economic system that had taught one Georgia farmer that he "better not accumulate much, no matter how hard and honest you work for it, as they—well you can't enjoy it.'"[6] With the frustrations of the past etched in their minds, black southerners headed north anticipating a future offering unparalleled potential.

Because historians have not examined the dynamics of the Great Migration, they have not understood how the migrants interpreted their situation and made decisions. The movement has been discussed mainly within the context of race riots, or the physical growth and institutional development of the black ghetto. Such studies tend to relegate migrants to a passive role, by examining unionization from the perspective of the established black community and dismissing newcomers as ignorant or naively manipulable.[7] Buffeted by the power and propaganda of employers, the appeals of unions, and the bourgeois perspective of the black middle class, newcomers supposedly broke strikes because they were pawns of employers, because they did not know better, or because they naturally followed the prevailing wind in the black community. The evidence, however, suggests that black migrants in Chicago packinghouses, influenced by conflicting forces, made their own decisions—and they made those decisions based on their experience, their perceptions of their situation, and their goals.

With the meat packing companies employing a sizeable plurality of black workers at any given moment, and the unions attempting to organize their plants actively recruiting black workers, the five-year campaign to unionize the stockyards affords special insight into the attitudes of black newcomers to Chicago. The Great Steel Strike of 1919, which attracted more attention nationally, and has since served as an apotheosis of the era's labor conflict, is less interesting in this context. Unlike the Stockyards Labor Council, the National Committee For Organizing Iron and Steel Workers made no special efforts to organize blacks, and did little to try to convince them that previous patterns of discrimination would be abandoned. Predictably, blacks remained largely outside the organization, although many in Chicago and elsewhere participated in the walkout on the first day of the "Great Strike." The packinghouses, more than the steel mills, provide a setting that affords an opportunity to understand how black workers from the South regarded their place in American industrial society.[8]

When the Stockyards Labor Council, a consortium of packinghouse unions formed under the auspices of the Chicago Federation of Labor, undertook to organize the Chicago stockyards in 1917, its leadership knew that black workers would be difficult to organize. Blacks had served as strikebreakers twice before in the stockyards, and now they constituted a significant and growing proportion of the work force. The leaders of the Council—especially John Fitzpatrick and William Z. Foster—not only recognized the necessity of including blacks in the stockyards unions, but also considered organizing blacks to be good union policy in general. Neither shared the extreme racist attitudes of Samuel Gompers and most other labor leaders associated with the American Federation of Labor. They appointed black organizers, lectured white members on the importance of accepting black workers into their unions, and appealed to black community institutions for support.[9]

They achieved a measure of success. Black men and women either born in the

North or resident there before 1916 joined at a rate comparable to white workers, perhaps as high as 90 percent by 1919. But the migrants—or "new men," as one black shop steward called them—were less receptive.[10]

Although it is difficult to count precisely the number of migrants who joined stockyards unions, evidence suggests that at least half of all black workers in the stockyards belonged at some point. Many of these approximately 6,000 union members were newcomers. A survey of dues payments, corroborated by testimony from black workers, suggests the pattern of black union membership: many black workers joined, but a large proportion let their dues lapse after a short time. They were interested in unions, but not committed to them.[11]

Union leaders disclaimed responsibility for their failure to attract the loyalty of black workers. "If the colored packing house worker doesn't come into the union," declared one official, "it isn't the fault of the Stock Yards Labor Council."[12] They had done all they could to reach out to blacks, and John Fitzpatrick, President of the Chicago Federation of Labor, especially deserves recognition for his sincerity. Fitzpatrick correctly identified the essence of the problem, but misunderstood its source. "The Southern negro," he lamented, "is different. We figure that his slavery days ended at about the time that he came up here to work in the Packing houses."[13] Fitzpatrick was right that migrants were "different," and that this difference partly explained their actions, but he was wrong in his assumption that the problem was their allegedly slavish personality. Contrary to conventional wisdom the migrants were not what sociologist George E. Haynes called "putty in the hands of three more or less conflicting interests"—employers, organized (white) labor, and politicians—who were assumed to be the real actors in the drama.[14] The men and women who had participated in the Great Migration had already taken a step that indicated that they had no intention of permitting other people to control their lives.

Fitzpatrick's passive migrants conform to the image his contemporaries and many subsequent scholars have held of the Great Migration, and, until recently, of Afro-American history in general. Supposedly the movement was leaderless, stimulated by white labor agents from northern industry who lured docile but dissatisfied black southerners to the North with lavish promises of higher wages. The movement then acquired "momentum," the argument continues, as migrants wrote enticing letters to friends and relatives still in the South. Unorganized, people left hurriedly, abandoning mules in half-plowed fields. This description does indeed roughly describe the experience of some migrants, but it is an inaccurate portrait of the movement as a whole.[15]

Few fields were left half-plowed. Many southern whites believed that migrants left precipitously because white opposition to the movement required that blacks remain circumspect about migration plans. Learning that supposedly lazy, unambitious, and indecisive black laborers were climbing aboard northbound trains, many southern whites assumed that outside agitators had plied gullible Negroes with unrealistic dreams attractive enough to induce them to depart irrationally and hurriedly. Even some blacks—especially notables with ties to white elites—mistakenly interpreted departures as rash, impetuous decisions since prospective migrants often hid their intentions until the last minute.[16]

But decisions to leave often were made thoughtfully, purposefully, and within the context of community debate. Many young black southerners had already widened their horizons and loosened ties to home through seasonal labor in southern sawmills, turpentine camps, and similar industries. Others learned about northern conditions without leaving home. They organized meetings to discuss the issue with other members of the community, or introduced the subject in church or in popular gathering places. Some organized migration clubs, which helped migrants to maintain ties while leaving, in addition to enabling them to take advantage of discounted group railroad fares. This activity took place within the context of a purposeful search for information. Black southerners asked railroad workers about cities at the other end of the line. They subscribed to northern black newspapers, especially the Chicago *Defender*, which circulated widely in the South and was often read aloud in homes, churches, barbershops, and poolrooms. Rather than passively accepting such information and then impulsively departing, many prospective migrants first wrote letters to the *Defender*, northern black institutions, or friends who had already left, asking for assistance or advice.[17]

Although many elements of this "migration network" have been identified by students of the exodus, its coherence and significance have, until recently, remained unexplored. Emphasis on the role of labor agents has reinforced images of the Great Migration as leaderless, organized only to the extent that it was shaped by northern employers and the invisible hand of the labor market. But the actual role of labor agents remains ambiguous. Recruiters for northeastern railroads helped to spark the migration in 1916; publicists for industries in cities not well known in the black South probably had a continuing influence in some southern cities, and in northern cities that had already attracted newcomers. But few black southerners ever encountered a recruiter, and only a handful of Chicago's migrants were recruited by labor agents. The legend of the "pass rider" was more influential than the reality, as rumors of labor agents contributed to the general sense of anticipation and hope which spread through the black South. Many workers who were recruited by agents had already decided to leave, and merely seized the opportunity for a free trip. And many so-called agents were among the recent migrants who returned home to visit after being told by a foreman that jobs were available for friends who might be convinced to come North. Such people might more appropriately be considered part of an indigenous communications network that lent coherence to the Great Migration.[18]

This dynamic of migration suggests that newcomers to Chicago were not as passive as unionist leaders suggested when they charged that the migration resulted mainly from the activities of labor agents employed by Chicago industrialists. That many black newcomers joined the stockyards organizing drive, and then decided that membership was not the best strategy, suggests that they approached the question of unionization no more passively than that of migration. Black workers acted according to their own assessments of the situation and their own interests, in some cases joining first in order to learn how membership might benefit them, and subsequently deciding that their interests lay elsewhere.

Nor were the migrants necessarily as ignorant of industrial relations issues as most contemporaries and many historians have assumed. If many shared the reaction of one newcomer who remarked, ''they didn't have no unions where I comed from—ain't nothin' there anyway but farmers,'' others had a least some notion of what was going on.[19] A few had carried North with them actual union experience, and they probably were among those who readily joined the stockyards unions. Unionized black dockworkers in New Orleans and craftsmen in scattered southern cities understood the benefits of organization. So did the 8,000 black workers who belonged to trade unions in the first decade of the twentieth century in the Birmingham, Alabama, district. Like the 700 black helpers who struck railroad shops in Marshall, Texas, during a wage dispute in 1916, these men, their families, and their friends were familiar with the advantages and the meaning of unionization.[20]

Rural black southerners also understood the value of collective action. The bloody riot near Helena, Arkansas, in 1919 was provoked by a meeting of an organization of sharecroppers. Some 10,000 to 17,000 black men had belonged to the Brotherhood of Timber Workers, which organized in 1910 and conducted a series of strikes in the southern woods between 1912 and 1914. Like the sawmill laborers who had participated in Knights of Labor strikes in Mississippi in 1889 and 1900, these men traveled frequently, many of them living in farm settlements as well as in labor camps. Through them, men and women with more limited experience learned about organization and strikes. A broader source of organizing lore lay among the 60,000 blacks who had joined the Knights of Labor in the 1880's, when black local assemblies were formed not only in southern cities, but also in smaller communities as well. The Colored Farmers Alliance, even if its claim of 1 million members was an exaggeration, also left a legacy of collective protest in the rural South after it disintegrated in the 1890's.[21] Much of this activity took place in parts of the South that later sent large numbers of migrants to Chicago, and involved sectors employing the mobile young men most likely to migrate and end up in packinghouses.

Migrants predisposed toward unionization, however, were a small minority. Most black southerners, if they knew anything about unions, had learned to be suspicious of organized labor. In southern cities where craft unions had achieved some power, white craftsmen frequently excluded black competitors. Where black carpenters, bricklayers, painters, and blacksmiths had such a secure foothold that their strikebreaking potential could not be ignored, unions organized them into separate—and powerless—locals. Black railroad men, a crucial link in the information network that had helped to spread the migration, circulated tales of equally problematic experiences with the railroad brotherhoods, which customarily demanded that blacks be replaced with whites.[22] Migrants aware of this correlation between successful union organization and loss of black jobs were likely to regard warily the appeals of the stockyards organizers. However, especially because there were black organizers involved in the Chicago campaign, migrants at least were prepared to listen, if not always to follow.

Union leaders later complained that they had been unable to transmit their message to black workers because, as William Z. Foster argued, "the firm opposition of the negro intellegensia" had created a barrier between the organizers and black workers.[23] Understanding the extent and meaning of that influence requires an examination of why certain institutions had standing among migrants. The dynamic of migration partly explains why migrants looked to these leaders and institutions for advice.

Union leaders argued that middle-class black Chicagoans acted as conduits for employer propaganda, and that corporate contributions to black institutions bought loyalty. The argument was not without validity, but it was generally overstated, especially with regard to the two most influential institutions—the *Defender* and the Chicago Urban League. It was most accurate with respect to the black branch of the Chicago YMCA. Through its Efficiency Clubs, the YMCA sought to inculcate loyalty to employers, as well as proper work habits. But while it provided a small cadre of anti-union leadership, the YMCA failed to reach a significant number of workers, especially among the migrants.[24]

More central to the lives of working-class black men and women was the church, which was also a source of cultural and institutional continuity for many migrants. A few of the largest churches operated employment bureaus, while some ministers at smaller "storefront" churches acted as hiring agents for employers. Some migrants had reorganized their old congregations and brought their former pastors to Chicago, and these ministers were likely to be especially influential because they provided continuity of leadership. Because most black church services were sermon-oriented, the minister was a critical source of information for churchgoers, especially southern migrants, accustomed to the centrality of the church in their secular lives.[25]

A few black ministers were pro-union, allowing organizers to speak to their congregations, permitting a church to be used for a meeting, or even preaching on "the benefits of unionization." These included Lacey Kirk Williams and John F. Thomas, who occupied influential pulpits at Olivet and Ebenezer Baptist Churches. With Olivet membership increasing from 3,500 to more than 9,000 between 1916 and 1922, Williams's voice was especially important. There is, however, no evidence that Williams exerted substantial efforts in the interest of unionization, although both steel and packinghouse organizing were discussed at his church. Thomas qualified his endorsements by cautioning worshippers to resist the message of the Industrial Workers of the World and other advocates of "revolution." Among those at the largest churches, only James Henderson of Institutional A.M.E. Church was willing to assist labor leaders in their efforts to secure meetings with black ministerial alliances.[26]

To the extent that they cared about the issue of unionization, pastors at most of Chicago's large black churches tended to agree with A.M.E. Bishop Archibald J. Carey that "the interest of my people lies with the wealth of the nation and with the class of white people who control it." This class of whites included Philip Armour, Gustavus Swift, Cyrus McCormick, and George Pullman, whose substantial contributions had rescued Carey's Quinn Chapel from foreclosure at the turn of the century. Carey remained a friend and political ally of packinghouse entrepreneurs and other industrialists. When black organizers began to build the Brotherhood of Sleeping Car Porters in the mid-1920s, he opposed even this effort to unionize black workers. Other churches had similar ties to Chicago employers. Ministers at struggling storefront churches often needed the income they could secure as labor agents for employers seeking strikebreakers. At churches so poor that their spiritual leaders supported themselves with outside jobs, labor trouble at the minister's workplace offered not only the opportunity to earn an employer's gratitude, but also to assist unemployed members of the congregation. In general, black churches provided employers, who had little other contact with black Chicago, with a means of communication with potential strikebreakers. It is not clear, however, that they represented an either unanimous or deeply committed voice opposed to union membership.[27]

Despite the continuing influence of the church, many black workers increasingly turned to secular institutions—especially the black press—for advice during the 1910s. The *Defender* had already won the trust of many migrants before they left the South. Printing stories about racial oppression in the South that black southerners knew to be true, but that few southern black newspapers could publish, the *Defender* had earned a reputation among its southern readers as a militant, fearless spokesman. After he had "read every space of" his first issue, one Texan wrote to the Chicago newspaper in 1917 that "I never dreamed that there was such a race paper published." Attempts by officials in many southern communities to suppress its distribution served only to validate its reliability. Many migrants came to Chicago, rather than another northern city, because of images gleaned from the *Defender*—and, because they inferred from its columns that it and the other Chicago black institutions it publicized could be depended upon for assistance. Increases in its local circulation suggest that after arriving in Chicago, newcomers continued to read the *Defender* or have it read to them.[28]

Although never reluctant to lecture migrants on any aspect of life in Chicago, the *Defender*, until 1920, avoided a firm position on unionism. Some editorials advised workers to join unions; other recited the virtues of company loyalty. Its fluctuating position defies neat categorization: the *Defender* considered trade unionism and collective bargaining useful; opposed strikes; labeled the American Federation of Labor unions discriminatory and left wing unions too radical; advised blacks to join unions if they would be treated as equals; and considered strike-breaking legitimate, especially during periods of high unemployment and as a means of entry into industries from which blacks previously had been excluded. Editor Robert Abbott acknowledged that employers had not always dealt fairly with blacks, but he admired industrialists, their ideas, and their ideals. And he remained wary of antagonizing the men who controlled jobs and philanthropic purses. Still, until it seemed certain that the organizing campaign was losing ground, Abbott also sought to avoid antagonizing union leaders. The right choice for a black worker, according to the *Defender*, was apparently the one most likely to increase the race's share of jobs.[29]

The message migrants read in the *Defender* was likely to encourage them to avoid involvement in labor conflicts, or, at best, to join unions but avoid committing themselves to a costly strike. Strikebreaking clearly had legitimate functions in the right time and place. Equally important, in its news columns the *Defender* simply ignored most union activity. When the 1921–22 strike finally began, it did not find its way into the *Defender* for three weeks.

The *Defender's* rhetorical ambivalence and tacit hostility contrasts sharply with attention the stockyards campaign received in the Chicago *Whip*. Founded in 1919, the *Whip* never attained influence comparable to the *Defender*, but by mid-1920 it had become a significant voice in the community. Devoting a much larger proportion of its space to labor issues than did the *Defender*, the *Whip* even carried a regular column by John Riley, a black organizer in the stockyards. Union rallies in the black community—ignored by the *Defender*—received publicity in the *Whip*, frequently on the front page. Although the editors also advised blacks to join unions "only when to their advantage," they stated unequivocally in 1919 their support for both the steelworkers' and stockyards unions. By the time of the 1921–22 packinghouse strike, however, the *Whip* had joined the *Defender* in ignoring the union campaign and meetings called by black organizers.[30]

What is most salient about the positions of these influential black voices, linking them to a broad consensus in the black community that was imperfectly understood by white unionists, is that they considered strikebreaking thinkable, even when either not practicable or not desirable. The scab unambiguously represented an evil to white unionists, but to many black strikebreaking had to be considered seriously—even if rejected. Where the *Butcher Workman* considered the strikebreaker "a two-legged animal with a corkscrew soul—a waterlogged brain, a combination backbone made of jelly and glue," the *Defender* saw instead a man who faced starvation, and reminded readers that "self-preservation is the first law of nature."[31] The means of self-preservation, however, was more of an open question than it seemed to white union leaders certain that black editors were tools of industrial interests.

It is unlikely that either newspaper's position, or treatment of the issue, was directly influenced by pressure from employers. Both the *Whip* and the *Defender* were primarily race newspapers and evaluated issues accordingly. Because the principle of unionization was secondary to the question of what stockyards unions could do for the black community, the editors could change their minds easily, depending on the power equation in the stockyards and the level of interest in the black community. When Abbott became convinced that the packers would win, he abandoned all attempts to maintain good relations with the unionists. When the *Whip* reached the same conclusion, its editors—who were younger than Abbott and less steeped in the capitalist values the *Defender* editor had imbibed at Hampton Institute—simply dropped the issue entirely.

The Chicago Urban League could not dispose of the unionization question so easily, but it similarly looked first to the interests of the black community, especially in terms of employment opportunities. Like the *Defender*, the Urban League commanded special influence among migrants, many of whom had read in the *Defender* about its services to newcomers. Described by one prospective migrant as "the society that helps colored emigrants," the League was a logical place for newcomers to turn when they needed assistance. It handed out cards at train stations, held meetings for newcomers, and maintained a centrally located store front. Although its patronizing and didactic attitudes towards migrants tended to discredit its advice on some matters, its counsel on economic issues was generally taken seriously— especially since it frequently had been the Urban League that had found a migrant a job, or had provided temporary economic assistance. In 1919 alone, 14,000 blacks found jobs in Chicago through the Urban League's placement office; and more than 20 percent of the city's black population used the League's services at least once that year.[32]

Although the League criticized both employers and unions for discrimination, its official position advised black workers to join unions whenever possible. Strike-breaking was advisable "only where the union affected had excluded colored men from membership." Strict adherence to these principles should have rendered the League's position on the packinghouse campaign unambiguously pro-union. More-over, the lesson some Urban League leaders drew from the 1917 East St. Louis riots was that black workers might contribute to racial peace by joining unions, rather than antagonize white co-workers.[33]

Chicago Urban League officials did indeed counsel black workers to join the stockyards unions. Executive Director Hill considered unionization the only solution to the black workers' insecurity in the industrial labor force, and spoke at the July, 1919, rally. Other influential figures in the organization were also sympathetic, with the Industrial Secretary arguing—privately—that "the best interest of colored men in the Yards in my belief is in union organization."[34] Yet, the League took care to avoid too strong a stance. Its middle-class leaders had ties to employers, and a large chunk of its budget came from packinghouse firms. As one League official later explained, the encouragement to join unions was "a statement we wanted to make clear-cut and unambiguous, yet not needlessly provocative." As long as the stockyards remained peaceful, the League could straddle the fence, even if it leaned slightly to the left.[35]

The Urban League discarded its careful balancing act sometime before the 1921–22 strike during which it quietly referred jobseekers to two struck packinghouse firms.[36] The new policy probably can be attributed to the race riot in late July, 1919, possible increased pressure from employers, the impact of the 1920–21 recession, and internal League politics. But the shift is not important here, because, by the time of the riot, most migrants had already decided not to join the union. Indeed, the riot was partly a result of this resistance, although it also further alienated blacks from white workers and their unions.

Although its financial ties and middle-class perspective certainly influenced its posture and limited its options, the Urban League also must be understood in terms of a world view dominated by the category of race. Like Abbott at the *Defender*, black Urban Leaguers looked first to the interests of race, and middle-class values interacted with but did not determine the substance of their race-consciousness. "The League is not opposed to unionism," explained a League spokesman, "but is interested primarily in the welfare of colored workers."[37] By 1921, it was clear that employers controlled the jobs and the money, and while managers could not be trusted to treat blacks equitably in matters of promotion, unions were no more trustworthy and had less to offer. Alliances with unions were a wartime luxury and ironically, perhaps even a wartime necessity in some cases. They lasted only so long as they did not require blacks to make the commitments and take the risks demanded by a strike. Given the psychological and material relationships between migration and jobs, such risks were unacceptable both to middle-class black leaders and to hopeful and ambitious newcomers.

Even while it was supporting unionization, however, the Urban League inhibited the organization of black workers, although perhaps unwittingly. It and other black institutions performed functions that could appear to render unions redundant. Both the League and the YMCA had industrial departments which worked with employers to solve problems involving black workers. "If you are having trouble with your employers," the League's cards and leaflets read, "call upon the Chicago League on Urban Conditions Among Negroes." A black worker with a complaint about a foreman would go to the Urban League whose representative could discuss the problem with a plant official. By providing a grievance procedure that offered direct links to management, the Urban League, and to a lesser extent, the YMCA, appropriated a crucial function of the trade union and they did it within a black institutional matrix. The Urban League, observed one white social worker, "furnished the leadership usually furnished by the federation."[38]

This competitive institutional function of the League was but a part of a broader phenomenon. Formal positions on unionization aside, Chicago's black institutional and commercial world inhibited the organization of its working class into unions. Unlike Back of the Yards, garment districts, and neighborhoods surrounding the steel mills, Chicago's "Black Belt" bore no special relationship to a particular industry. Its institutional development had preceded the entrance of its population into industry, and its culture was structured by neither the rhythms nor the social relations of a set of similar workplaces. Black workers had to be organized either outside the community or away from the immediacy of the workplace. The process of organizing white workers in Packingtown, which according to one historian, "took on the atmosphere of a Baptist camp meeting" at the height of the campaign, contrasted sharply with the task of stirring up enthusiasm among black workers, who had to be collared on train platforms and streetcars.[39] Black workers in unionizing industries were less likely to attend union meetings after work partly because they had to travel home; in nearly all cases they did not—and could not—live in the factory neighborhood.

Once a strike began, their communities experienced the conflict differently. In Back of the Yards, the 1921 strike was a community event. Women hurled bags of paprika at policemen. Crowds stoned homes of strikebreakers. Pastors, businessmen, lodges, and even neighborhood bankers donated provisions to strikers. Without overstating the level of community support for strikers in such neighborhoods, it is clear that unions were neighborhood—and often ethnic—institutions. In the "Black Belt," however, they were external to the community, seeking support both from workers and from middle-class leaders whose neighborhood orientation competed with unions, rather than enhanced the process of mobilization.[40] Unlikely to become a part of the black community, unions had even less chance of being perceived as external institutions that—like schools—were self-evidently beneficial and amenable to incorporation into Afro-American tradition. Their burden was inescapable in this context. They had to demonstrate that they were interracial institutions, able to offer blacks access to opportunities and power—access that was central to both the Great Migration itself and its support among northern black leaders. But the unions seemed to some blacks to be white institutions, primarily interested in the welfare of white workers. Black unionists, argued one workman, were "damn fools," and "nothing but a lot of white folk's niggers."[41]

Despite sincere efforts to organize blacks, including hiring black organizers, the Stockyards Labor Council could not bridge the cultural distance between white and black workers. Repeatedly—and often with the best intentions—union leaders offended black workers and the rest of the black community. Establishing a union local headquartered in the ghetto, thereby allowing blacks to sign up more easily and control their own affairs, seemed natural to unionists accustomed to ethnic locals. Besides, technically, blacks had the right to join other locals. Migrants knew, however, that the separate local also reflected the reluctance of many white unionists to accept blacks into their organizations.

Viewing what they encountered through the lens of their own experience, migrants logically interpreted the "colored local" as a sign of Jim Crow. In union newspapers (which printed "darky" anecdotes as fillers), organizing speeches, and even special appeals to blacks, white unionists betrayed a similar insensitivity and inability to avoid familiar symbols of racism. When the Chicago Federation of Labor defended its organizers who "had invited the negroes into the white man's unions," it unwittingly stated the essence of the problem.[42] To black workers, especially southerners who had migrated to escape white domination, the Stockyards Labor Council was a "white man's union." They understood its benefits, but also doubted that those benefits would be extended equally to white and black members.

White packinghouse workers contributed further to blacks' suspicions that unionization was actually a racial issue. Black workers had been among the strikebreakers in two previous packinghouse conflicts, as well as in other bitter strikes in Chicago. White workers had come to associate strikebreaking with blackness, and during a teamsters' strike in 1905, some blacks were attacked despite protestations that they were not involved in the conflict. It was enough, answered one assailant, that the victim was black. To many white packinghouse workers, blacks were "nigger scabs," a concept that offered a shorthand description of a scab race. White unionists were willing to accept the support and, in some cases, even the fellowship of black union members, but such individuals were considered exceptions; white unionists sharply distinguished them from others of their race. Black non-members were the targets of specifically racial epithets which were used as the simple word "scab" was used to describe white strikebreakers.[43]

Because of the words white workers used, migrants often interpreted invective based on nonunion status as racial insults, especially when white workers simply used the word "nigger" to describe a black nonunion man. When nonunion newcomers joined work gangs, whites refused to work with them because they were not union members; but the white workers—many of whom had a limited English vocabulary—often voiced their objection in racial terms. As one white worker, after some prodding, explained to the federal mediator, his refusal to work with "the colored fellows" actually referred only to those not wearing a union button.[44]

Migrants, accustomed to southern patterns of social relations, interpreted the walkouts as manifestations of the racial prejudice they had so often suffered in the South rather than tactics in a class conflict. Those who had heard about the exclusionary policies of craft and railway unions in the South were likely to draw the obvious analogy. In the South, power exerted by whites had limited their alternatives; indeed, the decision to migrate represented an attempt to break those constraints. Participants in the Great Migration had chosen to leave, against the wishes and threats of whites, and even the advice of many established black leaders. Many migrants resented being told now that they must join the union to keep a job. They had come North partly to be free to make choices themselves, and to be evaluated according to their performance rather than their relations with whites.

Between white workers and their organizations, on the one hand, and black southerners, on the other, lay a chasm unbridgeable by union rhetoric and the realities of class conflicts. As Abram Harris, a black economist, observed in 1925, "a few Marxist epigrams" would not sway black workers whose "experience and tradition" suggested an independent course.[45] Migrants recalled their experience with white working-class competition and individual relationships with both "good" and "bad" employers (or landlords *qua* employers), and remembered that vertical connections tended to be more useful than horizontal ones; and in this situation vertical connections were readily available through black institutions with links to employers. Whatever the benefits of unions, they were, as one migrant put it, "no good for the colored man."[46] They were white institutions.

This definition of industrial relations as an essentially racial issue related closely to the reasons migrants had come North. Observers and subsequent scholars generally enumerated laundry lists of dichotomous economic and social causes of the Great Migration, and then called the economic factors "primary," or "fundamental." Were this the case, migrants might have been more receptive to unionization appeals because higher wages would have been their prime consideration. Or, one might persuasively interpret their actions as the result of sheer intimidation by employers, against a group of hapless refugees from the series of economic disasters that struck the South between 1914 and 1917. The traditional emphasis on the role of labor agents in the Great Migration would only corroborate such a passive image of the migrants.[47]

But the Great Migration was neither a passive social process shaped by broad forces of macro-historical change, nor a movement narrowly rooted in simple and quantifiable causative factors. A careful look at the reasons migrants left their southern homes for northern cities reveals a broader motivation drawing on the migrants' comparison of their place in the circumscribed racial order in the South with the possibilities of participation in what they perceived to be the open industrial society of the North. Responding to what Alain Locke called "a new vision of opportunity," they considered the recently opened industrial jobs in the North their chance to share a world previously accessible only to whites. They conflated economic and social stimuli into what they called "bettering their condition." Their letters display countless variants of this theme: "Better his Standing"; "elevate myself"; "chance for advancement." They came North in search of something black Americans had once hoped they would win from emancipation: their rightful place as "part of the great whole of the mighty American nation," as John Mercer Langston had expressed it in 1866.[48] For most freedmen that place was to have been secured by landownership, and now a new generation looked instead to industry. But certain fundamental objectives remained unchanged—good schools, equal rights before the law, and equal access to community institutions. These constituted the foundation of freedom and citizenship. After two generations of economic, educational, social, and political stultification in the South, the North represented to many black southerners the final hope to attain what white Americans supposedly had—the opportunity as citizens to better their condition through hard work. "All I ask is give me a chance," wrote one Louisiana man, "and I will make good."[49]

Unionization offered one possible means of bettering their condition, and many migrants flirted with it—hence the large number who joined and then dropped out. But even if unions could win wage gains—and it was by no means clear that they could—migrants were more interested in securing and holding jobs, because factory work constituted a central aspect of their newly attained status. It seemed clear that employers controlled the jobs, and that white unions looked first to the interests of white workers. The record of industrialists on racial discrimination was no better than that of unions: until the war, blacks had been hired only as strikebreakers and had been laid off as soon as the conflict had ended. This time, however, employers had hired blacks before the strike, and the relationships black institutions had developed with employers seemed to offer some assurance that the jobs would be secure. At the very least, black institutions could be counted upon to lobby for black jobs.

The migrants' performance at work corroborates this interpretation of their intentions. E. P. Thompson, and other scholars who have followed in his tradition, have suggested that individuals new to industrial work generally resisted industrial work discipline.[50] Black migrants certainly faced a significant adjustment, as most of them had come from the rural South and were accustomed to an agricultural sense of time—the centerpiece of Thompson's model. Employers who hired newcomers from the South complained of lateness, absenteeism, and poor productivity. Distinctions drawn between northern and southern blacks suggest that the complaints cannot be dismissed summarily as racism.

Within a few years, employers were no longer complaining. Nearly all industrial managers interviewed by the Chicago Commission on Race Relations in 1920 reported satisfaction with black workers. A comparison of absentee and tardiness statistics from 1917 to 1919 in Chicago shows significant improvement among blacks, most of whom were recent arrivals.[51] There is no evidence that black workers resisted the pleas of employers and social workers to discard old work habits. Those work patterns were associated with a system of relationships that they had rejected by coming North, and they evinced no nostalgia for the past. As black southerners who had long been excluded from the economic mainstream, they felt that their new industrial jobs represented meaningful progress, rather than immiseration. They had come to Chicago to be industrial workers, and expected hard work and efficiency to bring rewards.

This is not to say that migrants who worked in packinghouses and other Chicago industries enjoyed their jobs, or did not understand that they were being exploited. But industrial work represented a foothold, and glances backward and forward suggested to migrants that they had already bettered their condition, and might continue to do so. Moreover, they interpreted exploitation in a manner different from white workers. They were being exploited, they perceived, not because they were workers, but because they were black. Having come North because it was better to be black in the North than in the South, they assessed their position in terms consonant with their experiences and their ambitions.

NOTES

Portions of this article have appeared in James R. Grossman, *Land of Hope: Chicago, Black Southerners, and the Great Migration* (Chicago: University of Chicago Press, 1989).   Reprinted by permission of University of Chicago Press.

1. Chicago *Whip*, 19 July 1919; *New Majority* (Chicago), 5 July and 9 August 1919 (hereafter cited as *NM*).

2. *NM*, 12 July 1919; *The Butcher Workman*, July 1919 (hereafter cited as *BW*); Carl Sandburg, *The Chicago Race Riots, July 1919* (New York: Harcourt, Brace and Howe, 1919), p. 47; *Whip*, 19 July 1919.

3. It is always difficult to estimate the size of crowds, and even more problematic to gauge the significance of a given turnout. In this case, union newspapers eschewed their usual practice of estimating the size of the meeting, and Carl Sandburg's estimate of 2,000 or 3,000 is less than the usual figures for Stockyards Labor Council rallies. Given Sandburg's proclivity for exaggeration, his figure should suggest a maximum; see Sandburg, *Chicago Race Riots*, p. 47. Many black Chicagoans had expected a riot to erupt on July 4; see William M. Tuttle, Jr., interview with Chester Wilkins, Chicago, 25 June 1969 (transcript in possession of Tuttle), p. 3. For an exaggerated description of the black community's response to the parade—which nevertheless suggests that there was some significant response—see "Negro Agitation," Military Intelligence Report (July 1919), p. 3, the U.S. Department of Justice, General Records, Box 14, Glasser File (RG 60, NA).

4. It is difficult to estimate the volume of migration to Chicago during this period. The census statistics, when controlled for deaths and births, yield a figure of 50,000 (61,000 between the 1910 and 1920 censuses), an estimate accepted by Allan Spear in his classic, *Black Chicago: The Making of a Negro Ghetto* (Chicago: University of Chicago Press, 1967). However, the 1920 census probably undercounted blacks, especially in cities, and because the 1910 census employed black enumerators, it is likely that its count is not as underestimated, and therefore, the difference between 1910 and 1920 is probably understated. Observers unanimously offer figures higher than 50,000. According to Emmett Scott, "daily counts," probably by the Chicago Urban League, indicate that 50,000 migrants arrived in Chicago between January, 1916, and June, 1917, alone. The Chicago Urban League estimated at the end of 1919 that the city's black population had increased 75,000 since 1913, most of which would have occurred during the war. Others, including Charles Johnson, Mary McDowell, and Carl Sandburg, offered estimates of 1916–1919 migration ranging from 65,000 to 75,000. Sandburg, who claimed that his estimates drew upon an exhaustive survey of forty local authorities, guessed that 150,000 migrants arrived in Chicago, with only 70,000 remaining permanently; his penchant for exaggeration, however, must be taken into consideration. See Otis Duncan and Beverly Duncan, *The Negro Population of Chicago: A Study of Residential Succession* (Chicago: University of Chicago Press, 1957), p. 33;

Spear, *Black Chicago*, p. 141; Emmett J. Scott, *Negro Migration During the War* (New York: Oxford University Press, 1920), p. 102; Chicago *Defender*, 13 December 1919, 31 January 1920; Charles S. Johnson, "Digest of Contributing Factors to Racial Outbreak July 29, 1919" (typescript, [c. 1920]), p. 1, National Urban League Records (NULR), Box 87, Series 6 (Library of Congress); Sandburg, *Chicago Race Riots*, pp. 5, 10.

    5. *Iron Age* 98 (28 June 1917): 1563–64.

    6. Letter to *Defender* (name withheld by request), 28 April 1917.

    7. For distinctive applications of the ghettoization framework, see David M. Katzman, *Before the Ghetto: Black Detroit in the Nineteenth Century* (Urbana: University of Illinois Press, 1973); Spear, *Black Chicago*; Kenneth L. Kusmer, *A Ghetto Takes Shape: Black Cleveland, 1870–1930* (Urbana: University of Illinois Press, 1976); Gilbert Osofsky, *Harlem: The Making of a Negro Ghetto*, 2d ed. (New York: Harper and Row, 1971); Gilbert Osofsky, "The Enduring Ghetto," *Journal of American History* 55, no. 2 (September 1968): 243–55. Different patterns of black community development can be found in Thomas C. Cox, *Blacks in Topeka, Kansas, 1865–1915: A Social History* (Baton Rouge: Louisiana State University Press, 1982); Douglas H. Daniels, *Pioneer Urbanites: A Social and Cultural History of Black San Francisco* (Philadelphia: Temple University Press, 1979); and George C. Wright, *Life Behind a Veil: Blacks in Louisville, 1865–1930* (Baton Rouge: Louisiana State University Press, 1985). For reviews of this historiography, see Joe William Trotter, Jr., *Black Milwaukee: The Making of an Industrial Proletariat, 1915–1945* (Urbana: University of Illinois Press, 1985), pp. 264–82; and Kenneth Kusmer, "The Black Urban Experience in American History," in *The State of Afro-American History*, Darlene C. Hine, ed. (Baton Rouge: Louisiana State University Press, 1986), pp. 91–122. The best study of a northern race riot during this period is William M. Tuttle Jr., *Race Riot: Chicago in the Red Summer of 1919* (New York: Atheneum, 1970); its chapter on the Great Migration is probably the most evocative and insightful chapter length treatment of the movement. See also Elliott M. Rudwick, *Race Riot at East St. Louis, July 2, 1917* (Carbondale: Southern Illinois University Press, 1964); David Levine, *Internal Combustion: The Races in Detroit, 1915–1926* (Westport, Conn.: Greenwood Press, 1976). Trotter's *Black Milwaukee*, by focusing on class formation rather than ghettoization as the central process in Afro-American urban history, has moved outside what he calls the "ghetto synthesis" and drawn attention to migrants as the central actors in the process of "proletarianization." But the focus is still the community, rather than the migrants themselves, and the process is viewed from the perspective of community development rather than the experience of the migrants. Two recent studies focusing on the migrants and their orientation toward work and unionization are Peter Gottlieb, *Making Their Own Way: Southern Blacks' Migration to Pittsburgh, 1916–1930* (Urbana: University of Illinois Press, 1987) and James R. Grossman, *Land of Hope: Chicago, Black Southerners, and the Great Migration* (Chicago: University of Chicago Press, 1989). The other major book-length historical study of the Great Migration, Florette Henri, *Black Migration: Movement North, 1900–1920* (Garden City: Anchor Press/Doubleday, 1975) adds narrative detail and argumentative force to Emmett Scott's classic *Negro Migration*, upon which it draws heavily for its framework. Its premise, that the Great Migration prepared black Americans to be "New Negroes," reads the movement backward rather than forward.

    8. On blacks and the steel strike of 1919, see Spear, *Black Chicago*, pp. 163–64; David Brody, *Steelworkers in America: The Nonunion Era* (Cambridge, Mass.: Harvard University Press, 1960), pp. 224–25; William Z. Foster, *The Great Steel Strike and Its Lessons* (New York: B. W. Huebsch, 1920), pp. 205–207; Sterling D. Spero and Abram L. Harris, *The Black Worker* (1931; reprint, New York: Atheneum, 1968), pp. 260–63; Horace R. Cayton and George S. Mitchell, *Black Workers and the New Unions* (Chapel Hill: University of North Carolina Press, 1939), p. 79; Gottlieb, *Making Their Own Way*, pp. 152, 156–64, 172. Cleveland (along with Wheeling, West Virginia) constituted an exception, in that its black steelworkers were "almost completely unionized." There, the Amalgamated Association did make a special effort to recruit them. It is also possible that, because black

Cleveland did not have the institutional framework found in black Chicago, the union did not face some of the competitive obstacles that I discuss below. See Kusmer, *A Ghetto Takes Shape*, pp. 186–87, 197.

9. For a detailed discussion of packinghouse organizing between 1917 and 1922, see David Brody, *The Butcher Workmen: A Study in Unionization* (Cambridge, Mass.: Harvard University Press, 1964), pp. 75–105. Earlier use of black strikebreakers in Chicago's stockyards is discussed in Alma Herbst, *The Negro in the Slaughtering and Meat-Packing Industry in Chicago* (Boston: Houghton Mifflin, 1932), pp. 14–19; Spero and Harris, *Black Worker*, pp. 264–68; Spear, *Black Chicago*, pp. 38–39; and Tuttle, *Race Riot*, pp. 114–20. On Foster and Fitzpatrick's recognition of the necessity of organizing blacks, see e.g., William Z. Foster, "How Life Has Been Brought into the Stockyards," *Life and Labor* 8, no. 4 (April 1918): 64; and Spero and Harris, *Black Worker*, p. 270. On AFL attitudes toward blacks, see Spero and Harris, *Black Worker*, pp. 17–22, 92; Ira de A. Reid, ed., *Negro Membership in American Labor Unions* (New York: Alexander Press, 1930), p. 104; Bernard Mandel, "Samuel Gompers and the Negro," *Journal of Negro History* 40, no. 1 (January 1955): 34–60; Marc Karson and Ronald Radosh, "The American Federation of Labor and the Negro Worker, 1894–1945," in Julius Jacobson, ed., *The Negro and the American Labor Movement* (Garden City: Anchor Books, 1968), pp.158–60.

10. "Arbitration between the Chicago Meat Packers and Their Employees," 20 June 1919, pp. 178, 290, Federal Mediation and Conciliation Service (FMCS), Records, File 33/864, RG 280 (Washington National Records Center, Suitland); Spero and Harris, *Black Worker*, p. 271.

11. "Arbitration between the Chicago Meat Packers and Their Employees," pp. 429, 456, 474, 491. For membership estimates, see Sandburg, *Chicago Race Riots*, p. 45; Chicago Commission on Race Relations (CCRR), *The Negro in Chicago: A Study of Race Relations and a Race Riot* (Chicago: University of Chicago Press, 1922), p. 413; A. Philip Randolph and Chandler Owen, "The Cause of and Remedy for Race Riots," *The Messenger* 2, no. 9 (September 1919): 18; Howard R. Gold and Byron K. Armstrong, *A Preliminary Study of Inter-Racial Conditions in Chicago* (New York: Home Missions Council, 1920), p. 14. Because observers stated that "most" black workers joined Local 651, it is unlikely that other locals included more than 2,000 black members.

12. *NM*, 12 July 1919.

13. Fitzpatrick quoted in Herbst, *Negro in Slaughtering and Meat-Packing*, p. 37. For evidence of Fitzpatrick's reputation among blacks, see the correspondence in John Fitzpatrick Papers, box 25 (Chicago Historical Society [CHS]).

14. U.S. Department of Labor, Division of Negro Economics, *The Negro at Work during the World War and During Reconstruction* (Washington, DC, Government Printing Office, 1921); the same statement can be found in a memo from Haynes to the Secretary of Labor, 27 August 1919, U.S. Department of Labor, File8/102e, Chief Clerk's File, RG 174 (Washington, DC, National Archives).

15. The "leaderless" image is an artifact of the overwhelming opposition to northward migration among the recognized black leadership in the South, especially at Tuskegee and similar institutions. Because black southerners with the greatest access to newspapers, speakers platforms, and the ears of whites, opposed the movement, even the most astute observers accepted the thesis. Du Bois quoted without dispute a Mississippi preacher's claim that "leaders of the race . . . had nothing to do with it." John Hope called the movement, "unled, unguided," and W. T. B. Williams of Tuskegee agreed that it was a "movement without organization or leadership." Black and white newspapers agreed that the movement was "headless," as did such influential students of the migration as Charles Johnson, Monroe Work, and Emmett Scott. See W. E. B. Du Bois, "The Migration of Negroes," *Crisis* 14, no. 2 (June 1917): 66; John Hope to W. T. B. Williams, 1 November 1919, W. T. B. Williams Mss., "1921" fol., box 6 (I am indebted to John Vernon for this quotation); U.S. Department of Labor, Division of Negro Economics, *Negro Migration, 1916–17* (Washington, DC, Government Printing Office, 1919), p. 95; *Southwestern Christian Advocate*, 9 March 1918,

reprint in NULR, box 86, Series 6; clipping from [Birmingham] *Age-Herald*, 21 March 1917, in Arthur Mitchell Papers, fol. 1, box 1, CHS; folder marked "Migration Study, Newspaper Extracts, 1916–1917," passim, NULR, box 87, Series 6; *Minutes of the University Commission on Race Questions* (1917), p. 42. For the consensus that the migration was "leaderless," see Tuttle, *Race Riot*, p. 93fn.

16. On Southern white opposition to northward black migration, see Grossman, *Land of Hope*, pp. 38–39, 43–55.

17. Grossman, *Land of Hope*; Gottlieb, *Making Their Own Way*, pp. 23–30, 40–59. On the *Defender*, see James R. Grossman, "Blowing the Trumpet: The Chicago *Defender* and Black Migration to Chicago During World War I," *Illinois Historical Journal* 78, no. 2 (Summer 1985): 82–96.

18. Johnson, "Beginning of the Exodus of 1916–1917," pp. 1, 7, and "Labor Agents," pp. 1–2, NULR, folder marked "Migration Study, Draft (Final) Chapters 7–13" [1917], box 86, Series 6; Scott, *Negro Migration during the War*, pp. 38–39, 53–55. For evidence of northern agents recruiting in Florida, see Jerrell Shofner, "Florida and the Black Migration," *Florida Historical Quarterly* 57, no. 3 (January 1979): 270–71. On recruitment of workers in industries in East Tennessee, but otherwise "spontaneous and unorganized" migration from that state, see Lester Lamon, *Black Tennesseans, 1900–1930* (Knoxville: University of Tennessee Press, 1977), p. 126. For evidence that industrialists in Pittsburgh, Milwaukee, and other northern cities sent agents south, see Gottlieb, *Making Their Own Way*, pp. 43–45, 55–59; and Trotter, *Black Milwaukee*, p. 46. Congressional hearings investigating the 1917 riot in East St. Louis turned up little actual evidence of black migrants carried north by labor agents; see Rudwick, *Riot in East St. Louis*, pp. 20, 166–70. On the influence of rumors about agents, see e.g., Charles Johnson, "Stimulation of the Movement," p. 5, NULR, "Draft." On the insignificance of the agents as factors in the decision to leave the South, see *Negro Migration*, p. 100; Johnson, "Jackson, Mississippi," p. 1, NULR, folder marked "Migration Study, Mississippi Summary," in box 86, Series 6.

19. *Negro in Chicago*, p. 424.

20. Spero and Harris, *Black Worker*, pp. 183–86; Johnson, "Meridian," p. 1, NULR, "Mississippi Summary"; Eugene Kinckle Jones to Secretaries of the Affiliated Organizations, 8 April 1918; and T. H. Dwelle to Jones, 11 April 1918, both in NULR, box 87, Series 6; Paul Worthman, "Black Workers and Labor Unions in Birmingham, Alabama, 1897–1904," *Labor History* 10, no. 3 (Summer 1969): 394–95; Paul Worthman and James Green, "Black Workers in the New South, 1865–1915," in Nathan I. Huggins, Martin Kilson, and Daniel M. Fox eds., *Key Issues in the Afro-American Experience* (New York: Harcourt, Brace, Jovanovich, 1971), vol. 2, p. 61; *Defender*, 7 October 1916.

21. Estimates on black membership in these organizations vary; I have presented a range or a conservative figure. Spero and Harris, *Black Worker*, pp. 331–33; Philip Foner, *Organized Labor and the Black Worker, 1619–1973* (New York: Praeger Publishers, 1974), pp. 49, 56, 115; Vernon H. Jensen, *Lumber and Labor* (New York: Farrar and Rinehart, 1945), pp. 87–91; Nollie Hickman, *Mississippi Harvest* (Oxford: University of Mississippi Press, 1962), pp. 236–37; August Meier and Elliott Rudwick, "Attitudes of Negro Leaders Toward the American Labor Movement from the Civil War to World War I," in *The Negro and the American Labor Movement*, p. 33; Martin Dann, "Black Populism: A Study of the Colored Farmers' Alliance Through 1891," *Journal of Ethnic Studies* 2, no. 3 (Fall 1974): 62–69.

22. John Dittmer, *Black Georgia in the Progressive Era, 1900–1920* (Urbana: University of Illinois Press, 1977), p. 30; Spero and Harris, *Black Worker*, 252–53; Lamon, *Black Tennesseans*, pp. 159–60, 162, 164; Lorenzo Greene and Carter Woodson, *The Negro Wage Earner* (Washington, DC: Association for the Study of Negro Life and History, 1930), pp. 186–92; Reid, *Negro Membership in American Labor Unions*, p. 43; George S. Mitchell, "The Negro in Southern Unionism," *The Southern Economic Journal* 2, no. 3 (January 1936): 26–33; Worthman and Green, "Black Workers in the New South," p. 62; "The Negro Railway Trainman and the U.S. Railway Labor Board," Abram L. Harris Papers,

Decision No. 307, Docket 138, Chicago, 4 November 1921, folder 16, box 43–1 (Washington, DC, Moreland-Spingarn Research Center, Howard University). See also William H. Harris, *The Harder We Run: Black Workers since the Civil War* (New York: Oxford University Press, 1982), pp. 46–48.

23. Foster, *The Great Steel Strike and Its Lessons*, p. 211.

24. On efficiency clubs, see "Arbitration between the Chicago Meat Packers and Their Employees," pp. 267–69, FMCS, File 33/864, RG 280; Cayton and Mitchell, *Black Workers and the New Unions*, pp. 392–93; George R. Arthur, *Life on the Negro Frontier* (New York: Association Press, 1934), p. 186; Arthur, "The Young Men's Christian Association Movement Among Negroes," *Opportunity* 1 no. 3 (March 1927): 17; *Defender*, 14 October 1922; *Whip*, 29 October 1921; Arthur to William J. Parker, 10 April 1920, Julius Rosenwald Papers, folder 6, box 44 (Regenstein Library, Univ. of Chicago).

25. For employment bureaus at Olivet, Metropolitan, Institutional, and New Trinity churches, see Olivet Baptist Church, *Facts and Figures* (Chicago, [1920]), p. 4, Papers of the Chicago Commission on Race Relations, 1919–1920 (microfilm), folder 6 (Illinois State Archives, Springfield); Ford S. Black comp., *Black's Blue Book: Directory of Chicago's Active Colored People and Guide to Their Activities* (Chicago: F. S. Black, 1921), pp. 80, 86; E. Jennings, "Institutional A.M.E. Church," Illinois Writers Project, "The Negro in Illinois" Vivian Harsh Collection, box 29 (Churches) (Carter G. Woodson Regional Library, Chicago); Joseph Logsdon, "Reverend Archibald J. Carey and the Negro in Chicago Politics," (Master's thesis, University of Chicago, 1961), pp. 17–18; *Whip*, 11 March 1922. A 1916 description of black Chicago observed that "nearly every colored church has an employment agency as one of its most active auxiliaries"; see Junius Wood, *The Negro in Chicago* (Chicago: Chicago Daily News, 1916), p. 9. On the general influence of Chicago's black churches, see Logsdon, "Reverend Archibald J. Carey," pp. 10–33; Carroll Binder, *Chicago and the New Negro* (Chicago: Chicago Daily News, 1927), p. 17.

26. "Mass Meeting, Tuesday, March 18" [Chicago, 1919], Broadside in Graphics Dept. CHS; *Whip*, 22 November 1919; Sandburg, *Chicago Race Riots*, p. 51; Myra Young Armstead, interview with Ida Mae Cress, 9 April 1985 (tape in possession of author); "Chicago Law and Order League, Hyde Park Protective Association," *Newsletter*, 21 December 1925, Claude Barnett Papers, folder 11, box 2, Section 12 ("Religion") (CHS); "[Report of] Meetings Held with Ministers in an Attempt to Secure Their Cooperation in the Interest of Community Welfare" [August 1920?], Fitzpatrick Papers, box 25 (CHS).

27. Harold Gosnell, *Negro Politicians: The Rise of Negro Politics in Chicago* (Chicago: University of Chicago Press, 1935), p. 320; Quinn Chapel A.M.E. Church, *120th Anniversary Record, 1847–1967* (Chicago, 1967), p. 25; Logsdon, "Reverend Archibald J. Carey," pp. 17, 43, 79–80; Richard R. Wright, *87 Years Behind the Black Curtain: An Autobiography* (Philadelphia: Rare Book Co., 1965), pp. 114–15; *Whip*, 14 May 1921; Wood, *Negro in Chicago*, p. 9; *Negro in Chicago*, pp. 415, 421–22; interviews with black ministers in South Chicago, Ernest W. Burgess Papers, folder 5, box 89, Section 3 ("Research") (Regenstein Library, University of Chicago); Cayton and Mitchell, *Black Workers and the New Unions*, pp. 255–56; Paul S. Taylor, *Mexican Labor in the United States*, vol. 2, p. 2, *Chicago and Calumet Region* (Berkeley: University of California Press, 1932), p. 93.

28. Emmett J. Scott comp., "Letters of Negro Migrants of 1916–1918," *Journal of Negro History* 4 (October 1919): 327; Grossman, "Blowing the Trumpet," pp. 82–95.

29. Grossman, *Land of Hope*, pp. 231–34.

30. *Whip*, 11 October 1919, 7 February 1920. Riley's column first appeared on 19 July 1919. It and articles by other union leaders continued to run until March 1920. For a comparison of space devoted to "industrial relations" in the *Whip* and *Defender*, see *Negro in Chicago*, p. 558.

31. Spero and Harris, *Black Worker*, pp. 281–82; *BW*, December 1921; *Defender*, 17 December 1921. For a classic image of the strikebreaker, see Jack London, "The Scab," in Philip Foner ed., *Jack London, American Rebel* (New York: Citadel Press, 1947).

32. Scott, "Letters of Negro Migrants," pp. 291, 294–95; Chicago Urban League, *Fifth*

Annual Report of the Chicago Urban League (Chicago, 1919), p. 2; Arvarh Strickland, *History of the Chicago Urban League* (Urbana: University of Illinois Press, 1966), p. 71. For notices of "strangers meetings" sponsored by the League, see *Defender*, 18 May, 20 July, 19 October 1918.

33. National Urban League, "The Way Out: A Suggested Solution of the Problems of Race Relations Adopted at the National Urban League Annual Conference, Detroit, Michigan, October 15–19, 1919" (typescript, 1919), NULR, box 5, Series 4. The Chicago Branch's similar position is indicated in Dorothy Crounse, Louise Gilbert, and Agnes Van Driel, "The Chicago Urban League" (Chicago, 1936), pp. 14–15, typescript in Chicago Urban League file, box 286, Records of the Welfare Council of Metropolitan Chicago (CHS). See also Eugene K. Jones, "Coming to the Front," *Opportunity* 4, no. 2 (February 1926): 44.

34. The Industrial Secretary was William Evans; see Evans to John T. Clark, October 7, 1920, Urban League of Pittsburgh Papers (Archives of Industrial Society, Hillman Library, University of Pittsburgh). (I am grateful to Peter Gottlieb for providing a copy of this letter, which he photocopied from the collection when it was still housed in the offices of the Urban League of Pittsburgh.) On Evans's ambivalence, see his "The Negro in Chicago Industries," *Opportunity* 1 no. 2 (February 1923): 15–16. On Hill's pro-union orientation, see T. Arnold Hill, "Recent Developments in the Problem of Negro Labor," *Proceedings of the National Conference of Social Work* 48 (1921): 322–23; A. Philip Randolph et al. to Hugh Frayne, February ?, 1926, Victor Olander Papers, folder 9, box 2 (CHS); T. Arnold Hill, "Address to the Executive Council of the American Federation of Labor," 4 May 1925, NULR, box 87, Series 6; Hill to Robert S. Abbott, 5 April 1926, NULR, box 1, Series 4; Hill to George C. Hall, 18 May 1925, NULR, box 28, Series 4. On George C. Hall's sympathy for unionization, see Strickland, *History of the Chicago Urban League*, p. 28; Sandburg, *Chicago Race Riots*, p. 50; *Defender*, 23 February 1918. On Charles Johnson, see [Charles S. Johnson], "Labor and Race Relations," *Opportunity* 4, no. 37 (January 1926): 4–5.

35. Horace Bridges, "The First Urban League Family," in Chicago Urban League, *Two Decades of Service* (Chicago, 1936), p. 6. The best data on the Urban League's funding sources are in the Julius Rosenwald Papers (Regenstein Library, Univ. of Chicago): see especially lists of donors in folders 13–14, box 9; W[illiam] C. G[raves] to Rosenwald, 26 November 1919, folder 15, box 9; T. Arnold Hill to Graves, 8 February 1921, 2 July 1921, 7 September 1921, and 2 February 1922, folder 16, box 9.

36. *Defender*, 13 May 1922.

37. *Negro in Chicago*, p. 432; the spokesman was probably William Evans.

38. Card distributed by Chicago Urban League, Arthur Aldis Papers, folder 6 (Univ. of Illinois, Chicago); T[homas] J. Woofter, "The Negro and Industrial Peace," *Survey* 45, no. 12 (18 December 1920): 421. See also Strickland, *History of the Chicago Urban League*, pp. 69–70; Claude Barnett, "We Win A Place in Industry," *Opportunity* 8, no. 3 (March 1929): 83.

39. James R. Barrett, *Work and Community in the Jungle: Chicago's Packinghouse Workers, 1894–1922* (Urbana: University of Illinois Press, 1987), p. 204; see also pp. 207–8; and Lizabeth Cohen, *Making a New Deal: Industrial Workers in Chicago, 1919–1939* (New York: Cambridge University Press, 1990), pp. 34, 45. For a more focused analysis of the relationship and the competition between unions and community institutions, see William Kornblum, *Blue Collar Community* (Chicago: University of Chicago Press, 1974).

40. Barrett, *Work and Community in the Jungle*, p. 258; Robert A. Slayton, *Back of the Yards: The Making of a Local Democracy* (Chicago: University of Chicago Press, 1986), pp. 94–95. Slayton's argument that "the entire community rallied to help those out of work" perhaps overstates the unanimity characterizing a community which also had strikebreakers within its midst, but the larger point stands nevertheless.

41. "Arbitration between the Chicago Meat Packers and Their Employees," pp. 221–28, FMCS, File 33/864, RG 280.

42. *NM*, 9 August 1919. The view of Local 651 as a Jim Crow institution is documented

in *Negro in Chicago*, p. 429. On the insensitivity of union newspapers, see *NM*, 1 November 1919, 20 December 1919, 6 and 13 November 1920, 16 December 1920, 16 and 23 April 1921, and 10 June 1922, *BW*, July 1920, and January 1921. The publications of the National Women's Trade Union League (published in Chicago) and the Illinois State Federation of Labor were scarcely interested in black workers; see *Life and Labor Bulletin*, 1921–1929; *Illinois State Federation of Labor Weekly News Letter* 6–9 (1920–1925).

43. Spero and Harris, *Black Worker*, pp. 132, 265; Tuttle, *Race Riot*, pp. 113, 116–22; Eric Hardy, "Relation of the Negro to Trade Unionism" (Master's thesis, University of Chicago, 1911), pp. 35–36.

44. Arbitration between the Chicago Meat Packers and Their Employees," pp. 103, 131–32, 148, 150–57, 177, FMCS, File 33/864, RG 280.

45. Abram L. Harris, "A White and Black World in American Labor and Politics," *Journal of Social Forces* 4 (December 1925): 380.

46. *Negro in Chicago*, p. 424.

47. The seminal studies in this context are Scott, *Negro Migration During the War*, and *Negro Migration*. For an emphasis on natural disasters and the labor market, see Robert Higgs, "The Boll Weevil, the Cotton Economy, and Black Migration: 1910–1930," *Agricultural History* 50, no. 2 (April 1976): 335–50. The most notable exception to this framework was for many years Clyde Kiser, *Sea Island to City: A Study of St. Helena Islanders in Harlem and Other Urban Centers* (New York: Columbia University Press, 1932). The most recent, and most successful, departure from the tradition of viewing the migrants as historical objects rather than subjects is Gottlieb, *Making Their Own Way*. See also Henri, *Black Migration*. An insightful critique of the "push-pull" framework can be found in Neil Fligstein, *Going North: Migration of Blacks and Whites from the South, 1900–1950* (New York: Academic Press, 1981), pp. 65–66.

48. Alain Locke, ed., *The New Negro: An Interpretation* (New York: Albert and Charles Boni, 1925), p. 6; Scott, "Letters," pp. 298–99, 303, 306, 315; Emmett J. Scott, comp., "Additional Letters of Negro Migrants of 1916–1918," *Journal of Negro History* 4 (October 1919): 439; George E. Haynes, "Migration of Negroes into Northern Cities," *Proceedings of the National Conference of Social Work* 44 (1917): 496. Langston is quoted in Leon F. Litwack, *Been in the Storm So Long: The Aftermath of Slavery* (New York: Alfred A. Knopf, 1979), p. 539.

49. Scott, "Additional Letters," p. 428. On the importance of these perquisites of citizenship to emancipated slaves, see Litwack, *Been in the Storm So Long*, p. 547.

50. E. P. Thompson, "Time, Work-Discipline, and Industrial Capitalism," *Past and Present* 38 (December 1967), pp. 56–97; Herbert Gutman, *Work, Culture, and Society in Industrializing America: Essays in American Working-Class and Social History* (New York: Knopf, 1976), pp. 3–78.

51. Helen Sayre, "Making Over Poor Workers," *Opportunity* 2 (February 1923): 17–18; *Fourth Annual Report of the Chicago Urban League* (Chicago, 1920), p. 8; *Negro at Work During the World War and Reconstruction*, pp. 50–51; *Negro in Chicago*, pp. 372–78; George E. Haynes, "Negroes Move North, II," *Survey* 48 (January 1919): 458; Sayre, "Negro Women in Industry," *Opportunity* 2, no. 20 (August 1924): 243–44; Gold and Armstrong, *Preliminary Study*, pp. 11, 13–14; J. O. Houze, "Negro Labor and the Industries," *Opportunity* 1, no. 1 (January 1923): 21; Woofter, "The Negro and Industrial Peace," p. 420; William L. Evans, "An Inquiry into the Working Conditions of Colored Workmen Employed by the Argo Corn Products & Refining Company, Argo, Illinois, 1920," p. 2, NAACP Records, "Jan. 5–April 24, 1922" folder, box C-320 (Library of Congress, Washington DC); "Memorandum 'A'," enclosed in letter from T. Arnold Hill to Walter F. White, 14 November 1919, NAACP Records, "Sept.–Dec., 1919" folder, box C-319; "Conference on the Negro in Industry," Committee on Industry, Chicago Commission on Race Relations, 23 April 1920, Rosenwald Papers, folder 5, box 6.

Getting There, Being There
African-American Migration to Richmond, California, 1910–1945

Shirley Ann Moore

The history of African-Americans in California has been overlooked until recently, even though blacks have had a vital impact on California's political, economic, social, and cultural fabric since the early days of Spanish conquest and rule in the eighteenth century. The San Francisco Bay area became an important center for African-American life in the state by the turn of the century and grew in significance as World War II accelerated black migration to the area. Richmond, California, located in the eastern portion of the San Francisco Bay, became a central economic and residential center to thousands of black people who migrated to the area seeking work and advancement in Richmond's Kaiser shipyards during the 1940s.

Although black people had lived and worked in Richmond from its founding in 1905, their presence and deeds virtually have been cloaked in invisibility by census takers, city officials, and early historians. Richmond's black population of 29 in 1910 grew to 270 by 1940 and, by 1945, the migration of over 100,000 black people to the San Francisco Bay area swelled Richmond's black population by 5,000 percent—or over 7,000 people. This brief study of African-American migration to Richmond, California, is an attempt to illuminate some of the strategies and networks that blacks developed and utilized in their quest for a better life in the Golden State in the decades before and during the boom years of World War II.[1]

The manner in which African-Americans arrived in California during the nineteenth century varied, but once there, all shared an ambiguous social status. Blacks were among the yankee immigrants who sailed to California on New England trading ships during the Mexican era (1821–1848). Black sailors frequently jumped ship at reprovisioning ports along the California coast and then made their way to the small black communities in San Francisco or Sacramento.[2]

During the gold rush era that commenced in 1849, some blacks made their way to California as traders or were brought by white slave owners to work the teeming gold fields. The passage in 1852 of California's Fugitive Slave Law only underscored the precarious status of African-Americans in the state because the selectively-enforced law threatened all blacks with a return to slavery. After 1865 and the passage of the Thirteenth Amendment, which abolished slavery, blacks in California began to think of themselves as residents of the state and the black population began to increase. Between 1850 and 1860, the African-American presence grew from just over 1,000 to almost 5,000, with the majority concentrated in San Francisco and Sacramento. By 1910 black Californians numbered almost 22,000 with the largest two communities being located in Los Angeles in the southern part of the State and San Francisco in northern California.[3]

For the first part of the nineteenth century San Francisco remained the center of black life in Northern California, but, by the late nineteenth and first decade of the twentieth century, the end of the Spanish-American War, labor disputes, and the earthquake and fire of 1906 led a significant portion of the black population to move out of San Francisco to the East Bay. Thus cities like Oakland, Alameda, and Richmond became important cities for African-Americans in northern California. Black people who settled in Richmond during this time were attracted by the numerous industries that city fathers had wooed to the city in their quest to build Richmond into the "Pittsburgh of the West." For example, the Santa Fe Railroad established a San Joaquin Valley line connecting its southern transcontinental route to Richmond, thus making that city a transportation and employment center in the East Bay. Standard Oil came to Richmond in the first decade of the twentieth century, as did the Pullman Coach Repair Company and numerous foundries, factories, and canneries. These industries offered employment opportunities for workers living in all parts of the Bay area.[4]

Early in its history Richmond therefore became an employment resource for African-Americans who migrated to California, whether they settled in the city or chose to live in the larger and more sophisticated cities of Oakland, Berkeley, or San Francisco. In 1910 Richmond's black population of 29 was far smaller than either that of San Francisco (1,642) or Oakland (3,055). The majority of pre–World War II migrants settled in Richmond from the South and Midwest. Seen in a national context, some of Richmond's early black settlers arrived in the city as part of the Great Migration that swept through black communities across the southern United States beginning in 1890 and continuing through the 1920s. Of the estimated 700,000 African-Americans who took part in that massive pre–World War II movement, about 35,000 settled in California and other states of the Far West.[5]

Like many blacks who left the South during that period, some early black Richmondites accomplished their migration in stages, leaving the rural South, settling in southern cities, moving to the North or Midwest, and finally striking out for California. The census of 1910 indicates that several black Richmond residents were part of that migration, coming from Mississippi, Texas, North Carolina, and Pennsylvania. Each stage of migration represented a quest for economic and social advancement and, at the same time, each stage helped to educate the migrants to urban customs and industrial discipline.[6]

African-Americans left their southern homes fleeing drought, floods, insect infestations, disfranchisement, racial oppression, and violence in search of economic opportunity and freedom. The "push" of racism and poverty and the "pull" of California's reputation for freedom and opportunity were important factors in black migration to Richmond. However, blacks who settled in Richmond were not passive victims pushed and pulled in a drama beyond their control. Their decision to migrate and their migrational behavior demonstrate that African-Americans developed strategies to gain a measure of autonomy in their lives and remained active agents in shaping their participation in the urban industrial workforce. Their strategies and networks served to facilitate the goals of economic and social advancement.

Some early black residents utilized kinship, friendship, and employment networks to accomplish their moves. As early as 1919, Joseph Griffin, a farmer in St. Landry Parish, Louisiana, moved his entire family out to Richmond. Griffin family members maintain that, in 1919, Joseph Griffin's plow unearthed a "box full of money" that had been "buried for a long time" in the Louisiana fields he worked. Shortly after the discovery, Mr. Griffin called his family together and instructed them to "pack up for California." The Griffin family purchased property in Richmond and their home became a "way station" for other family members and friends who also wanted to leave their homes and settle in California. Matthew and William Malbrough, two brothers from Louisiana, decided that they "could make more money and provide better" for their families in California than they could working as muleskinners in their home state. Thus, on counsel of a cousin already living in Berkeley, the Malbrough brothers made the long trip out to the Golden State by train, staying with their relatives in Berkeley until they found employment in a Richmond factory. Within a year, they were able to send for the rest of the family still in Louisiana.[7]

Louis Bonaparte, Sr., another early Richmond resident, worked as a Pullman porter on the Missouri Pacific Railroad in Louisiana and first came to Richmond on a vacation pass in the 1920s. Impressed with the "freedom that colored" people seemed to enjoy in California, he decided to make Richmond his permanent home in 1924. As a Pullman porter Mr. Bonaparte served as a kind of "scout" for other prospective migrants who wanted to come to the area. His favorable reports about the city induced others to come out. Similarly, Charles Henry Thurston, a migrant to Richmond in the 1940s, learned of the employment opportunities in Richmond through his Baptist church choir activities in his home state of Mississippi. He "traveled all over the South" for choir conventions discussing the "pros and cons" of migrating out to California with other church people. Mr. Thurston moved out in 1943 and boarded with church friends in Oakland before moving to Richmond to work in the wartime Ford Motor Company that had located in the city in 1931. Thus, early black Richmond residents, like thousands of others who comprised the Great Migration, made an informed decision to leave their old homes, relying on their personal and kinship networks to help in their transition to the urban industrial West.[8]

Despite their hopes for economic advancement and great social freedom, however, prewar black migrants quickly realized that their economic opportunities would be limited by constraints of law and custom. Although African-Americans in California had won citizenship rights in the nineteenth century, they still were prevented from exercising those rights fully. For example, black children were assigned to predominantly black schools; black families were confronted with "restrictive covenants" which barred them from buying property or living in certain neighborhoods; blacks were refused service in public accommodations; and black job seekers were denied employment outside the "traditional" spheres of service, domestic and unskilled labor. The census of 1910 indicates that black men in Richmond did indeed find themselves relegated to unskilled labor. Their wages, while "better than down South," were less than those of whites doing comparable work. Pay ranged from 25¢ to 50¢ an hour for blacks working in industries such as the Santa Fe Railroad, Pullman, Certainteed Manufacturing, and various foundries and canneries in and around the city.[9]

Competition for jobs among black workers was so keen that one prewar black resident explained that "you'd have to wait for somebody to die" to get hired by the industries. Unlike certain white ethnic immigrants who worked in Eastern factories and industries in the late nineteenth and early twentieth centuries, prewar black Richmond workers encountered little success in utilizing kinship or friendship referrals for industrial employment. White immigrants benefited from stereotypes which characterized them as willing, untiring, and docile workers and bosses eagerly hired them and their relatives with the same "traits" to feed the labor-hungry industries of the East and Midwest.

In contrast, black urban industrial workers encountered "negative stereotypes" which branded them as "inefficient, unsuitable and unstable," and made factory owners reluctant to "take a chance" on hiring them. Black industrial workers in Richmond therefore found themselves operating within a marginal employment environment in which kinship and friendship networks had little influence. For the most part they were "on their own." William Malbrough recalled that the practice of a black employee "putting in a good word" to a supervisor for a relative or friend was not effective in securing employment. To get work, he declared, "you'd just get out and get going place to place. Depending on where business was good, that's where you would go."[10]

Irene Malbrough Batchan noted that Richmond industries would hire blacks "if you were just brute strength, they could hire you for lifting pieces of steel but if you had a little bit of education, [they would not hire you]." Walter Freeman, Jr. worked at a Richmond manufacturing company where most of the black men "hand pull[ed] 1200-pound bales of rags. They would take a hook, put it in the bale, pull it down and bring it in.'' Blacks worked in several local foundries where the work was particularly hard. Irene Malbrough Batchan recalled that men who did foundry work "could take the iron for about twenty years before breaking down, hernia. I'm talking about what the men did!'' Although white workers might perform the same arduous work, they could aspire to move up the employment ladder. Black workers had no such option.[11]

Black women also were limited to arduous, low-paying, unskilled labor in pre–World War II Richmond. Female workers fit into the typical employment pattern of domestic service that generally characterized urban employment for black women across the country. The 1910 census indicates that black women who worked outside the home served as domestic workers in the affluent suburban and hill communities surrounding Richmond. Black women found that they could more readily obtain work as maids, cooks, and laundresses, than could black men who were often only marginally employed as seasonal or "occasional" workers in Richmond's industries. Irene Malbrough Batchan, who settled in Richmond in 1926, noted that black women who "weren't too old . . . were working cleaning up white folks' kitchen, cleaning [and] cooking.'' In 1915 Jessie Freeman (wife of Walter Freeman, Sr.) worked as a cook for a white family in San Francisco, coming home to Richmond only on weekends. In 1939 Richmond resident Mattie Slocum was the "biggest breadwinner in the family" thanks to her "live-in" domestic job in Orinda (a white suburb of Oakland, California) which permitted her to come home "every once in a while.''[12]

In contrast to black men, black female domestic workers in Richmond, like their counterparts studied by Borchert in the alley communities of Washington, DC, often served as liaisons between their community and the white world in which they worked, expanding economic opportunity and social contact for themselves and for black men whose access to the white sphere was even more limited. For example, Irene Malbrough Batchan recalled that "if they [white employers] liked the way the women would work in their homes or did ironing, they might throw some work to your husband or son or something from time to time.'' Jessie Freeman worked as a cook for a white doctor's family in San Francisco and "picked up lots of good medical sense,'' to try out on her occasionally ailing children. George and Ida Johnson, prewar Richmond residents, worked for a wealthy white East Bay financier who "taught" them "all about the stock market" and warned them of the impending crash in 1929. The financial tip proved only of passing interest to the Johnsons, however, since they "didn't have any money invested anyway.''[13]

Black workers in Richmond soon discovered that low-paying employment was not limited to industrial or domestic service, however. Black Richmondites found employment in the city's agricultural sector as well. Similar to Southern cities like Birmingham, Atlanta, and New Orleans, which were in transition from rural to urban at the turn of the century, Richmond's rural character continued to coexist with its industrial aspirations until World War II changed everything. Richmond resident Ivy Reid Lewis, whose family settled in the city in the 1930s, recalled that black residents nicknamed North Richmond "Cabbage Patch" because of the numerous Portuguese- and Italian-owned vegetable farms located there. Farm owners often hired black Richmondites with horses or mules to "do a little plowing or truck farming for them." For their efforts these agricultural workers received $3 to $5 a day or, as William Malbrough recalled, "whatever they thought you were worth." Additionally, some black residents augmented their income by raising and marketing dairy animals, poultry, and produce at home.[14]

On the eve of World War II, Richmond's unofficial but widespread practice of residential segregation through restrictive covenants had forced most of the black population of 270 into the North Richmond area. Because the city limits ran through the center of the neighborhood, one portion of the community lived inside city limits, while the rest remained in the unincorporated county portion. North Richmond lacked adequate police and fire protection, had few paved roads or street lights, and was in close proximity to the garbage dump. In this respect Richmond resembled other black urban communities which also suffered from inadequate city services and undesirable housing conditions. Kusmer, for example, identified the problem of restrictive covenants and housing segregation as being responsible for pushing Cleveland's 8,500 blacks "down the road to the ghetto." Borchert suggests that similar discrimination and flight by white property owners caused Washington, DC's 20,000 black alley residents to cluster in run-down, ill-served alley residences, and Bodnar's study of black Pittsburgh relates a similar pattern of community formation before World War II.

However, while the seeds of ghetto formation had been planted in prewar Richmond, the black neighborhoods in that city did not take on the contours of Eastern ghettos until the wartime boom of the 1940s when black newcomers flooded into the city and whites abandoned the area. Before World War II most black Richmondites maintained that Richmond offered them more social and economic freedom than the Jim Crow South despite the constraints which kept them on the lowest rung of the city's economic and social ladder. In general they enjoyed the "California lifestyle" and expressed no regrets about coming out to the Golden State. Most believed that positive change would come about gradually, but they never doubted their decision to migrate from their home states of the South.[15]

World War II changed the assumptions of gradualism for blacks and whites throughout the United States and in Richmond as well. From 1942 to 1945, 340,000 black people poured into California from all over the United States, with the largest number coming from Louisiana, Mississippi, Texas, Oklahoma, and Arkansas. Approximately 125,000 moved to the San Francisco Bay Area, with some 14,000 settling in Richmond. The war had a profound impact on every aspect of life in the city. It changed economic and social relationships, increased racial segregation, forged an uneasy alliance between black oldtimers and newcomers, and expanded the black urban industrial workforce. This transformation was precipitated by the location of the Kaiser shipyards in Richmond. As the federal government stepped up the pace of military preparedness during 1940, Congressional attention shifted to California where climate, open spaces, and natural resources made it an ideal site for military production. Thus, the government decided to invest almost half of its $70 billion national defense budget in the Golden State. Federal spending rejuvenated southern California's languishing aircraft industry and greatly expanded the shipbuilding capabilities of northern California.[16]

As aggressive western industrialists successfully landed lucrative government contracts, an infusion of over $3 billion worth of shipbuilding orders converted sleepy northern California coastal towns like Sausalito, Vallejo, and Richmond into bustling defense industry centers. Industrialists like Henry J. Kaiser, having successfully completed construction of the Grand Coulee Dam in Washington, enlisted the "good offices" of Bank of America's A. P. Giannini to influence the Roosevelt administration in his bid for contracts to construct thirty British merchant ships for Roosevelt's "arsenal of democracy." Richmond developer Fred Parr then persuaded Kaiser to locate his new enterprise at Richmond Harbor, California's second-largest port. Construction on the first shipyard began in early 1941 and, by year's end, four yards covered almost 900 acres. Kaiser shipyards became the most important and pervasive wartime industry in the city, employing over 150,000 workers, some 25,000 of whom were black. Yet, from the beginning, the yards proved to be a mixed blessing to the city. On one hand, they provided the industrial base that city officials had sought since the city's incorporation in 1905; but, on the other hand, the yards attracted thousands of workers whose needs severely strained city resources and disrupted established patterns of city life.[17]

Wartime labor needs sparked a Western population migration paralleling that of the gold and silver rushes of the nineteenth and early twentieth centuries. Of the 8 million people who moved west of the Mississippi in the decade of the 1940s, nearly one-half came to the Pacific coast. California received 3.5 million new residents, swelling the population from 6,907,000 in 1940 to 10,586,000 in 1950. Between 1940 and 1945, over 340,000 black people migrated to California. Over one-third settled in the San Francisco Bay Area. Richmond's black population increased 5,000 percent by 1943 to 5,673, and, by 1945, over 14,000 black people resided in Richmond. On average, these black migrants were young (23.13 years); more females (53 percent) than males (47 percent) made the journey; and most black migrants were married.

Blacks who came to Richmond during the war years represented the middle stratum of their southern communities. Theirs was not a migration of DuBois' "talented tenth" as early scholars like Carter Woodson postulated about the First Great Migration. Nor was their decision to leave the South only a reaction to political oppression. Rather, it appears that black migration to Richmond during World War II fits the pattern of migration suggested by historian Clyde Kiser in which southern-born blacks gradually expanded their employment parameters in ever-widening circles of secondary migration. This process saw black people move from the rural South to southern urban centers, to the cities of the North, and finally to the urban West.

Thus, migration to Richmond was part of a process begun in the nineteenth century and accelerated in the 1940s. Prewar black residents like Matthew Malbrough, who came out from the South to secure work in Richmond's early industries, represent the first wave of that process in the city. The influx of black migrants to Richmond's wartime shipyards only extended and intensified that process. African-American workers in the 1940s, continuing a pattern established in the last century, left their southern homes for work in defense industries of the North and Midwest and extended their area of migration and job opportunity to include the cities of the West. California became the destination of choice for the majority of black migrants, and Richmond's Kaiser shipyards attracted a significant portion of the African-American newcomers during World War II.[18]

Getting to Richmond proved almost as complex as the urban industrial experiences the migrants encountered upon arrival in the city. In addition to official recruitment efforts, black migrants relied on personal networks to inform and assist them in their move. Although official recruiting efforts by the Kaiser yards accounted for thousands of African-Americans coming to Richmond, black migrants tended to utilize their own friendship, kinship, and social channels to facilitate their migration from the South. Less than a year after launching its first ship, Kaiser initiated an intensive recruitment drive in June of 1942. Employing innovative recruitment techniques, Kaiser and the Richmond Chamber of Commerce distributed over 30,000 "job fact sheets" to hundreds of United States Employment Service Offices nationwide urging able-bodied men to come out to the shipyards. In an effort to fill its daily quota of 150 new workers, Kaiser stationed special shipyard "spotters" along the California border to direct newcomers to the Richmond yards.

After the passage of Executive Order 8802 banned race discrimination in defense industries, black workers accelerated their influx into the state. Hoping to capitalize on blacks' preference for wartime work in California, Kaiser shipyards in Richmond dispatched recruiters throughout the South to scour the area specifically for black workers, the last remaining untapped labor resource available to the labor-hungry wartime shipyards. Placing newspaper advertisements in the local papers and plastering black neighborhoods with brightly colored recruitment flyers, Kaiser made specific appeals to African-Americans residing in the South. Recruiting literature stressed Kaiser's pay benefits and minimal skill requirements, in addition to extolling the virtues of California's climate and recreational facilities. Margaret Starks, who moved to Richmond in 1943, recalled that a Kaiser recruitment advertisement in her home town newspaper in Pine Bluff, Arkansas, "caught my eye." Showing it to her husband, she urged him to "go to California and get a job [then] send for me later."[19]

Though official recruiting channels were important to black migration to Richmond during the 1940s, unofficial networks of church associations, railroad workers, and kinship and friendship ties helped to spread the news of Richmond's opportunities to potential migrants. Church affiliation contributed to the dissemination of employment news to southern blacks contemplating a move westward. For example, Charles Henry Thurston, who came to Richmond in 1943 from Jackson, Mississippi, was influenced by his participation in Baptist church choir conventions throughout the South. His son, Bill Thurston, recalled that Charles Henry "knew people from all over the state; he had been all over the state singing. I'm sure someone told him or my uncle that there was work [in Richmond]." Debating the "future of black people" in Mississippi with other "church people" as he traveled from one singing engagement to another, Charles Henry Thurston concluded that Richmond offered more promise for his family than did Mississippi. In 1943 he and his brother boarded the train in Jackson for Oakland, California. The two men lived with church friends who had settled in Berkeley a few years earlier. After landing a job with the Ford Motor Company in Richmond making steel plates for military vehicles, Mr. Thurston saved enough money to send train fare to his wife and son who joined him in 1944.[20]

Carrying the message of job opportunities up and down the Southern Pacific and Santa Fe Lines, Richmond- and Oakland-based railroad porters and maids helped persuade family and friends in the South to make the move. Louis Bonaparte, a retired railroad porter residing in Richmond since the 1920s, found that "people looked up to railroad workers everywhere," and their views about "what to do" and "where to go" were given considerable weight. In addition to this "word-of-mouth" persuasion, correspondence networks also provided powerful inducements for migration. Similar to black correspondence networks of the First Great Migration in the late nineteenth and early twentieth centuries, glowing letters from bay area newcomers to their loved ones at home played a large role in getting people to leave their homes in the South. One black newcomer to Richmond explained: "My brother came out here in 1942. He sent letters and said that wages was good and that we could get some good paying jobs. He wrote a lot of letters and we decided we would come out here and work in the shipyard." Another shipyard worker was persuaded to come to Richmond by letters from a former co-worker: "I had a friend out here who used to work at the lumber mill with me. . . . He wrote me to come out here and get one of these defense jobs." The two men became co-workers again in the Richmond shipyards.[21]

Thus, church membership, family, friends, and co-workers made up the personal recruiting networks that led some 25,000 black newcomers to work in Richmond's shipyards and nearly 7,000 to settle in the city by 1945. While the majority of them sought to extend their economic opportunities through migration from unskilled, agricultural labor to work in the urban industrial sector, black people also left their homes for reasons as complex and personal as the racial and social milieu of the Jim Crow South. For example, economic and social mobility was a persuasive factor in bringing many black men and women out from the South. The opportunity to earn a living outside the "traditional" sphere proved to be a powerful attraction for many. An ex-farmer from the South summed up the feelings of many black migrants who wanted to break free of old patterns: "It looked like just about everybody was going into the army or doing war work [so] I sold my tools and mules and come out to Richmond."[22] Similarly, Richmond's shipyards presented black women with the opportunity to break out of the low-paying domestic service rut Jim Crow imposed on them in the South. One Marshall, Texas migrant explained:

> You see, I am a colored woman and I am forty-two years old. Now you know that colored women don't have a chance for any kind of job back there [Texas] except in somebody's kitchen working for two or three dollars a week. I have an old mother and a crippled aunt to take care of. . . . I went to work for Kaiser and saved enough money to bring my aunt and mother out here.[23]

Decent wages and social mobility notwithstanding, some migrants struck out for Richmond because the threat of violence which permeated most aspects of race relations in the South had become intolerable. For instance, a black laborer in a Mobile, Alabama, shipyard decided to leave his hometown for Richmond not so much for the higher wages, but because "they had this riot there [Mobile] and a lot of the colored workers got beat up and I was afraid to go back in the yard . . . " Having endured a terrifying night in which "white men rode around . . . [and] threw rocks at our houses," he and his wife joined a group of black Mobile residents who were preparing to leave for Richmond: "I didn't even wait for my check. . . . [We] just decided to leave." Despite the "good pay" and greater freedom offered in California, the Richmond newcomer declared, "I don't guess I would have ever come out here unless they had had that riot."[24]

Although black migrants to Richmond readily admitted that "things were better than down South," conditions in Richmond's shipyards and in the city itself were far from ideal for African-Americans who worked and lived there. Black newcomers initially met a chilly reception from many longtime black residents who feared the newly arrived blacks, whom they characterized as uneducated, abrasive, and "lower class," would jeopardize their tenuous position in Richmond's economic and social hierarchy. Todd Iverson, the Deputy Probation Officer for Alameda County, adjacent to Richmond's Contra Costa County, explained that black migrants' "aggressive" reputation stemmed from the fact that their newly acquired status as vital war workers made them, "independent of [white] natives to find jobs." Determined never to go back to the deference and accommodation that marked their lives in the South, many black newcomers defended against any infringement on their newfound freedom by acting "rough, very ready to fight and to use any method to win." Thus, longtime black residents who believed any change in racial relations would evolve gradually, viewed newcomer assertiveness as evidence of brash, "lower class breeding and behavior," destined to destroy the economic and social gains blacks had managed to achieve. Wilbur Wheat, a migrant to Richmond in 1942, suggested that jealousy also motivated the friction between black newcomers and longtime residents since "they who was here [black longtime residents] wasn't doing much of anything when they that come [black migrants] started doing [some]thing, making a little progress. They didn't like it very much."[25]

The intraracial class conflict that developed between oldtimers and newcomers had at its core contrasting assumptions about the rate and scope of racial progress. However, as the black population swelled during the war years and racial constraints tightened on the entire African-American population in Richmond, both groups were compelled to come together to push for an end to racial discrimination. Just as black people began to settle into California's urban centers, municipalities from Los Angeles to San Francisco responded to their influx by establishing more stringent social, political, and economic restrictions on all black residents, newcomers and longtime residents alike. For example, residential restrictions tightened so that blacks became concentrated in the North Richmond section, with little chance of moving from that burgeoning ghetto. Little "privileges" enjoyed by black prewar residents, such as cashing paychecks at white-owned downtown stores, or being buried in the "white" cemetery, were curtailed as more black residents settled in the city. In contrast to prewar public schools in which the small number of black students appear to have enjoyed equal treatment from teachers and administrators, black school children in the 1940s were increasingly segregated in lower level classes in the city's public schools and labelled "slow learners" and "trouble-makers" by school officials who were not inclined or able to deal with the huge increase in students, black and white. Black Richmondites of the 1940s found that the local newspaper and the police department began to characterize criminal activity in racial terms, giving a distorted picture of black criminal activity and stigmatizing the entire community.[26]

Longtime Richmond residents, white and black, often attributed racial friction in the city and in the workplace to the influx of southern whites ("Okies") whom residents believed brought with them a cultural baggage of race prejudice. Even though "Okies" suffered the scorn of longtime resident whites because of their "twangy" speech and "unsophisticated" dress and behavior, the influx of black migrants to the city resulted in white residents labelling all blacks as ignorant, "pushy" nuisances who no longer knew their "place." Black newcomers and longtime residents alike quickly saw that white migrants found it easier to assimilate into the city's economic and social mainstream. White newcomers might need their "rough edges worn off" before they were assimilated, but, in contrast to African-Americans, few compulsory obstacles to employment and advancement stood in the way of their transition. All of this represented hardening white attitudes which blacks also encountered in the workplace.[27]

For black Richmondites entry into the urban industrial workforce proved to be a prolonged and shaded process beginning in the prewar years and accelerating in World War II. Wartime opportunities resulted in a notable but limited advancement in the economic sector but this "shift upward" could not be sustained once the shipyards and other defense industries shut down in the postwar period. Moreover, although the vast majority of African-Americans who migrated to Richmond during World War II experienced a distinct "shift upward" in economic status, skills, and occupation, a small number of black migrants experienced a decline in those areas because of persistent racial discrimination in the defense industries. Some non-agricultural black workers arrived in the yards with professional training or skills from urban centers of the South yet suffered a "downward thrust into unskilled labor" upon entry into Richmond's industrial workforce.

A University of California study of fifty unemployed black shipyard workers conducted in 1947 suggests that a number of black migrants had acquired professional and industrial training and a degree of urban sophistication from living and working in the urban South. Southern cities such as New Orleans, Mobile, Houston, Pine Bluff, Jackson, and Oklahoma City provided these migrants with their first encounters with life in a non-agricultural work environment. These black workers had previously held occupations such as carpenter, compress machine operator, stonecutter, welder, truck driver, clerk, sheet metal worker, cement handler, and stationary fireman. In addition, a few black newcomers had earned their livings as school teachers and principals in southern schools. Freed from the planting-cultivation-harvest cycle imposed by farming, a number of migrants attained a higher educational level (eighth grade) than did newcomers from rural areas of the same states. This contrasts with the popular image of all black migrants as unlettered, rural peasants.[28]

Although the Depression of the 1930s crippled the nation's economy and imposed hardship and deprivation on Americans of all races, African-Americans, generally precariously clinging to the bottom rung of the economic ladder, suffered especially hard. Despite this fact, Richmond's black population actually increased during the Depression years, growing from just 48 in 1930 to 270 in 1940. The increase in the city's black population can be explained by several factors. California's reputation continued to attract black migrants who felt they didn't have much to lose by "riding the rails," "driving," or walking to the Golden State to pursue a better life. The state's mild climate, agricultural employment, and reputation for "easy living" still made it an attractive destination for the Depression-Era unemployed and African-Americans joined their white counterparts in pouring into the state seeking work. Most black newcomers who settled in the city during the 1930s looked to the scaled-back but still functioning industries for employment. Most had managed to avoid closure by reducing shifts and cutting wages. The Ford assembly plant actually moved to Richmond in 1931 and became the city's largest employer after Standard Oil. Unlike Standard Oil, Ford hired black workers, who remained last hired and first fired.

Moreover, African-Americans in Richmond relied on a well-developed network of church, benevolent, and other community institutions as a "safety-net" to see them through. For example, church-related "feeding stations," "clean-clothes" closets, and food drives contributed to community cohesiveness and spirit. The growth of the African-American community during the hard years of the 1930s suggests a high degree of stability, self-esteem , and hope for the future that existed among African-Americans in Richmond despite their small numbers. Their optimism seemed to be confirmed when Kaiser Shipyards located in the city in 1940.

When the war opened up defense jobs on the west coast, African-Americans once again migrated from the urban South seeking greater economic opportunity only to find their occupation potential rigidly circumscribed by discriminatory hiring policies in the shipyards and other defense industries in Richmond. For the most part, skilled black migrants were barred from working at their previously acquired crafts in Richmond during and after the war boom. Thus, for a minority of African-American migrants entry into Richmond's urban industrial sector meant a decrease in occupational status and prestige but an increase in economic earnings. Charles Henry Thurston, a school teacher and principal in Jackson, Mississippi, was representative of this group. He migrated from Jackson and found defense work in the Richmond Ford plant. Although Mr. Thurston's pay of $50 to $60 a week at Ford represented a "vast amount more" than his salary as an educator in Mississippi, his family viewed his new position as "definitely a step down." However, they pragmatically accepted his new status: "Credentialing was very loose in the South [and Richmond schools] did not hire black teachers. He couldn't have taught in Richmond anyway. The best thing he could do was forget the prestige and make the money."[29]

Thousands of black workers were thus compelled to adopt a similarly realistic attitude toward their employment opportunities, yet racial discrimination and hostility in Richmond's wartime industries made even that path difficult for black workers. For example, in her study of Oakland, California's Moore shipyards in the 1940s, Katherine Archibald concluded that an undercurrent of racial tension constantly simmered beneath the veneer of wartime unity in bay area shipyards, and the Kaiser yards in Richmond were not exempt. Black shipyard worker Wilbur Wheat expressed the frustration of many blacks who came to Richmond during the war: "Some whites were nice, [but] like all peckerwoods [they] couldn't stand being around colored people. They would do anything to mess you up!"[30]

While many white workers disliked working alongside of blacks in the shipyards, Kaiser management appears to have exacerbated the situation by deferring to the racially exclusionary policies of the shipyard unions, letting them establish wage and promotional policies which discriminated against black workers in return for labor stability and productivity. African-Americans, regardless of skill level, ability, or training, found restrictive, union-enforced limitations placed on employment and promotions. While the Machinists', Painters' and Shipfitters' Unions all maintained exclusionary policies, the much larger Boilermakers' Union erected the greatest obstacles to black advancement. Controlling yard hiring with the tacit consent of management, Local 513 of the Boilermakers' Union came under condemnation from the director of the local office of the United States Employment Services Agency who flatly stated: "The hiring practices of the Boilermakers' Union have prevented Negro men and women from being employed in shipyards at Richmond solely because they are Negroes."[31]

The policies of Local 513 had the effect of keeping blacks' wages lower and barring them from better-paying jobs in the yards. Wilbur Wheat explained that he quit his job as a "leaderman" rather than be assigned to a segregated, "all colored crew" since union policy would not let a black person head a racially mixed crew. After passing the welder's test "with flying colors," longtime bay area resident and civil rights activist, Frances Mary Albrier, had her application turned down at Kaiser because the company "had not yet set up an auxiliary [union] to take in Negroes." Undeterred, Mrs. Albrier threatened to sue Kaiser if she were not permitted to join Local 513 and work at her trade in the shipyards. Mrs. Albrier was permitted to work at Kaiser, but white union officials sent her dues to the black auxiliary at Moore shipyard in Oakland, thus technically maintaining union segregation.[32]

Increasing black challenges to the system resulted in a half-measure of appeasement in 1943 when Kaiser established a segregated, "auxiliary" union for black workers who demanded union membership at Richmond. Local A-36, the Kaiser auxiliary, allowed black workers to pay union dues, but black auxiliary members were barred from voting on union policy or receiving other union benefits. Despite its segregated beginnings, however, Local A-36 represented an important step in the urban industrial process for most black workers. It gave them a sense of empowerment that went beyond their numbers and became an institution in which both black longtime residents and black migrants could come together in the common cause of breaking down employment barriers. The auxiliary placed over 10,000 African-American workers in shipyard and other positions during its first year of operation. In addition to shipyard employment, Local A-36 found jobs for a number of women in the city's newly expanded Recreation Department and spent a substantial portion of its resources on improving living conditions in North Richmond, home of most black Richmond residents.[33]

By 1943 black Richmondites had begun to wage fights against the auxiliaries. They joined with other black workers in a nationwide boycott of auxiliaries, refusing to pay dues. The Richmond NAACP, established in 1944 by a black newcomer and a longtime resident, became the fastest growing and most militant branch of the

Association on the west coast. The Richmond NAACP grew out of black shipyard workers' anti-discrimination activities in 1944 in which blacks picketed and sat-in at the union hall, attempted mass registration at the white unions, and staged several rent strikes to dramatize unequal treatment in federal housing projects. In addition, black Richmondites joined in a landmark lawsuit brought against the auxiliaries by Joseph James, a black shipyard worker at the Marin shipyards, across the Bay from Richmond. When the Supreme Court ruled in favor of black workers, striking down auxiliary unions in 1945, black Richmond residents began to believe that a new day was dawning. Bill Thurston expressed the sentiments of many: "For the first time you had poor black people from the South working with the union and all kinds of people who knew the ropes. It made them feel like they could do something too. It wouldn't be the same old story."[34]

Thus, optimism for the future springing from a growing sense of political and economic empowerment kept black workers streaming into Richmond's shipyards despite the persistence of racial tension and discrimination in the workplace. Pay, health, and safety benefits continued to make Kaiser attractive for most black workers. Although the company boasted that the average worker received $61 a week and had enough left over to save, the most skilled union workers received a minimum wage of $1.00 to $1.12 an hour for an eight hour shift, barely enough to cover the high cost of wartime living. Black workers, most often classified in the unskilled, non-union categories earned about 88¢ to 95¢ per hour on an eight hour shift.

The innovative Kaiser health plan, introduced in 1942 after influenza and pneumonia epidemics devastated the shipyard workforce, became very popular with all workers. For a weekly membership fee of 50¢ some 87 percent of the workers received "preventive protection, complete hospital, medical and surgical care; ambulance service and emergency treatment." For some black (and white) workers Kaiser's medical plan represented the first professional health care they had ever received. Finally, the Richmond shipyards maintained a reputation for safety that appealed to black and white workers. Frances Mary Albrier, a black welder in one of the yards, explained that the yards "were not cluttered up with a lot of beams and things in the walkways which you had to walk over and drag your welding hose over like at Moore's [Oakland] Shipyards."[35]

All these elements, pay, health and safety considerations, and a growing political strength, transmitted a sense of progress and empowerment to black workers in Richmond, but the most important factor in forging a black urban industrial workforce in Richmond was the daily work experience of black shipyard employees. Approximately 80 percent of Kaiser's black workers were initially employed as unskilled or semi-skilled trainees, but innovative shipyard assembly techniques permitted the majority of black employees to work in areas that had once required considerable technical training and skill. They became experts not in shipbuilding but in "performing one small job out of the total."

Black workers found their labor in demand, most for the first time in their lives.

While it was possible to "just show up" and be put to work "picking up scraps" as Wilbur Wheat did in 1942, those who aspired to be welders or burners received additional training in the government-sponsored programs offered at local high schools, or enrolled in the seven- to ten-day trainee programs established by Kaiser in the yards. More commonly, black workers received training at the unofficial "ten-day schools" which sprang up in home garages all over the area and were taught by workers who had only recently learned the tasks themselves. Even the ferry that brought workers across the Bay from San Francisco maintained a floating welding school which the shipyard workers called "Ferryboat College."[36]

Thus, African-American workers managed to carve out passageways through which they entered the new urban industrial workforce. Although shipyard employment experiences conditioned the struggles and the urbanization of blacks in Richmond and acquainted them with the industrial process, many black workers, along with their white colleagues, found it difficult to submit to the strict regimentation of the shipyards. Kaiser's innovative assembly line techniques and training programs shaped an efficient and highly productive industrial workforce, turning out ships at a truly astounding rate. Those same innovations, however, generated discontent among a significant portion of the workforce. Required to perform repetitive, boring tasks which demanded intense concentration, many workers believed themselves to be merely interchangeable parts in the vast shipyard machinery. Shipyard workers therefore protested this regimentation with a variety of strategies. Historian Patricia Cooper, writing about immigrant workers in the cigar industry in the late nineteenth and early twentieth centuries, has described such strategies as a "work culture" representing an unwritten system of rules and work attitudes that enabled workers to preserve self-esteem and derive a degree of autonomy and power in the workplace. Black workers in Richmond of the 1940s also developed and participated in a shipyard work culture to help them combat the regimentation and depersonalization that pervaded the urban industrial environment.[37]

Frustration with shipyard bureaucracy caused many workers to register their discontent by attempting to entangle the corporation in its own paperwork. Statistics compiled for the shipyards during the peak employment period of 1943 show that the yards experienced a turnover of 24,000 people a month. Much of this represented requests for transfers to other Kaiser yards. To counter such high figures, the federal government imposed the threat of military draft for any worker found guilty of requesting job transfers without "sufficient reason." Wilbur Wheat found himself in conflict with the new law after he requested a transfer to another yard in protest of his assignment as a "leaderman" of an "all colored crew" in Yard 2. His white supervisor denied the transfer and tried to intimidate Mr. Wheat by threatening to have him drafted if he did not return to work. Mr. Wheat explained, "married with one kid I didn't figure they would put me in the Army." Employing the "standard remedy" of industrial workers everywhere, Wilbur Wheat simply quit his job altogether.[38]

Short of quitting, shipyard workers registered their discontent with regimentation by "just not showing up." The United States Employment Service calculated that "avoidable absenteeism" in the yards ran at about 10 percent a day, or about 10,000 people. On Sundays the figure could easily reach as high as 18,000. While much of the absenteeism might reflect inadequate transportation and housing conditions, many workers felt entitled to "mental health" breaks to alleviate the strain of working in the round-the-clock shipyards. Black workers, many newly arrived from the rural South, were particularly reluctant to relinquish what Herbert Gutman has called "premodern work habits" and the cultural sanctions sustaining them. Like European immigrants of the turn of the century, many black shipyard workers viewed their unauthorized absences as a way of reaffirming their cultural value system which placed great emphasis on kinship, friendship, and religious ties. For instance, Margaret Starks, a migrant from Pine Bluff, Arkansas, and called by some black residents the "Mayor of North Richmond," reported that "lots of the people from the South resented having to work on Sundays no matter how much money they made. They didn't think it was right so honey, they didn't do it. Sunday was kept for church, family and kinfolks." Even the less devout had reservations about Sunday work. Some considered it a "family day," made for renewing kinship and friendship ties.[39]

Some black workers refused to give up their traditional Friday and Saturday night socializing in Richmond and Oakland clubs and taverns, which in many cases provided the only opportunity for black adults to relax, listen to their kind of music, and meet the opposite sex. Although Kaiser sponsored baseball and other organized activities for its employees, the majority of workers preferred their own recreational pursuits. Trotter has shown that black laborers employed in Milwaukee's tanning industry in the 1920s and 1930s routinely reported late to work rather than forgo the enjoyment of recreation in the main black community, which was difficult to reach by public transportation. Black shipyard workers in Richmond in the 1940s also chose not to forfeit their social life for a "record of stability and regularity" in the industrial workforce when to do so meant sacrificing customs which they considered vital to their self-worth and independence. Richmond shipyard workers, like their white immigrant and black migrant counterparts in the East and Midwest fifty years earlier, found that the impersonal quality of the urban industrial experience demanded that they maintain the cultural and social traditions.[40]

Shipyard work culture involved other more surreptitious opposition to regimentation and often took place under the noses of shipyard supervisors. Bob Geddins, a songwriter and founder of the bay area's only black record company in the 1940s (Big Town Records), worked in Shipyard 2 in 1943. Mr. Geddins frequently auditioned prospective blues and gospel singers "right there in the [hull of the] ships," and noted that "you could do a lot of other things in the yards, too." For example, Joseph Malbrough, who worked as a "rigger foreman" explained that prostitution became a fact of life in the yards and prostitutes did a brisk business with workers who had money "burning a hole in their pockets." At least one worker took a more dramatic stand against regimentation when Kaiser managers attempted to "boost morale" by piping music into the yards via loudspeaker. The frustrated worker cut the loudspeaker wires "every other day for two months" until his arrest by the FBI. He confessed his deeds saying that the continuous flow of "march tunes" and other music had become just so much intolerable "noise."[41]

Yet even though shipyard workers struggled against racism and regimentation, the financial rewards offered by Kaiser had a mitigating effect on their discontent. Thousands of black workers continued to pour through the shipyard gates, replacing those who left for other work. Shipyard employment represented an upgrading of skills and status for the majority of black workers, even if not for all. Black newcomers, who brought few industrial skills with them, grew in industrial skill, urban sophistication, and political awareness through their struggles in the shipyards and in the community. Richmond proved to be a place of opportunity and challenge for black residents who found themselves confronted with a hardening wall of discrimination in the boom town atmosphere of World War II.

The history of African-Americans in Richmond from 1910 to 1945 reveals that migration was part of an ongoing black strategy for attaining greater economic and social opportunity in the urban industrial workforce and gaining power in their lives. Black newcomers to the city and black longtime residents, far from being helpless victims of the events that transformed their lives, were active agents in shaping their transition to the urban industrial workforce. Their efforts revitalized and empowered the entire black community despite the intraracial class fragmentation that initially threatened group solidarity. Through their multi-dimensional living and work experience in wartime Richmond, black residents developed an expanded perspective of their power as workers in and residents of an urban industrial community. Even though their wartime economic "shift upward" could not be sustained once the shipyards closed down, black Richmondites, like African-Americans nationwide, utilized their newly developed perspective and empowerment to forge a postwar civil rights movement that substantially challenged the system which kept them from achieving their goals of economic and social advancement.

NOTES

1. Kenneth G. Goode, *California's Black Pioneers: A Brief Historical Survey* (Santa Barbara: McNally and Loftin, 1973), pp. 1–24.

2. Goode, *California's Black Pioneers*, pp. 12–25, 62–66; W. Sherman Savage, "The Negro in the Westward Movement," *Journal of Negro History* 25 (1940): 533–34; Robert F. Heizer and Alan F. Almquist, *The Other Californians: Prejudice and Discrimination under Spain, Mexico and the United States to 1920* (Berkeley, 1977), pp. 120–28.

3. Edward E. France, "Some Aspects of the Migration of the Negro to the San Francisco

Bay Area since 1940'' (Ph.D. diss., University of California, 1962), pp. 18–19; Goode, *California's Black Pioneers*, p. 109; Lawrence P. Crouchett, Lonnie G. Bunch, III, and Martha Kendall Winnacker, *The History of the East Bay Afro-American Community, 1852–1977* (Oakland: Northern California Center for Afro-American History and Life, 1977), pp. 9–10, 17.

4. Crouchett, Bunch, and Winnacker, *The History of the East Bay Afro-American Community*, pp. 9–10, 17.

5. *Thirteenth Census of the United States (1910). Statistics for California Supplement*, pp. 118, 1614; Florette Henri, *Black Migration, Movement North, 1900–1920: The Road from Myth to Man* (Garden City: Anchor Press/Doubleday, 1975), pp. 49–51.

6. Henri, *Black Migration*, pp. 49–51.

7. Joseph Griffin III (Richmond resident since the 1930s), interview with the author, 29 November 1987; Joseph Malbrough (Richmond resident since the 1920s), interview with the author, 18 August 1985; Wilbur Wheat and Vesper Wheat (Richmond residents since 1942), interview with the author, 24 January 1987 (Wilbur Wheat's sister, Georgie Wheat Bonaparte, was married to Louis Bonaparte). The story of the buried ''box full of money'' has been part of Griffin family lore for generations, but its authenticity is difficult to assess. It is significant to a discussion of black migration, however, because it suggests that, even before the massive infusion of black settlers during the World War II era, African-Americans viewed migration to the Golden State as the logical and desirable outcome to a change in economic status.

8. This paragraph and the preceding one based on Mildred Hudson Slocum, daughter of Girtha Hudson, interview with author, 17 November 1987; Bill Thurston, Richmond resident since 1944 and son of Charles Henry Thurston, interview with author, 10 September 1983.

9. Irene Malbrough Batchan, Richmond resident since the 1920s, interview with author, 14 September 1985. For an overview of racial discrimination in California, see Goode, *California's Black Pioneers*, especially pp. 106–119. Also see *Thirteenth Census of the United States (1910)*; Walter Freeman, Jr., Richmond resident since 1915, interview with author, 28 November 1987; Slocum, 17 November 1987; George Johnson, Richmond resident since the 1930s, interview with author, 13 August 1985.

10. William Malbrough, Richmond resident since 1924, interview with author, 14 September 1985. For a discussion of the impact of negative and positive stereotypes on European immigrant and African-American employment opportunities, see John Bodnar, Roger Simon, and Michael P. Weber, *Lives of Their Own: Blacks, Italians and Poles in Pittsburgh, 1900–1960* (Urbana: University of Illinois Press, 1982), pp. 556–65.

11. Batchan, 14 September 1985; Freeman, 18 November 1987; Slocum, 17 November 1987.

12. *Thirteenth Census of the United States (1910)*; Freeman, 28 November 1987; Slocum, 17 November 1987; Johnson, 13 August 1985.

13. For a concise history of domestic service in the United States, see David M. Katzman, *Seven Days a Week: Women and Domestic Service in Industrializing America* (1978; reprint, Urbana: University of Illinois Press, 1981), pp. 24–26, 46, 55, 65–94, 221–22, 266–79; James Borchert, *Alley Life in Washington: Family, Community, Religion and Folk Life in the City, 1850–1970* (Urbana: University of Illinois Press, 1980), pp. 168–95; Kenneth L. Kusmer, *A Ghetto Takes Shape, Black Cleveland, 1870–1930* (Urbana: University of Illinois Press, 1980), pp. 84–88, 109, 195; Batchan, 14 September 1985; Freeman, 28 November 1987; Johnson, 13 August 1985.

14. *Thirteenth Census (1910). Statistics for California Supplement*, pp. 644–45; Ivy Reid Lewis, Richmond resident since the 1930s, interview with author, 29 July 1987; Malbrough, 14 September 1985; Freeman, 28 November 1987.

15. Hubert Owen Brown, ''The Impact of War Worker Migration on Richmond Public Schools, 1940–1945'' (Ph.D. diss., Stanford University, 1973), p. 41; Kusmer, *A Ghetto*

Takes Shape, pp. 45–52; Borchert, *Alley Life*, pp. 7, 29–56; Bodnar et al., *Lives*, pp. 70–82; Batchan, 18 August 1985; Edwin P. "Red" Stephenson, *Transition: White Man in a Black Town* (Berkeley: University of California Regional Oral History Office, 1975), p. 28; Lewis, 29 July 1987.

16. Gerald D. Nash, *The American West Transformed: The Impact of the Second World War* (Bloomington: Indiana University Press, 1985), pp. 8–10, 17–19, 25–26, 66–70; John E. Wiltz, *From Isolation to War, 1931–1941* (New York: Thomas Y. Crowell, 1968), pp. 67–97.

17. William Sokol, "From Workingman's Town to All American City: The Socio-Political Economy of Richmond California during World War Two" (unpublished monograph, Richmond Public Library, June, 1971), p. 12; Joseph C. Whitnah, *A History of Richmond, California, the City That Grew from a Rancho* (Richmond: Chamber of Commerce, 1944), pp. 117–19; Nash, *American West*, pp. 27, 66–70; Joseph Fabry, *Swingshift: Building the Liberty Ships* (San Francisco: Strawberry Hill Press, 1982), p. 150.

18. Whitnah, *History of Richmond*, p. 119; Brown, "Impact of War Worker," p. 1; Charles Johnson, *The Negro War Worker in San Francisco* (San Francisco: n.p., 1944), pp. 2, 5, 7; Bodnar et al., *Lives*, pp. 31–37; Carter G. Woodson, *A Century of Negro Migration* (1918; reprint, New York: Russell and Russell, 1969), pp. 11, 21, 46–91; Clyde Kiser, *Sea Island to City: A Study of St. Helena Islanders in Harlem and Other Urban Centers* (1932; reprint, New York: AMS Press, 1969), pp. 149–52.

19. Sokol, "Workingman's Town," p. 20; Stephenson, *Transition*, p. 25; *The Kaiser Story* (Oakland: Kaiser Industries, 1968), p. 31; Margaret Starks, Richmond resident since 1943, interview with author, 2 April 1988.

20. Thurston, 10 September 1983.

21. Wheat and Wheat, 24 January 1987; Cy W. Record, "Characteristics of Some Unemployed Negro Shipyard Workers in Richmond California" (unpublished monograph, Library of Economic Research, University of California, September 1947), pp. 9, 31. For the role of kinship and friendship correspondence networks in European immigration to the United States, see Herbert G. Gutman, *Work, Culture and Society in Industrializing America* (New York: Vintage Books, 1976); Bodnar et al., *Lives*, pp. 41–42. Thomas Bell's novel, *Out of This Furnace* (Pittsburgh: University of Pittsburgh Press, 1976 ed.), provides a fictionalized but historically faithful account of life and kinship ties among Slovak immigrants in Pennsylvania's steel industries; see especially parts 1–3, pp. 3–258.

22. Record, "Characteristics," p. 31.

23. Ibid., p. 30.

24. Ibid., p. 31.

25. Charles Radcliffe Fulweiler, "A Preliminary Investigation of the Accommodation Mechanism as a Factor in the Clinical Study of the Negro Adolescent" (Master's thesis, University of California, Berkeley, 1951), pp. 24–25; Brown, "Impact of War Worker," p. 3; Wheat and Wheat, 24 January 1987.

26. Wheat and Wheat, 24 January 1987; Lewis, 29 July 1987; Stephenson, *Transition*, p. 28; *The Richmond Independent*, 14 February 1944, 17 May 1944, and 10 August 1943; Robert Wenkert, *An Historical Digest of Negro-White Relations in Richmond, California* (Berkeley: University of California Survey Research Center, 1967), pp. 27–30; Brown, "Impact of War Worker," p. 185.

27. Nash, *American West*, p. 70; Brown, "Impact of War Worker," p. 121; "Richmond Took a Beating," *Fortune* magazine, February 1945, p. 267. For a detailed and insightful analysis of the "Okie" experience in California, see James Nobel Gregory, "The Dust Bowl Migration and the Emergence of an Okie Subculture in California, 1930–1950" (Ph.D. diss., University of California, Berkeley, 1983).

28. Record, "Characteristics," pp. 19–21, 26, 32; Joe William Trotter, Jr., *Black Milwaukee, the Making of an Industrial Proletariat, 1915–1945* (Urbana: University of Illinois Press, 1985), especially pp. xii, 54.

29. Thurston, 10 September 1983.

30. Katherine Archibald, *Wartime Shipyard: A Study in Social Disunity* (Berkeley: University of California Press, 1947), pp. 3–4; Wheat and Wheat, 24 January 1987.

31. Brown, "Impact of War Worker," p. 173.

32. Wheat and Wheat, 24 January 1987; Frances Mary Albrier, *Determined Advocate for Racial Equality* (Berkeley: University of California Regional Oral History Office, 1977–78), pp. vi, 132–33.

33. Auxiliary Lodge Number 36 of the International Brotherhood of Boilermakers, Iron Shipbuilders and Helpers of America (Local A-36); *We Also Serve* (Berkeley: Tilghman Press, 1945), p. 25.

34. Cleophus Brown, Richmond resident since the 1930s and co-founder of the Richmond NAACP, interview with author, 18 October 1987; Nash, *American West*, pp. 92–93; Brown, "Impact of War Worker," p. 176; Philip S. Foner, *Organized Labor and the Black Worker, 1619–1981* (New York: International Publishers, 1981), pp. 248–49; Charles Wollenberg, *Golden Gate Metropolis: Perspectives in Bay Area History* (Berkeley: University of California Institute of Governmental Studies, 1985), p. 249; Thurston, 10 September 1983.

35. Sokol, "Workingman's Town," pp. 29–30, 36; Kaiser Industries, *The Kaiser Story*, pp. 27, 31, 33; Brown, "Impact of War Worker," pp. 42–43; Record, "Characteristics," pp. 43–45; *A Booklet of Illustrated Facts* (Richmond: Permanente Metals Corporation, 1944), pp. 30, 35; Albrier, *Determined Advocate*, pp. vi, 128a, 130–31.

36. Record, "Characteristics," p. 11; Nash, *American West*, p. 98; Kaiser Industries, *The Kaiser Story*, pp. 27, 31; Sokol, "Workingman's Town," pp. 29–30; Albrier, *Determined Advocate*, pp. vi, 128a, 130–1031; Wheat and Wheat, 24 January 1987.

37. Patricia Cooper, *Once a Cigar Maker: Men, Women and Work Culture in American Cigar Factories, 1900–1919* (Urbana: University of Illinois Press, 1987), pp. 2, 41–74, 65–66.

38. Boilermakers, Iron Shipbuilders, and Helpers of America, *Richmond Arsenal of Democracy* (Berkeley: Tilghman Press, 1947), p. 100; Sokol, "Workingman's Town," pp. 38–39, 52–53; Wheat and Wheat, 24 January 1987.

39. U.S. Congress, House of Representatives, Committee on Merchant Marines and Fisheries, Subcommittee, *Hearings on Shipyard Profits*, 78th Congress, 2d Session, vol. 5 (Washington, DC: Government Printing Office, 1944), p. 856; Sokol, "Workingman's Town," pp. 51–52; Nash, *American West*, p. 39; Gutman, *Work, Culture and Society*, pp. 14–29; Starks, 2 April 1988.

40. Trotter, *Black Milwaukee*, p. 62.

41. Bob Geddins, interview with author, 8 May 1987; Tom Mazzolini, "Living Blues Interview: Bob Geddins," *Living Blues Magazine*, September/October, 1977, pp. 19–30; Malbrough, 18 August 1985; Sokol, "Workingman's Town," p. 81.

Black Migration to the Urban Midwest
The Gender Dimension, 1915–1945

Darlene Clark Hine

The significance of temporal and spatial movement to a people, defined by and oppressed because of the color of their skin, among other things, defies exaggeration. Commencing with forced journeys from the interior of Africa to the waiting ships on the coast, over 11 million Africans began the trek to New World slave plantations that would, centuries later, land their descendants at the gates of the so-called "promised lands" of New York, Philadelphia, Chicago, Cleveland, Detroit, Milwaukee, and Indianapolis. The opening page of a privately published memoir of a black woman resident of Anderson, Indiana, captures well this sense of ceaseless movement on the part of her ancestors. D. J. Steans observed that "the backward trail of relatives spread from Indiana to Mississippi, crisscrossing diagonally through several adjoining states. Whether the descendants came ashore directly from Africa to South Carolina or were detoured by way of islands off the coast of Florida is unknown."[1]

For half a millennium black people in the New World have been, or so it seems, in continuous motion, much of it forced, some of it voluntary and self-propelled. Determined to end their tenure in the "peculiar institution," or die trying, thousands of blacks fled slavery during the antebellum decades, as the legendary exploits of Harriet Tubman and Frederick Douglass testify. Large numbers of blacks challenged, with their feet, the boundaries of freedom in the aftermath of the Civil War. Many moved west to establish new black towns and settlements in Kansas and Oklahoma in the closing decades of the nineteenth century. Others attempted to return to Africa.[2] To understand both the processes of black migration and the motivations of the individuals, men and women, who comprised this human tide is to approach a more illuminating portrait of American history and society. Central to all of this black movement was the compelling quest for that ever so elusive, but distinctly American property: freedom and equality of opportunity.

Long a riveting topic, studies of the Great Migration abound. Indeed, recent histories of black urbanization, especially those focused on key midwestern cities and towns—Chicago, Cleveland, Detroit, Milwaukee, and Evansville, Indiana—pay considerable attention to the demographic transformation of the black population, a transformation which began in earnest in 1915 and continued through the

World War II crisis.[3] As enlightening and pathbreaking as most of these studies are, there remains an egregious void concerning the experiences of black women migrants. This brief essay is primarily concerned with the gender dimension of black migration to the urban Midwest. It raises, without providing a comprehensive answer, the question, how is our understanding of black migration and urbanization refined by focusing on the experiences (similar to men in many ways, yet often unique) of the thousands of southern black women who migrated to the Midwest between the two World Wars? A corollary question concerns the nature of the relations between those black women who migrated out of the lower Mississippi Valley states and those who stayed put. It is also important to shed light on the phenomenon of intraregional migration for there was considerable movement of women between the midwestern cities and towns.

By 1920 almost 40 percent of Afro-Americans residing in the North were concentrated in eight cities, five of them in the Midwest: Chicago, Detroit, Cleveland, Cincinnati, and Columbus, Ohio. The three eastern cities with high percentages of black citizens were New York, Philadelphia, and Pittsburgh. These eight cities contained only 20 percent of the total northern population. Two peaks characterized the first phase of the Great Black Migration: 1916–1919 and 1924–1925. These dates correspond to the passage of more stringent anti-immigration laws, and the years in which the majority of the approximately 500,000 southern blacks relocated northward.[4]

Clearly the diverse economic opportunities in the midwestern cities served as the major pull factor in the dramatic black percentage increases registered between 1910 and 1920. Detroit's black population rose an astounding 611.3 percent. More precisely put, Detroit's Afro-Americans attracted by the jobs available at the Ford, Dodge, Chrysler, Chevrolet, and Packard automobile plants, increased from 5,741 in 1910 to 120,066 in 1930. Home of the northern terminus of the Illinois Central Railroad, the *Chicago Defender*, meat packing, and mail order enterprises, Chicago was not outdone. The Windy City's black population, which in 1910 numbered 44,103, jumped to 233,903 in 1930.[5]

Drawn to midwestern jobs, throughout the First World War era, the numbers of black males far exceeded female migrants. Thus the black population of midwestern cities, unlike in most eastern and southern cities, did not reflect a majority of females. Until the differences between the processes and consequences of migration to black men and to black women are fully researched no comprehensive synthesis or portrait of the migrants is possible. Many unexplored dimensions of black migration and urbanization still beg attention. In addition to the good studies of political and cultural developments in Chicago, for example, more work needs to be done on the relation between migration and the development of black social, political, economic, and religious institutions in other midwestern cities. Although historians Peter Gottlieb and James Borchert have stressed the continuity between black life in the South and in northern cities, we do not yet understand fully the mechanisms by which this continuity was achieved, or its meaning.[6] It is perhaps fair to suggest that black women played a critical role in the establishment of an array of black institutions, especially the churches and mutual aid organizations that gave life in northern cities a southern flavor. Historian Elizabeth Clark-Lewis, although addressing Washington, DC, directly, argues, "The growth of African-American churches in Washington, then, was a direct consequence of the steady influx of these working-class (former live-in) women. They strongly supported church expansion because their participation in the church activities further separated them from the stigma of servitude."[7]

Still in need of refinement is our understanding of the connection between migration and black social-class formation and between migration and the rise of protest ideologies which shaped the consciousness of the "New Negro," not only in Harlem, but also in midwestern cities. We need studies of the relation between migration and family reorganization, and between migration and sex-role differentiation in the black communities, especially in terms of religious activity; and of the development of new types of community-based social welfare programs. Moreover, we need micro-studies into individual lives, of neighborhoods, families, churches, and fraternal lodges in various cities. Examination of these themes makes imperative an even deeper penetration into the internal world of Afro-Americans. Perhaps even more dauntingly, to answer fully these questions requires that the black woman's voice and experience be researched and interpreted with the same intensity and seriousness accorded that of the black man.

Information derived from statistical and demographic data on black midwestern migration and urbanization must be combined with the knowledge drawn from the small, but growing, numbers of oral histories, autobiographies, and biographies of twentieth century migrating women. Court records of legal encounters, church histories, black women's club minutes, scrapbooks, photographs, diaries, and histories of institutions ranging from old folks' homes, orphanages, businesses, and Phillis Wheatley Homes to local YWCAs yield considerable information on the lives of black women migrants to and within the middle western region. Actually these sources, properly "squeezed and teased" promise to light up that inner world so long shrouded behind a veil of neglect, silence, and stereotype, and will quite likely force a rethinking and rewriting of all of black urban history.

A perusal of the major studies of black urbanization reveals considerable scholarly consensus on several gender-related themes. Scholars generally acknowledge that gender did make a difference in terms of the reasons expressed for quitting the South, and affected the means by which men and women arrived at their northern destinations. Likewise, scholars concur that men and women encountered radically divergent socioeconomic and political opportunities in midwestern cities. Gender and race stereotyping in jobs proved quite beyond their control and was intransigent in the face of protest. Scholars agree that black women faced greater economic discrimination and had fewer employment opportunities than black men. Their work was the most undesirable and least remunerative of all northern migrants. Considering that their economic condition or status scarcely improved or changed, for many women migrants were doomed to work in the same kinds of domestic service jobs they had held in the South, one wonders why they bothered to move in the first place. Of course there were significant differences. A maid earning $7 a week in Cleveland perceived herself to be much better off than a counterpart receiving $2.50 a week in Mobile, Alabama. A factory worker, though the work was dirty and low status, could and did imagine herself better off than domestic servants who endured the unrelenting scrutiny, interference, and complaints of household mistresses.[8]

It is clear that more attention needs to be directed toward the noneconomic motives propelling black female migration. Many black women quit the South out of a desire to achieve personal autonomy and to escape from sexual exploitation both within and outside of their families and from sexual abuse at the hands of southern white as well as black men. The combined influence of domestic violence and economic oppression is key to understanding the hidden motivation informing major social protest and migratory movements in Afro-American history.[9]

That black women were very much concerned with negative images of their sexuality is graphically and most forcefully echoed in numerous speeches of the early leaders of the national organization of black women's clubs. Rosetta Sprague, the daughter of Frederick Douglass, declared in an address to the Federation of Afro-American Women in 1896:

> We are weary of the false impressions sent broadcast over the land about the colored woman's inferiority, her lack of noble womanhood. We wish to make it clear in the minds of your fellow country men and women that there are no essential elements of character that they deem worthy of cultivating that we do not desire to emulate that the sterling qualities of purity, virtue, benevolence and charity are no more dormant in the breast of the black woman than in the white woman.[10]

Sociologist Lynda F. Dickson cautions that "recognition of the major problem—the need to elevate the image of black womanhood—may or may not have led to a large scale club movement both nationally and locally."[11] It cannot be denied, however, that "the most important function of the club affiliation was to provide a support system that could continually reinforce the belief that the task at hand—uplifting the race, and improving the image of black womanhood was possible."[12] A study of the history of the early twentieth century black women's club movement is essential to the understanding of black women's migration to the middle western towns and cities and the critical roles they played in creating and sustaining new black social, religious, political, and economic institutions. These clubs were as important as the National Urban League and the NAACP in transforming black peasants into the urban proletariat.[13]

This focus on the sexual and the personal impetus for black women's migration neither dismisses nor diminishes the importance of economic motives, a discussion of which I will return to later. Rather, I am persuaded by historian Lawrence Levine's reservations. He cautions, "As indisputably important as the economic motive was, it is possible to overstress it so that the black migration is converted into an inexorable force and Negroes are seen once again not as actors capable of affecting at least some part of their destinies, but primarily as beings who are acted upon—southern leaves blown North by the winds of destitution."[14] It is reasonable to assume that many were indeed "southern leaves blown North," and that others were more likely self-propelled actors seeking respect, space in which to live, and a means to earn an adequate living.

Black men and women migrated into the Midwest in distinctive patterns. Single men, for example, usually worked their way North, leaving farms for southern cities, doing odd jobs, and sometimes staying in one location for a few years before proceeding to the next stop. This pattern has been dubbed "secondary migration." Single black women, on the other hand, as a rule, traveled the entire distance in one trip. They usually had a specific relative—or fictive kin—waiting for them at their destination, someone who may have advanced them the fare and who assisted with temporary lodging and advice on securing a job.[15] Amanda Jones-Watson, a fifty-year-old resident of Grand Rapids, Michigan, and three-time President of the still functioning Grand Rapids Study Club, founded in 1904, migrated from Tennessee in 1936 in her 30s. She recalls asking her uncle, who had just moved to Grand Rapids, to send her a ticket. She exclaimed, "I cried when it came. I was kidding. My sister said, 'Amanda, what are you worried about? You can always come back if you don't like it.' " Jones-Watson was fortunate. Her uncle was headwaiter at the Pantlind Hotel. She continued, "I got a job as a maid and was written up in a local furniture magazine for making the best bed at the Pantlind."[16]

For Sara Brooks, a domestic, the idea that she should leave Alabama and relocate in Cleveland in 1940 originated with her brother. He implored his sister, "Why don't you come up here? You could make more here." Brooks demurred, "Well, I hadn't heard anything about the North because I never known nobody to come no further than Birmingham, Alabama, and that was my sister-in-law June, my husband's sister." A single mother of three sons and a daughter, Brooks eventually yielded to her brother's entreaties, leaving her sons with her aging parents. She recalled, "But my brother wanted me to come up here to Cleveland with him, so I started to try to save up what little money I had. . . . But I saved what I could, and when my sister-in-law came down for me, I had only eighteen dollars to my name, and that was maybe a few dollars over enough to come up here. If I'm not mistaken it was about a dollar and fifteen cent over."[17]

The influence and pressure of family members played a substantial role in convincing many ambivalent young women to migrate. A not so young sixty-eight year old Melinda left her home in Depression-ridden rural Alabama to assist her granddaughter in childrearing in Anderson, Indiana. Even when expressing her plans to return home once her granddaughter was up and about, somehow Melinda knew that the visit would be permanent. Grounded largely in family folklore, D. J. Steans declared that Melinda had labored hard at sharecropping, besides taking in washing and ironing. Even after her sixty-second birthday, she was still going strong. Many weeks she earned less than 50¢, but she was saving pennies a day for her one desire to travel north to visit her great-grandchildren.[18]

Some women simply seized the opportunity to accompany friends traveling north. Fired from her nursing job at Hampton Institute, in Hampton, Virginia, Jane Edna Hunter packed her bags determined to head for Florida. She never made it. According to Hunter, "en route, I stopped at Richmond, Virginia, to visit with Mr. and Mrs. William Coleman, friends of Uncle Parris. They were at church when I arrived; so I sat on the doorstep to await their return. After these good friends had greeted me, Mrs. Coleman said, 'Our bags are packed to go to Cleveland, Jane. We are going to take you with us.' " Jane needed little persuasion. She exclaimed, "I was swept off my feet by the cheerful determination of the Colemans. My trunk, not yet removed from the station, was rechecked to Cleveland."[19] Hunter arrived in the city on May 10, 1905 with $1.75 in her pockets, slightly more than Sara Brooks brought with her thirty-five years later.

The different migratory patterns of black males and females reflect gender conventions in the larger society. A woman traveling alone was surely at greater risk than a man. After all, a man could and did, with less approbation and threat of bodily harm, spend nights outdoors. More importantly, men were better suited to defend themselves against attackers. However, given the low esteem in which the general society held black women, even the courts and law officials would have ridiculed and dismissed assault complaints from a black female traveling alone, regardless of her social status. Yes, it was wise to make the trip all at once, and better still to have company.

Although greater emphasis has been placed on men who left families behind, black women, many of whom were divorced, separated, or widowed, too left loved ones, usually children, in the South when they migrated. Like married men, unattached or single black mothers sent for their families after periods of time ranging from a month to even several years. Actually, I suspect that a great number of women who migrated into the Midwest probably left children, the products of early marriages or romantic teenage liaisons, with parents, friends, and other relatives in the South. It would be exceedingly difficult, if not impossible to develop any statistical information on this phenomenon. Nevertheless, the oral history of Elizabeth Burch of Fort Wayne, Indiana, offers poignant testimony of a child left behind:

I was born [December 20, 1926 in Chester, Georgia] out of wedlock to Arlena Burch and John Halt. My mother went north and that's where they—all of it began in a little town called Albion, Michigan and she went back south to have me. . . . Aunt Clyde that's my mother's sister, she was the baby and that was a little town called Albion, Michigan. That's where I was conceived at. That's where my mother went when she left Georgia. My mother decided well she go back up north. She married just to get away from home to go back north and this guy was working as a sharecropper and he had made enough money that year that he was willing to marry my mother and take her back up north. . . . So they left me with Miss Burch—Miss Mattie Elizabeth Burch, namesake which was my grandmother and that's where I grew up at and years passed and years went through I was just on the farm with my grandparents.[20]

The difficulty of putting aside enough money to send for their children placed a tremendous strain on many a domestic salary. It took Sara Brooks almost fifteen years to reconstitute her family, to retrieve her three sons left behind in Orchard, Alabama. With obvious pride in her accomplishment, Brooks explained, "The first one to come was Jerome. . . . Then Miles had to come because my father didn't wanna keep him down there no more because he wouldn't mind him. . . . Then Benjamin was the last to come." Brooks summed up her success, "So I come up to Cleveland with Vivian, (her daughter) and after I came up, the rest of my kids came up here. I was glad—I was VERY glad because I had wanted em with me all the time, but I just wasn't able to support em, and then I didn't have no place for them, either, when I left and come to Cleveland cause I came here to my brother."[21]

Arguably, inasmuch as so many midwestern black women were absentee mothers—that is, their children remained in the South—their actual acculturation into an urban life style became a long, drawn out, and often incomplete, process. On the other hand, as historians Peter Gottlieb and Jacqueline Jones persuasively maintain, black women served as critical links in the "migration chain."[22] They proved most instrumental in convincing family members and friends to move north. This concept of women as "links in a migration chain" begs elaboration. I suspect that it is precisely because women left children behind in the care of parents and other relatives that they contributed so much to the endurance and tenacity of the migration chain. Their attachment to the South was more than sentimental or cultural. They had left part of themselves behind.

Parental obligations encouraged many black women migrants to return south for periodic visits. Burch recalled that "My mother would come maybe once a year—maybe Christmas to visit" her in Georgia from Ft. Wayne.[23] Still other midwestern women returned perhaps to participate in community celebrations, family reunions, and to attend religious revivals. Of course, such periodic excursions southward also permitted display of new clothes and other accoutrements of success. Before she made the journey to Cleveland, Sara Brooks admitted delight in her sister-in-law's return visits. "I noticed she had some nice-lookin little clothes when she come back to Orchard to visit. She had little nice dresses and brassieres and things, which I didn't have. . . . I didn't even have a brassiere, and she'd lend me hers and I'd wear it to church."[24] Indeed, Brooks's recollections raise a complex question—To what extent and how does the woman's relation to the South change over the course of the migrant's life? When do migrants move from being southerners in the North to southern northerners?

Unable, or unwilling, to sever ties to or abandon irrevocably the South, black women's assimilation to urban life remained fragmented and incomplete. It was the very incompleteness of the assimilation, however, which facilitated the south-ernization of the Midwest. Vestiges of southern black culture were transplanted and continuously renewed and reinforced by these women in motion. The resiliency of this cultural transference is reflected in food preferences and preparation styles, reliance on folk remedies and superstitions, religious practices, speech patterns, games, family structures and social networks, and music, most notably, the blues.[25] The southernization of urban midwestern culture was but one likely consequence of the migration chain women forged. In short, although unattached black women migrants may have traveled the initial distance to Chicago, Cleveland, Detroit, or Cincinnati, in one trip, as long as offspring, relatives, and friends remained in the south, psychological and emotional relocation was much more convoluted and, perhaps, more complicated than heretofore assumed.

Discussions of the marital status and family obligations—specifically whether the women migrants had children remaining in the South—are indirectly, perhaps, related to a more controversial topic of current interest to historians of nineteenth century black migration and urbanization. In his study of violence and crime in post–Civil War Philadelphia, Roger Lane suggests that there was a marked decline in black birthrates in the city near the turn of the century. He attributes the decline in part to the rising incidence of syphilis which left many black women infertile. He notes that, "In Philadelphia in 1890 the black-white ratio was .815 to 1,000, meaning that black women had nearly 20 percent fewer children than whites, a figure that in 1900 dropped to .716 to 1,000, or nearly 30 percent fewer." Lane concludes, "All told, perhaps a quarter of Philadelphia's black women who reached the end of their childbearing years had at some time had exposure to the diseases and habits associated with prostitution. This figure would account almost precisely for the difference between black and white fertility in the city."[26]

Without reliance on the kinds of statistical data Lane employs in his analysis, the oral histories and autobiographies of midwestern black women migrants suggest an alternate explanation, though often overlooked, in discussions of black birth decline. Sara Brooks, mother of five children, was still in her childbearing years when she embraced celibacy. She declared, "See, after Vivian was born I didn't have no boyfriend or nothin, and I went to Mobile, I didn't still have no boyfriend in a long time. Vivian was nine years old when Eric come. . . . But after Eric came along, I didn't have no boyfriend. I didn't want one because what I wanted, I worked for it, and that was that home.'' Brooks had realized her dream in 1957 with the purchase of her home and the reuniting of all of her children under one roof.[27]

For women, ignorant of effective birth control or unable to afford the cost of raising additional children alone, sexual abstinence was a rational choice. It should be pointed out that often deeply held religious convictions, disillusionment with black men, a history of unhappy and abusive marriages, adherence to Victorian ideals of morality, a desire to refute prevalent sexual stereotypes and negative images of black women as a whole, or even an earlier unplanned pregnancy may have informed many a decision to practice sexual abstinence among adult black women. Only latent acceptance of the myths concerning the alleged unbridled passions and animalistic sexuality of black women prevent serious consideration of the reality and extent of self-determined celibacy. Meanwhile, until we know more about the internal lives of black women, the suggestion of abstinence or celibacy as a factor limiting births should not be dismissed.

The fact that women who migrated north produced fewer children than their southern counterparts warrants further investigation. It is not enough to argue that prostitution, venereal disease, and infanticide account for declining black births in urban settings. Many other factors, in addition to abstinence, offer fruitful and suggestive lines of inquiry. Some scholars have asserted that children in urban as opposed to rural settings had rather insignificant economic roles and therefore their labor was not as important to family survival.[28]

As black women became more economically sufficient, better educated, and more involved in self-improvement efforts, including participation in the flourishing black women's club movement, they would have had more access to birth control information.[29] As the institutional infrastructure of black women's clubs, sororities, church groups, and charity organizations took hold within black communities, they gave rise to those values and attitudes traditionally associated with the middling classes. To black middle-class aspirants, the social stigma of having many children would have, perhaps, inhibited reproduction. Furthermore, over time, the gradually evolving demographic imbalance in the sex ratio meant that increasing numbers of black women in urban midwestern communities would never marry. The point is simply this, that not dating, marrying, or having children may very well have been a decision—a deliberate choice, for whatever reason—that black women made. On August 23, 1921, Sarah D. Tyree wrote tellingly about her own decision not to date. Tyree had a certificate from the Illinois College of Chiropracty, but was, at the time, taking care of aged parents and her sister's children in Indianapolis. She confided to her sister living in Muskegon, Michigan:

I have learned to stay at home lots. I firmly believe in a womanly independence. Believe that a woman should be allowed to go and come where and when she pleases alone if she wants to, and so long as she knows who is right, she should not have to worry about what others think. It is not every woman who can turn for herself as I can, and the majority of women who have learned early to depend upon their male factors do not believe that their sister-woman can get on alone. So she becomes dangerously suspicious, and damagingly tongue-wagging. I have become conscious of the fact that because I am not married, I am watched with much interest. So I try to avoid the appearance of evil, for the sake of the weaker fellow. I do not therefore go out unaccompanied at night. There are some young men I would like to go out with occasionally if it could be understood that it was for the occasion and not for life that we go. I don't care to be bothered at any time with a fellow who has been so cheap and all to himself for 5 or 6 years I have all patients [sic] to wait for the proper one to play for my hand.[30]

Moreover, social scientists Joseph A. McFalls, Jr., and George S. Masnick persuasively argue that blacks were much more involved in birth control than previously assumed. They contend, "The three propositions usually advanced to support the view that birth control had little, if any, effect on black fertility from 1880 to 1940—that blacks used 'ineffective' methods, that blacks did not practice birth control 'effectively,' and that blacks used birth control too late in their reproductive careers to have had much of an effect on their fertility—simply have no empirical or even a priori foundation. There is no reason now to believe that birth control had little impact on black fertility during this period."[31] Not to be overlooked are the often chronic health problems overworked, undernourished, and inadequately-housed poor black women undoubtedly experienced, especially during the Depression. In discussing the morbidity and mortality rates of blacks in Chicago, Tuttle observes that,

Chicago's medical authorities boasted of the city's low death rate, pointing to statistics which indicated that it was the lowest of any city in the world with a population of over one million. Their statistics told another story as well, however, and it was that Chicago's blacks had a death rate which was twice that of whites. The stillbirth rate was also twice as high; and the death rate from tuberculosis and syphilis was six times as high; and from pneumonia and nephritis it was well over three times as high. . . . The death rate for the entire city was indeed commendable, but the statistics indicated that the death rate for Chicago's blacks was comparable to that of Bombay, India.[32]

One more observation about the declining birth rate among northern black women should be made. Here it is important to note the dichotomy between black women who worked in middle- and working-class occupations. Middle-class working women, regardless of color, had fewer children than those employed in blue collar jobs. The professional and semi-professional occupations most accessible to black women during the years between the world wars included teaching, nursing, and social work, on the one hand, and hairdressing or dressmaking, on the other. In some of the smaller midwestern communities and towns, married women teachers, race notwithstanding, lost their jobs, especially if the marriage became public knowledge or the wife pregnant. At least one black woman school teacher in Lafayette, Indiana, confided that she never married, though she had been asked, because in the 1930s and 1940s to have done so would have cost her the position. The pressure on the small cadre of professional black women not to have children was considerable. The more educated they were, the greater the sense of being responsible, somehow, for the advance of the race and of black womanhood. They held these expectations of themselves and found them reinforced by the demands of the black community and its institutions. Under conditions and pressures such as these, it would be erroneous to argue that this is the same thing as voluntary celibacy. Nevertheless, the autonomy, so hard earned and enjoyed to varying degrees by both professional women and personal service workers, offered meaningful alternatives to the uncertainties of marriage and the demands of childrearing. The very economic diversity—whether real or imagined—that had attracted black women to the urban Midwest, also held the promise of freedom to fashion socially useful and independent lives beyond family boundaries.

None of this is to be taken as a categorical denial of the existence of rampant prostitution and other criminal activity in urban midwestern ghettos. Too many autobiographies and other testimony document the place and the economic functions of prostitution in urban society to be denied. Indeed, Jane Edna Hunter's major contribution to improving black women's lives in Cleveland—the establishment of the Phillis Wheatley boarding homes—stemmed from her commitment to provide training, refuge, and employment for young migrating women who were frequently enticed or tricked into prostitution as a means of survival. She remarked on her own awakening, "the few months on Central Avenue made me sharply aware of the great temptations that beset a young woman in a large city. At home on the plantation, I knew that some girls had been seduced. The families had felt the disgrace keenly—the fallen ones had been wept and prayed over. . . . Until my arrival in Cleveland I was ignorant of the wholesale organized traffic in black flesh."[33]

Young, naive country girls were not the only ones vulnerable to the lure of seduction and prostitution. Middle-aged black women also engaged in sex for pay, but for them it was a rational economic decision. Sara Brooks did not disguise her contempt for women who bartered their bodies. She declared, while commenting on her own struggle to pay the mortgage on her house, "Some women woulda had a man to come and live in the house and had an outside boyfriend too, in order to get the house paid for and the bills." She scornfully added, "They meet a man and if he promises em four or five dollars to go to bed, they's grab it. That's called sellin your own body, and I wasn't raised like that."[34]

Prostitution was not the only danger awaiting single migrating black women. Police in many midwestern towns seemed quick to investigate not only black men but women who appeared suspicious. Historian James E. DeVries records several encounters between black women and the police in Monroe, Michigan. "In January 1903, Gertie Hall was arrested after acting in a very nervous manner on the interurban trip from Toledo. An investigation by Monroe police revealed that Hall was wanted for larceny in Toledo, and she was soon escorted to that city." In another incident four years later involving fifteen-year-old Ahora Ward, also from Toledo, DeVries notes that she was "picked up and taken to jail. . . . As it turned out, she had been whipped by her mother and was running away from home when taken into custody."[35]

There exists a scholarly consensus about the origins and the destinations of the overwhelming majority of black migrants throughout the period between 1915 and 1945. Before turning to a discussion of the economic impetus, or the pull factors, for black women's migrations, I would like to interject another rarely explored "push" factor, that is, the desire for freedom from sexual exploitation, especially rape by white men, and to escape from domestic abuse within their own families. A full exploration of this theme requires the use of a plethora of sources including oral testimonials, autobiographies, biographies, novels, and court records. The letters, diaries, and oral histories collected by the Black Women in the Middle West Project and deposited in the Indiana Historical Society contain descriptions of domestic violence which fed the intraregional movement of black women who had migrated from southern states. Elizabeth Burch explained why she left Ft. Wayne for Detroit, "And my mother—and my stepfather—would have problems. He would hit my mother and so, you know, beat upon my mother . . . but he never did beat up on me. My mother would say—'Well you just don't put your hands on her. You better not, hear.' " To avoid these scenes Burch moved to Detroit but later returned to Ft. Wayne.[36]

Similarly Jane Pauline Fowlkes, sister of the above-mentioned Sarah Tyree, was granted a divorce from her husband, Jess Clay Fowlkes in Muskegon, Michigan, in 1923 and returned to her family and sister in Indianapolis. Granted the decree because her husband was found "guilty of several acts of extreme cruelty," Fowlkes retained custody of all three children.[37]

While Sara Brooks's experiences are hardly representative, they are nevertheless suggestive of the internal and personal reasons black women may have had for leaving the South. Brooks vividly described the events that led her to leave her husband for the third and final time. When she ran away from home the last time, she didn't stop running until she reached Cleveland almost a decade later. "When he hit me," she said, "I jumped outa the bed, and when I jumped outa the bed, I just ran. . . . I didn't have a gown to put on—I had on a slip and had on a short-sleeved sweater. I left the kids right there with him and I went all the way to his father's house that night, barefeeted, with that on, on the twenty-fifth day of

December. That was in the dark. It was two miles or more and it was rainin. . . . I walked. And I didn't go back.''[38]

For whatever reasons Sara Brooks, Melinda, Jane Edna Hunter, and others wound up in the various midwestern cities, they expected to work and to work hard, for work was part of the definition of what it meant to be a black woman in America, regardless of region. The abundant economic opportunities, or "pull factors," especially in automobile plants and, during the War, in the defense industries, had been powerful inducements for black male migrants. The dislocation of blacks in southern agriculture, the ravages of the boll weevil, floods, and the seasonal and marginal nature of the work relegated to them in the South were powerful "push" factors. Taken together these factors help us to understand why 5 percent of the total southern black population left the South between 1916 and 1921.[39]

Black women shared with black men a desire for economic improvement and security. They too were attracted to midwestern cities, specifically those with a greater diversity of women's jobs. The female occupational structure of Chicago, for example, held the promise of more opportunity for black women than did the much more heavy industry dependent Pittsburgh.[40] Black men, however, were not as constrained. To be sure, the majority of neither group expected to secure white collar jobs or managerial positions. None were so naive as to believe that genuine equality of opportunity actually existed in the North or the Midwest, but occasionally black women migrants did anticipate that more awaited them in Cleveland and Chicago than an apron and domestic servitude in the kitchens of white families, segregated hotels, and restaurants. Most were disappointed. Author Mary Helen Washington recalled the disappointment and frustration experienced by her female relatives when they migrated to Cleveland:

> In the 1920s my mother and five aunts migrated to Cleveland, Ohio from Indianapolis and, in spite of their many talents, they found every door except the kitchen door closed to them. My youngest aunt was trained as a bookkeeper and was so good at her work that her white employer at Guardian Savings of Indianapolis allowed her to work at the branch in a black area. The Cleveland Trust Company was not so liberal, however, so in Cleveland she went to work in what is known in the black community as "private family."[41]

Scholars concur that, while black women secured employment in low level jobs in light industry, especially during the World War I years when overseas immigration came to a standstill, this window of opportunity quickly closed with the end of hostilities. Florette Henri calculates that "immigration dropped from 1,218,480 in 1914, to 326,700 in 1915, to under 300,000 in 1916 and 1917, and finally to 110,618 in 1918." This drop and the draft made it possible for black women to squeeze into "occupations not heretofore considered within the range of their possible activities," concluded a Department of Labor survey in 1918.

Thus the percentage of black domestics declined between 1910 and 1920, from 78.4 percent to 63.8 percent in Chicago, and from 81.1 percent to 77.8 percent in Cleveland.[42]

The study of migrations from the perspective of black women permits a close examination of the intersection of gender, class, and race dynamics in the development of a stratified work force in midwestern cities. During the war years a greater number of black women migrants found work in midwestern hotels as cooks, waitresses, and maids, as ironers in the new steam laundries, as labelers and stampers in Sears Roebuck and Montgomery Wards mail order houses, as common laborers in garment and lampshade factories, and in food processing and meat packing plants. But even in these places, the limited gains were short lived and easily erased. As soon as the War ended and business leveled off, for example, both Sears and Wards immediately fired all the black women.[43] In 1900 black women constituted 4 percent of the labor force in commercial laundries; by 1920 this figure had climbed to 6 percent. As late as 1930 a little over 3,000 black women, or 15 percent of the black female labor force in Chicago were unskilled and semi-skilled factory operatives. Thus over 80 percent of all employed black women continued to work as personal servants and domestics. Historian Allan H. Spear points out that "negro women were particularly limited in their search for desirable positions. Clerical work was practically closed to them and only a few could qualify as school teachers. Negro domestics often received less than white women for the same work and they could rarely rise to the position of head servant in large households."[44]

In Milwaukee, especially during the Depression decades, black women were, as historian Joe Trotter observes, "basically excluded from this narrow industrial footing; 60.4 percent of their numbers labored in domestic service as compared to only 18.6 percent of all females."[45] To be sure, this was down from the 73.0 percent of black women who had worked as domestics in Milwaukee in 1900.[46] A decline of 13 percent over a forty-year period—regardless of from what angle it is viewed— is hardly cause for celebration.

Many reasons account for the limited economic gains of black women as compared to black men in midwestern industries. One of the major barriers impeding a better economic showing was the hostility and racism of white women. The ceiling on black women's job opportunities was secured tight by the opposition of white women. White females objected to sharing the settings, including hospitals, schools, department stores, and offices. Now 90, Sarah Glover migrated with her family to Grand Rapids, Michigan, from Alabama in 1922, where they had jobs working in the coal mines. Although she would in later years become the first practical nurse in the city, during her first seventeen years as a maid at Blodgett Hospital, she scrubbed the floors. After completing her housekeeping chores she'd voluntarily help the nurses. She reminisced, "The nurses used to call me 'Miss Sunshine' because I would cheer up the patients. I'd come over and say you look good today or crack a joke. That used to get most of them smiling again." In spite of her good work record, excellent human relations skills, and eagerness, hospital officials deemed it a violation of racial rules and thus rejected Glover's appeal to become a nurse's aid.[47]

Historians Susan M. Hartmann and Karen Tucker Anderson convincingly demonstrate that while white women enjoyed expanded employment opportunities, black women continued to be the last hired and first fired throughout the Depression and World War II years. Employers seeking to avert threatened walkouts, slowdowns, and violence caved into white women's objections to working beside or, most particularly, sharing restroom and toilet facilities with black women.[48] To be sure, many employers, as was the case with the Blodgett Hospital in Grand Rapids, harbored the same racist assumptions and beliefs in black inferiority, but camouflaged them behind white women's objections.

The black media was not easily fooled by racist subterfuges and remained keenly attuned to all excuses that rationalized the denial of job opportunities to black women. In its official organ, *Opportunity*, National Urban League officials catalogued the thinly-veiled justifications white employers offered when discriminating against women:

> "There must be some mistake"; "No applications have heretofore been made by colored"; "You are smart for taking the courses, but we do not employ coloreds"; "We have not yet installed separate but equal toilet facilities"; "A sufficient number of colored women have not been trained to start a separate shift"; "The training center from which you come does not satisfy plant requirements"; "Your qualifications are too high for the kind of job offered"; "We cannot put a Negro in our front office"; "We will write you . . . but my wife needs a maid"; "We have our percentage of Negroes."[49]

Trotter did, however, discover instances when the interests of white women occasionally promoted industrial opportunities for black women. "The white women of the United Steelworkers of America Local 1527, at the Chain Belt Company, resisted the firm's proposal for a ten-hour day and a six-day week by encouraging the employment of black women."[50] In a classic understatement, historian William Harris hesitantly asserts, "Black women apparently experienced more discrimination than black men in breaking into nonservice jobs."[51]

In their study of labor unions in Detroit, August Meier and Elliott Rudwick reveal that more than white women's hostility accounts for the employment discrimination and the job segregation black women encountered in the automobile industries. Throughout the World War II era, the Ford Motor Company hired only a token number of black women. According to Meier and Rudwick, "Black civic leaders and trade unionists fought a sustained and energetic battle to open Detroit war production to black women, but because government manpower officials gave discrimination against Negro females low priority, the gains were negligible when compared with those achieved by the city's black male workers." By March 1943, for example, the Willow Run Ford Plant employed 25,000 women, but less than 200 were black. Apparently, Ford was not alone or atypical in these anti-black women hiring practices. Both Packard and Hudson employed a mere half dozen each at this time. Most of those employed in the plants, as was to be expected, worked in various service capacities—matrons, janitors, and stock handlers. Meier and Rudwick point out that ''As late as the summer of 1943 a government report termed the pool of 25,000 available black women the city's 'largest neglected source of labor.' ''[52]

Much more work needs to be done on the migration of black women. As difficult as the task may prove, historians must begin to probe deep into the internal world and lives of these women, who not only were Detroit's largest neglected source of labor, but also remain the largest neglected, and still most obscure, component of Afro-American history. It is not enough to study black women simply because they are neglected and historically invisible. Rather it is incumbent that we examine and interpret their experiences, for what this new information yields may very well bring us closer to a comprehensive and more accurate understanding of all of American history from colonial times to the present.

NOTES

1. D. J. Steans, *Backward Glance: A Memoir* (Smithtown, NY: Exposition Press, 1983), p. 1.

2. Thomas C. Cox, *Blacks in Topeka, Kansas, 1865–1915* (Baton Rouge: Louisiana State University Press, 1982); Nell Irvin Painter, *Exodusters: Black Migration to Kansas after Reconstruction* (New York: W. W. Norton, 1977); Quintard Taylor, ''The Emergence of Black Communities in the Pacific Northwest, 1865–1910,'' *Journal of Negro History* 64 (1979): 342–45; Janice L. Ruff, Michael R. Dahlin, and Daniel Scott Smith, ''Rural Push and Urban Pull: Work and Family Experience of Older Black Women in Southern Cities, 1880–1910,'' *Journal of Social History* 16 (Summer 1983): 39–48; James O. Wheeler and Stanley D. Brunn, ''Negro Migration into Southwestern Michigan,'' *Geographical Review* 58 (April 1968): 214–30. For a description of the development of eight all-black towns in northern communities of more than 1,000 population, see Harold M. Rose, ''The All-Negro Town: Its Evolution and Function,'' *Geographical Review* 55 (1965): 362–81. Edwin S. Redkey, *Black Exodus: Black Nationalism and Back-to-Africa Movements, 1890–1969* (New Haven: Yale University Press, 1969), pp. 150–94; Wilson Jeremiah Moses, *The Golden Age of Black Nationalism 1850–1925* (New York: Oxford University Press, 1978), pp. 83–102.

3. Allan H. Spear, *Black Chicago: The Making of a Negro Ghetto, 1890–1920* (Chicago: University of Chicago Press, 1967); Peter Gottlieb, *Making Their Own Way: Southern Blacks' Migration to Pittsburgh, 1916–1930* (Urbana: University of Illinois Press, 1987); Kenneth Kusmer, *A Ghetto Takes Shape: Black Cleveland, 1870–1930* (Urbana: University of Illinois Press, 1976); Joe William Trotter, Jr., *Black Milwaukee: The Making of an Industrial Proletariat, 1915–45* (Urbana: University of Illinois Press, 1985); Darrel E. Bigham, *We Ask Only a Fair Trial: A History of the Black Community of Evansville, Indiana* (Bloomington: Indiana University Press, 1987); Florette Henri, *Black Migration: Movement North, 1900–*

1920 (New York: Anchor Press, 1975); Richard Walter Thomas, "From Peasant to Prole-tarian: The Formation and Organization of the Black Industrial Working Class in Detroit, 1915–1945" (Ph.D. diss., University of Michigan, 1976).

4. Trotter, *Black Milwaukee*, p. 25; Thomas, "From Peasant to Proletarian," pp. 6–7; Henri, *Black Migration*, pp. 52, 69. For a general overview of the historiography of black urbanization see, Kenneth Kusmer, "The Black Urban Experience in American History," in *The State of Afro-American History: Past, Present, and Future*, Darlene Clark Hine, ed. (Baton Rouge: Louisiana State University Press, 1986), pp. 91–122. In an important study of women in Chicago, historian Joanne J. Meyerowitz comments on the different migratory patterns of black and white women: "Black women followed different paths of migration to Chicago. In 1880 and in 1910, the largest group of black women adrift in Chicago, almost half, came from the Upper South states of Kentucky, Tennessee, and Missouri. A smaller group of migrants listed birthplaces elsewhere in the South. In 1880, one-fourth of black women adrift came from the states of the Deep and Atlantic Coastal South; in 1910, almost one-third. During and after World War I, the stream of migrants from Mississippi, Alabama, Georgia, and other parts of the Deep South swelled to a flood"; Joanne J. Meyerowitz, *Women Adrift: Independent Wage Earners in Chicago, 1880–1930* (Chicago: University of Chicago Press, 1988), p. 10.

5. Henri, *Black Migration*, p. 69; August Meier and Elliott Rudwick, *Black Detroit and the Rise of the UAW* (New York: Oxford University Press, 1979), pp. 5–7; Spear, *Black Chicago*, pp. 129–30.

6. Gottlieb, *Making Their Own Way*; James Borchert, *Alley Life in Washington: Family, Community, Religion, and Folklife in the City, 1850–1970* (Urbana: University of Illinois Press, 1980), p. 237; Borchert stresses throughout his study "the strong continuities not only between slave and alley culture, but also between alley culture and both rural and urban black cultures of the third quarter of the twentieth century" (p. 237–78). Also see Kusmer, "The Black Urban Experience," p. 113; Dianne M. Pinderhughes, *Race and Ethnicity in Chicago Politics: A Reexamination of Pluralist Theory* (Urbana: University of Illinois Press, 1987); St. Clair Drake and Horace R. Cayton, *Black Metropolis: A Study of Negro Life in a Northern City* (New York: Harcourt, Brace & World, 1945; rev. edition, 1970).

7. Elizabeth Clark-Lewis, " 'This Work Had a End': African-American Domestic Work-ers in Washington, D.C., 1910–1940," *"To Toil the Livelong Day": America's Women at Work, 1780–1980*, Carol Groneman and Mary Beth Norton, eds. (Ithaca: Cornell University Press, 1987), pp. 196–212, especially p. 211.

8. Clark-Lewis, " 'This Work Had a End,' " p. 198–99; David M. Katzman, *Seven Days a Week: Women and Domestic Service in Industrializing America* (New York: Oxford University Press, 1979), pp. 219–21.

9. Darlene Clark Hine, "Rape and the Inner Lives of Black Women in the Middle West: Preliminary Thoughts on the Culture of Dissemblance," *Signs: Journal of Women and Culture in Society* 14 (Summer 1989): 912–20.

10. H. F. Kletzing and William F. Crogman, *Progress of a Race* (1987; reprint, New York: Negro University Press, 1969), p. 193.

11. Lynda F. Dickson, "Toward a Broader Angle of Vision in Uncovering Women's History: Black Women's Clubs Revisited," *Frontiers* 9, no. 2 (1987): 62–68, especially p. 67.

12. Ibid., p. 67.

13. See Moses, *The Golden Age of Black Nationalism*, chapter 5, "Black Bourgeois Feminism versus Peasant Values: Origins and Purposes of the National Federation of Afro-American Women," pp. 103–31; Darlene Clark Hine, *When the Truth Is Told: Black Women's Culture and Community in Indiana, 1875–1950* (Indianapolis: National Council of Negro Women, Indianapolis Section, 1981), pp. 49–78.

14. Lawrence W. Levine, *Black Culture and Black Consciousness: Afro-American Folk Thought from Slavery to Freedom* (New York: Oxford University Press, 1977), p. 274.

15. Gottlieb, *Making Their Own Way*, pp. 46–49, 52; Jacqueline Jones, *Labor of Love, Labor of Sorrow: Black Women, Work, and Family from Slavery to the Present* (New York: Basic Books, 1985), pp. 159–60.

16. Carol Tanis, "A Study in Self-Improvement," *Grand Rapids Magazine* 42 (January 1987): 41–44 (quote on p. 43). The complete records and minute books of the Grand Rapids Study Club are located in the Grand Rapids Public Library, Grand Rapids, Michigan. They are among the most thorough and extensive records, spanning the years between 1920s to the early 1980s, of a midwestern regional black women's club I have found.

17. Sara Brooks, *You May Plow Here: The Narrative of Sara Brooks*, Thordis Simonsen, ed. (New York: Touchstone Edition, Simon and Schuster, 1987), pp. 195–96.

18. Steans, *Backward Glance*, p. 17.

19. Jane Edna Hunter, *A Nickel and a Prayer* (Cleveland: Elli Kani Publishing Co., 1940), pp. 65–66. Hunter's papers are located at the West Reserve Historical Society, Cleveland, Ohio.

20. The Maddy Bruce Story, 18 May 1984, transcript, Deborah Starks Collection, box 1, folder 4, Oral Histories, Black Women in the Middle West (BWMW) Project, Ft. Wayne, Indiana (Indiana Historical Society, Indianapolis, Ind.). There is considerable confusion surrounding the spelling of the name in the transcript. Sometimes her name is spelled Burch, which is the way she spelled it in the text of the oral history. The listing of the oral history, however, is under Bruce. For the sake of consistency in the narrative, I refer to her as Burch.

21. *You May Plow Here*, pp. 211–14, 216–17.

22. Gottlieb, *Making Their Own Way*, pp. 49–50; Jones, *Labor of Love, Labor of Sorrow*, pp. 156–60. Also see Earl Lewis, "Afro-American Adaptive Strategies: The Visiting Habits of Kith and Kin among Black Norfolkians during the First Great Migration," *Journal of Family History* 12 (1987): 407–20.

23. The Maddy Bruce Story.

24. Brooks, *You May Plow Here*, p. 195.

25. LeRoi Jones, *Blues People: The Negro Experience in White America and the Music That Developed from It* (New York: William Morrow and Co., 1963), pp. 105–107; Sandra R. Leib, *Mother of the Blues: A Story of Ma Rainey* (Amherst: University of Massachusetts Press, 1981), pp. 21–22, 78–79; Daphne Duval Harrison, *Black Pearls: Blues Queens of the 1920s* (New Brunswick, NJ: Rutgers University Press, 1988), pp. 18–21.

26. Roger Lane, *The Roots of Violence in Black Philadelphia, 1860–1900* (Cambridge: Harvard University Press, 1986), pp. 130, 158–59.

27. Brooks, *You May Plow Here*, pp. 206, 109. For a provocative discussion of earlier black women who also practiced abstinence, see Rennie Simson, "The Afro-American Female: The Historical Context of the Construction of Sexual Identity," in *The Powers of Desire: The Politics of Sexuality*, Anne Suitow, Sharon Thompson, and Christine Stansall, eds. (New York: Monthly Review Press, 1983), pp. 229–35. Simson's observations warrant quoting at length: "[Harriet] Jacob's attempt to maintain control over her life is also shown in her pattern of living after her escape to freedom in the North. She mentioned no sexual attachments and relied on herself for financial support. [Elizabeth] Keckley too learned self-reliance. A brief marriage with a Mr. Keckley ended in divorce as she found him 'a burden instead of a helpmate.' No children issued from this marriage as Keckley did not wish to bring any more slaves into the world and thus fulfill her function as a breeder. When her marriage was terminated she said of her husband, 'Let charity draw around him the mantle of silence.' Keckley never mentioned another sexual relationship and, like Jacobs, she remained self-supporting for the rest of her life" (p. 232). For a discussion along the same vein see Darlene Clark Hine, "Female Slave Resistance: The Economics of Sex" in *The Western Journal of Black Studies* 3 (Summer 1979): 123–27. For additional insight into incidences of domestic violence in the aftermath of emancipation, see Ira Berlin, Steven F. Miller, and Leslie F. Rowland, "Afro-American Families in the Transition from Slavery to Freedom," *Radical History Review* 42 (November 1988): 89–121, especially pp. 99–100.

28. Stewart E. Tolnay, "Family Economy and the Black American Fertility Transition," *Journal of Family History* 11, no. 3, (1986): 272–77.

29. The Minute Book of the 1935 meetings of the Grand Rapids Study Club notes that among other issues, one topic earmarked for discussion was birth control. On 10 January 1935 the Study Club met to discuss "Public Institutions-Prisons, Asylums, Hospitals, etc." The question that focused the discussion was, "Who belongs in Prison—Habitual Drunkard? Prostitutes? Homosexual? Non-supporter?" Box 1 (Grand Rapids Public Library, Grand Rapids, Michigan); Gerda Lerner, "Early Community Work of Black Club Women," *Journal of Negro History* 59 (1974): 158–67. For a probing examination of black club women's work and institution building in one midwestern city, see Earline Rae Ferguson, "The Woman's Improvement Club of Indianapolis: Black Women Pioneers in Tuberculosis Work, 1903–1938," *Indiana Magazine of History* 84 (September 1988): 237–61.

30. Sarah Darthulin Tyree to Jennie P. Fowlkes, 23 August 1921. Frances Patterson Papers, box 1, folder 2, BWMW Project (Indiana Historical Society, Indianapolis, IN).

31. Joseph A. McFalls, Jr., and George S. Masnick, "Birth Control and the Fertility of the U.S. Black Population, 1880 to 1980," *Journal of Family History* 6 (Spring 1981): 103.

32. William M. Tuttle, Jr., *Race Riot: Chicago in the Red Summer of 1919* (New York: Atheneum, 1982), p. 164.

33. Hunter, *A Nickel and a Prayer*, p. 68. Also see, for a judicious discussion of white and black prostitution, Ruth Rosen, *The Lost Sisterhood: Prostitution in America, 1900–1918* (Baltimore: The Johns Hopkins University Press, 1982). See Thomas Connelly, *The Response to Prostitution in the Progressive Era* (Chapel Hill: University of North Carolina Press, 1980), pp. 48–66, for a discussion of the relations between prostitution and European immigration.

34. Brooks, *You May Plow Here*, p. 219.

35. James E. DeVries, *Race and Kinship in a Midwestern Town: The Black Experience in Monroe, Michigan, 1900–1915* (Urbana: University of Illinois Press, 1984), pp. 90–91.

36. The Maddy Bruce Story, 18 May 1984.

37. Divorce Decree: Jesse Clay Fowlkes vs. Jane Pauline Fowlkes, 12 April 1923 Frances Patterson Papers, box 2, folder 3 (Indiana Historical Society, Indianapolis, IN). J. C. Fowlkes was ordered to pay $7.50 per week for the support of the children.

38. Brooks, *You May Plow Here*, p. 219. For an insightful historical analysis of the meaning of wife-beating and battered women's resistance, see Linda Gordon, *Heroes of Their Own Lives: The Politics and History of Family Violence, Boston 1880–1960* (New York: Viking Press, 1988), pp. 250–88.

39. Gerda Lerner, *Black Women in White America: A Documentary History* (New York: Vintage Books, 1973), pp. 238–39; Jones, *Labor of Love*, pp. 161–64; Gottlieb, *Making Their Own Way*, pp. 107–9.

40. Spear, *Black Chicago*, pp. 29, 34, 155; Henri, *Black Migration*, pp. 142, 168.

41. Mary Helen Washington, *Invented Lives: Narratives of Black Women, 1860–1960* (New York: Anchor Press, 1987), p. xxii.

42. Henri, *Black Migrations*, p. 52.

43. Spear, *Black Chicago*, pp. 151–55, Henri, *Black Migration*, pp. 143–44.

44. Spear, *Black Chicago*, p. 34.

45. Trotter, *Black Milwaukee*, pp. 14, 47, 81, 171, 203.

46. Trotter, *Black Milwaukee*, p. 174.

47. Tanis, "A Study in Self Improvement," p. 42.

48. Susan M. Hartmann, "Women's Organizations during World War II: The Interaction of Class, Race, and Feminism," in *Woman's Being, Woman's Place: Female Identity and Vocation in American History*, Mary Kelley, ed. (Boston: G. K. Hall, 1979); Karen Tucker Anderson, "Last Hired, First Fired: Black Women Workers during World War II," *Journal of American History* 64 (June 1982): 96–97.

49. George E. DeMar, "Negro Women Are American Workers, Too," *Opportunity* 21

(April 1943): 41–43, 77. For a description of the stratified workforce in Milwaukee, see Trotter, *Black Milwaukee*, pp. 159, 171. Trotter notes that, "Where black females worked in close proximity to whites, the work was stratified along racial lines. At the Schroeder Hotel, for example, black women operated the freight elevator, scrubbed the floors, and generally performed the most disagreeable maid's duties. Conversely, white women worked the passenger elevator, filled all clerical positions, and carried out light maid's duties" (p. 159).

50. Trotter, *Black Milwaukee*, p. 174.

51. William H. Harris, *The Harder We Run: Black Workers since the Civil War* (New York: Oxford University Press, 1982), p. 64.

52. August Meier and Elliott Rudwick, *Black Detroit and the Rise of the UAW* (New York: Oxford University Press, 1979), pp. 136, 153–54. Joe Trotter also notes that in spite of vigorous efforts to extend the benefits of the FEPC to black women, the Fair Employment Practices Committee focused upon traditionally white female-dominated industries. Yet, he notes, the complaints of black women of racial discrimination in heavy industries like Allis Chalmers, Nordberg, and Harnishchfeger were "frequently dismissed by the FEPC due to insufficient evidence, although some of their charges were as potently documented as those of black men." Trotter, *Black Milwaukee*, p. 171.

Conclusion
Black Migration Studies
The Future

Joe William Trotter, Jr.

As suggested by the foregoing essays, black migration was indeed a complicated process. Its full comprehension requires an appreciation for changing interpretations and for new sources, approaches, and theoretical perspectives. Despite important progress in this direction, however, several interrelated issues remain open for further investigation: the gender dimension, variation from city to city, larger social, cultural, and political implications, comparative ethnic and racial perspectives, interdisciplinary questions, and the problem of synthesis.

As we have seen in this volume, emphases on southern black kin, friend, and community networks illuminate the role of black women in the migration process. As Earl Lewis notes in his essay on Norfolk blacks, "women served as the primary kinkeepers." Yet, in her telling critique of the literature, Darlene Clark Hine's essay challenges us to move beyond the role of women in the communications and travel networks. She urges us to identify and evaluate: 1) gender specific motivations for moving; 2) the impact of black female migration on black urban life; and 3) the larger implications of black female migration for understanding American urban and social history.[1]

Uncovering the gender dimension of black population movement is an enormous order. No less than black men, it involved a variety of women at different stages of the life cycle, and with different motives for migrating, different regional and subregional origins, and different destination points. Moreover, as Clark Hine concludes, it is necessary to integrate the new findings into our larger understanding of black migration, urbanization, and the development of industrial America. Only then will we gain a more comprehensive and accurate portrait of American history.[2]

In his recent essay, "The Black Urban Experience in American History," Kenneth Kusmer calls attention to the variable impact of the Great Migration on different cities. Black migration, he says, has been "much more complex than one would realize from looking at a few major industrial centers during the World War I period."[3] Key to this variation was the changing character of a city's economy, and its place in the national network of cities. An excellent illustration of the variable impact of the black migration is the experience of blacks in Evansville, Indiana.

During the late nineteenth century, Evansville was a booming commercial and increasingly industrial city. Yet its black population dropped from 7,500 in 1900 to less than 6,300 in 1910, and stagnated at less than 7,000 until World War II. Improved rail connections between the South and North opened up greater employment opportunities for blacks in cities like Chicago, Cleveland, and Detroit than in Evansville. Thus, as historian Darrel E. Bigham suggests, Evansville seemed "a less logical terminus for southern blacks seeking to make a new start." As blacks in other northern cities entered industrial jobs in the era of the Great Migration, Evansville's black men and women remained primarily in the common labor, domestic, and personal service sector.[4]

While the black population of some cities like Evansville experienced stagnation during the era of the Great Migration, other black communities of substantial prewar growth actually declined and sometimes virtually disappeared. The coaltowns of Muchakinock, Haydock, and especially Buxton in southern Iowa provide perhaps the most extreme examples. In 1900, the Consolidation Coal Company created Buxton as a model coal mining town. Within five years, blacks from Virginia, Missouri, and parts of Iowa made up about 55 percent of the town's 5,000 residents. However, by World War I, the black population dropped to 40 percent; it continued to drop as the coal industry declined in the postwar years, and disappeared during the 1920s. According to historians Dorothy Schwieder, Joseph Hraba, and Elmer Schwieder, the Iowa towns of Buxton, Muchakinock, and Haydock had served as distribution points for blacks moving to all parts of the northern United States.[5]

The larger social, cultural, and political implications of the Great Migration are also unclear. As suggested by changing perspectives on black urban history (as discussed in the introductory essay of this collection), some scholars accent the relationship between migration and race relations, ghettoization, or proletarianization. Moreover, whatever the perspective, some emphasize continuity, while others stress a significant break with the past. In his book (more so than in this volume) Gottlieb accents the persistence of southern attitudes and consciousness among black newcomers to Pittsburgh. Like peasant migrants to industrial cities throughout the world, he argues, black migrants sought northern wages in order to sustain a traditional "southern" way of life. Even blacks who settled permanently "in fact lived, worked, socialized, and worshipped primarily among other blacks from the South."[6] Only future generations would become "wholly" northern urban-industrial men and women; for the old generation sustained a rich pattern of visitations between Pittsburgh and the nearby South.

Grossman thrusts the issue of citizenship and industrial democracy to the forefront of his analysis. In his book on the subject, he emphasizes the Great Migration as an emerging watershed in the ongoing civil rights struggle. According to Grossman, for many, the Great Migration was a symbolic reorientation of their aspirations from the world of southern agriculture to the world of northern industries. In short, "many migrants viewed migration as an opportunity to share the perquisites of American citizenship."[7]

In order to fully understand the larger meaning of the black migration, we will need more research on the complicated relationship between migration, ghettoization, and class formation on the one hand, and a broad range of institutional, political, and cultural changes within the black community on the other. Part and parcel of this agenda must be closer attention to the precise relationship between those who left and those who stayed behind. For some migrants never even left the South, as suggested by black migration to Norfolk and southern West Virginia.[8]

More comparative studies of African-Americans and European immigrants are also essential. A variety of studies conducted over the past decade points the way.[9] In their ground-breaking study *Lives of Their Own* (1982), social historians John Bodnar, Roger Simon, and Michael Weber compared the experiences of African-Americans, Italians, and Poles in Pittsburgh between 1900 and 1960. Focusing on industrial development between 1880 and 1920, Olivier Zunz offers a comparative assessment of blacks and white ethnic groups in Detroit. Unfortunately, however, Zunz, Bodnar, and others paint a highly pathological portrait of blacks, deemphasize their indispensable, even if weak, institutional life, and portray them in more individualistic, atomistic, and, in the case of Zunz, ahistorical terms than seems warranted by the evidence.[10]

While Bodnar, Zunz, and others have charted important new ground, we need additional studies that approach the comparative issue from the vantage point of African-American history. Then we will be able to retain the focus on the important role of black culture and power while acknowledging ethnic and racial differences. Moreover, the importance of structural constraints should receive proper weight alongside attitudinal and cultural factors. In their illuminating essay, "A Tale of Three Cities: Blacks, Immigrants, and Opportunity in Philadelphia, 1850–1880, 1930, 1970," for example, Theodore Hershberg and his colleagues argue that the experiences of white immigrants and blacks were shaped "by three distinct opportunity structures and ecological forms, and three distinct settlement patterns," corresponding roughly to the early industrializing city, the industrial city, and the post-industrial city of recent times.[11]

Comparative studies, however, should not be confined to the experiences of black Americans and white immigrants. They should also extend to analyses of black and white Americans, as well as black and nonwhite immigrants who migrated from overseas.[12] For not all immigrants were white, nor all internal migrants black.

Black migration in comparative perspective, perhaps more than other subjects in American and African-American history, will require greater interdisciplinary research. Demography, economics, geography, political science, sociology, psychology, and anthropology all will need closer attention from historians of black population movement. It is clear that closer attention to changing social science techniques, theory, and interpretations of the subject will reward our efforts. Over the past two decades, black migration has emerged as a critical theme in a variety of social science disciplines. Studies by anthropologists Carol Stack, Ulf Hannerz, and Charles A. and Betty Lou Valentine, all provide important contributions to our understanding of black kin, friend, and communal networks in the migration and resettlement of blacks in cities. By the mid-1970s, geographers like Richard L. Morrill, O. Fred Donaldson, Harold Rose, and John Frazer Hart had made their pioneering contributions to the locational aspects of black population movement. At the same time, demographers, economists, and sociologists like Reynolds Farley, William Vickery, Neil Fligstein, and others helped to deepen our understanding of black migration in historical perspective.[13]

In our efforts to expand our interdisciplinary grasp of the black migration, however, we should appreciate the problems of particular disciplinary traditions, struggles, and new departures. As social historian John Modell has recently noted, over the past several decades economics, political science, sociology, and parts of anthropology have mathematicized their modes of inquiry, while somewhat later anthropology, portions of political science, and sociology emphasized hermeneutic methods.[14] Research on black migration is evidently undergoing comparable changes. In 1977, for example, William Vickery noted that prevailing economic studies of black migration were "few, poor in quality, and over thirty years old." The techniques employed were "crude, mainly correlation analysis." Thus, Vickery advanced "multiple regression" techniques, which require more specialized skills than correlation methods, as his major tool of analysis.[15] In short, the scholar of black urban migration should be aware of the potential pitfalls as well as the rewards of eclecticism.

As we deepen our interdisciplinary grasp of the Great Migration, it should provide a framework for a larger synthesis of black migration in historical perspective. Of course the volume, nature, and underlying causes of black population movement varied significantly over time and space. From the colonial period through the antebellum era, enslaved Africans and later African-Americans (supplemented by a few free blacks) experienced forced migration from one agricultural region or locale to another.[16] Blacks moved from the tobacco region of the upper South, dominant during the colonial period, to the cotton areas of the southwest during the nineteenth century.[17]

The Civil War and Reconstruction radically transformed the social, economic, and political context of black migration. Spurred by the presence of federal troops, the ending of chattel slavery, the enactment of full citizenship legislation, and the increasingly hostile white reaction to black freedom, black population movement accelerated. Yet, after emancipation, blacks would continue to tread paths from farm to farm. As historian Nell Painter notes in her careful study of the black migration to Kansas in 1879, "The Exodus was a rural-to-rural migration, at least in intent, whereas the later movement was rural-to-urban." After the turn of the century, Painter succinctly notes, "the Afro-American quest for land subsided, or turned into a hunt for jobs."[18]

Despite the shadow of the plantation before World War I, the urbanization of African-Americans had deep historical roots. It reached back through the Civil War and Reconstruction to the antebellum and colonial periods. In his research on blacks in the seaport cities of British and later Revolutionary America, Gary Nash locates the roots of black urban migration and proletarianization deep in the colonial period.[19]

During the emancipation fervor that swept Revolutionary America during the late eighteenth century, black migration to the northern seaport cities of Boston, New York, and Philadelphia escalated. According to Nash, the growing movement of blacks to these cities "increased the urban bias already characteristic of black life in the colonial period."[20]

Under the impact of the Civil War and Reconstruction, black migration to American cities increased. Black population movement to cities during this period helped to shape the subsequent pattern. As Emancipation historian Armstead L. Robinson argues, the mass migrations of World War I "tended to follow paths already laid out by these preexisting migration patterns rather than breaking entirely new ground."[21] Nonetheless, as suggested by the essays in this volume, the two World Wars and the Great Depression would again alter the specific context, magnitude, and directions of black migration. Moreover, from the end of World War II through the mid-1960s, the technological revolution in southern agriculture, the emergence of the welfare state, and the militant civil rights and Black Power movements of blacks themselves, all would help to complete the long-run transformation of blacks from a predominantly rural proletariat to a predominantly urban working class.[22]

Distributed almost equally between the South on the one hand and the North and West on the other, by the 1970s the black urban migration had run its course. According to demographer Phillip Hauser, increases in black urban population were now "mainly due to births." Sociologist William J. Wilson suggests the meaning of this recent trend, when he states that: "For the first time in the twentieth century, the ranks of blacks in central cities are no longer being replenished by poor immigrants. This strongly suggests that, other things being equal, the average socioeconomic status of urban blacks will show a steady improvement, including a decrease in joblessness, and with this a decrease in crime, out-of-wedlock births, single-parent homes, and welfare dependency."[23]

Sociologists like William J. Wilson are correctly concerned with the policy implications of recent shifts in black migration, but historians can facilitate understanding by showing how recent trends emerged out of the past, changed, and took on different forms and meaning. Peter Gottlieb's essay in this volume offers provocative ideas about similarities and differences between patterns of black migration before, during, and after the Great Migration. Using illustrations from the Pittsburgh metropolitan region, he suggests that the migration of World War I and the 1920s was a migration of hope, initiative, and courage, as young southern blacks struck out for a new life in northern cities. Conversely, according to Gottlieb, the migration of the post-World War II era was one of relative despair, resignation, and few opportunities, as technological changes in southern agriculture intersected with a sluggish steel industry and overwhelmed the capacity of black migration networks to function in traditional ways. Indeed, he argues, blacks who moved in the latter period were as much refugees as migrants, for they were "uprooted in a sense that earlier migrants had not been." As Gottlieb well knows, however, he offers tantalizing and suggestive, but insufficient, evidence to support his comparative propositions.[24] Yet, the essays in this volume show that even within the same epoch (let alone different periods characterized by different social dynamics), black migration operated differently under certain conditions, at certain times, and in certain places than in others.

In short, a historical synthesis of black migration should shed light on both continuities and discontinuities in black population movement over long periods of time. It would carefully assess patterns of black migration under first commercial, then industrial, and finally post-industrial capitalism. Only by analyzing the black migration in historical perspective will we be able to fully understand the formation and transformation of the black community in urban America. Thus, the essays in this volume not only suggest the slow emergence of black migration studies as a subfield, but also, and perhaps most importantly, the outlines of a larger synthesis. Although a number of salient issues remain unresolved, it is to be hoped that this book will help to stimulate critical rethinking, discussion, and research.

NOTES

1. See above, "Black Migration to the Urban Midwest: The Gender Dimension, 1915–1945" by Darlene Clark Hine.
2. Cf. Joanne Meyerowitz, "Women and Migration: Autonomous Female Migrants to Chicago, 1880–1930," *Journal of Urban History* 13, no. 2 (Feb. 1987): 147–68; Cynthia Neverdon-Morton, *Afro-American Women of the South and the Advancement of the Race, 1895–1925* (Knoxville, TN: University of Tennessee Press, 1989), pp. 59–77; Jacqueline Jones, *Labor of Love, Labor of Sorrow: Black Women, Work, and the Family from Slavery to the Present* (New York: Basic Books, 1985), pp. 152–95; Gerda Lerner, ed., *Black Women in White America: A Documentary History* (New York: Vintage Books, 1972).
3. Kenneth Kusmer, "The Black Urban Experience in American History," in *The State of Afro-American History: Past, Present and Future*, Darlene Clark Hine, ed. (Baton Rouge: Louisiana State University Press, 1986), pp. 111–12.
4. Darrel E. Bigham, *We Ask Only a Fair Trial: A History of the Black Community of Evansville, Indiana* (Bloomington and Indianapolis: Indiana University Press, 1987), pp. xi–xiii, 109, 153–73. For other variations, see Thomas C. Cox, *Blacks in Topeka, Kansas, 1865–1915: A Social History* (Baton Rouge: Louisiana State University Press, 1982); Douglas H. Daniels, *Pioneer Urbanites: A Social and Cultural History of Black San Francisco* (Philadelphia: Temple University Press, 1980); Spencer Crew, "Black Life in Secondary Cities: A Comparative Analysis of the Black Communities of Camden and Elizabethtown, New Jersey, 1860–1920" (Ph.D. diss., Rutgers University, 1978); James E. DeVries, *Race and*

Kinship in a Midwestern Town: The Black Experience in Monroe, Michigan, 1900–1915 (Urbana: University of Illinois Press, 1984); Robert P. Stuckert, "Black Populations of the Southern Appalachian Mountains,"*Phylon* 48, no. 2 (Summer 1987): 141–51; and Ronald L. Lewis, "From Peasant to Proletarian: The Migration of Southern Blacks to the Central Appalachian Coalfields," *Journal of Southern History* 55, no. 1 (Feb. 1989): 77–102.

5. Dorothy Schwieder, Joseph Hraba, and Elmer Schwieder, *Buxton: Work and Racial Equality in a Coal Mining Community* (Ames, IA: Iowa State University Press, 1987), pp. 3–12, 209.

6. Peter Gottlieb, *Making Their Own Way: Southern Blacks' Migration to Pittsburgh, 1916–30* (Urbana: University of Illinois Press, 1987), p. 210.

7. James R. Grossman, *Chicago, Black Southerners, and the Great Migration* (Chicago: University of Chicago Press, 1989), p. 8.

8. Earl Lewis, *In Their Own Interests: Race, Class, and Power in Twentieth Century Norfolk* (Berkeley: University of California Press, 1991); Joe William Trotter, Jr., *Coal, Class, and Color: Blacks in Southern West Virginia, 1915–32* (Urbana: University of Illinois Press, 1990). Cf. George C. Wright, *Life Behind a Veil: Blacks in Louisville, 1865–1930* (Baton Rouge: Louisiana State University Press, 1985).

9. For comparative research on blacks and white immigrants, see John Bodnar, Roger Simon, and Michael P. Weber, *Lives of Their Own: Blacks, Italians, and Poles in Pittsburgh, 1900–1960* (Urbana: University of Illinois Press, 1982); Theodore Hershberg et al., "A Tale of Three Cities: Blacks, Immigrants, and Opportunity in Philadelphia, 1850–1880, 1930, 1970," in T. Hershberg, *Philadelphia: Work, Space, Family, and Group Experience in the Nineteenth Century* (New York: Oxford University Press, 1981), pp. 461–91; Stanley Lieberson, *A Piece of the Pie: Black and White Immigrants since 1880* (Berkeley: University of California Press, 1980); Stephan Thernstrom, *The Other Bostonians: Poverty and Progress in the American Metropolis, 1880–1970* (Cambridge: Harvard University Press, 1973). Also see Olivier Zunz, *The Changing Face of Inequality: Urbanization, Industrial Development, and Immigrants in Detroit, 1880–1920* (Chicago: University of Chicago Press, 1982); and Caroline Golab, *Immigrant Destinations* (Philadelphia: Temple University Press, 1977).

10. Bodnar, Simon, and Weber, *Lives of Their Own*, pp. 7, 77–78; Zunz, *The Changing Face of Inequality*, pp. 6, 372–98.

11. Hershberg, et al., "A Tale of Three Cities." See also Lieberson, *A Piece of the Pie*, pp. 9–10.

12. Neil Fligstein, *Going North: Migration of Blacks and Whites from the South, 1900–1950* (New York: Academic Press, 1981), pp. 1–19; Ronald Takaki, *Strangers from a Different Shore: A History of Asian Americans* (Boston: Little, Brown and Company, 1989); Ira De A. Reid, *The Negro Immigrant: His Background, Characteristics and Social Adjustment, 1899–1937* (New York: Columbia University Press, 1939); Alejandro Portes and Robert L. Bach, *Latin Journey: Cuban and Mexican Immigrants in the United States* (Berkeley: University of California Press, 1985); and Lucie Cheng and Edna Bonacich, *Labor Immigration under Capitalism: Asian Workers in the United States before World War II* (Berkeley: University of California Press, 1984).

13. See Norman E. Whitten and John F. Szwed, eds., *Afro-American Anthropology: Contemporary Perspectives* (New York: Free Press, 1970); Robert T. Ernst and Lawrence Hugg, eds., *Black America: Geographic Perspectives* (Garden City, NY: Anchor Books, 1976); Jamshid A. Momeni, *Demography of the Black Population in the United States: An Annotated Bibliography with a Review Essay* (Westport, CT: Greenwood Press, 1983); Reynolds Farley, *Growth of the Black Population: A Study of Demographic Trends* (Chicago: Markham Publishing Company, 1970); Daniel O. Price, *Changing Characteristics of the Negro Population* (Washington, DC: Government Printing Office, 1969); Flora Gill, *Economics and the Black Exodus: An Analysis of Negro Emigration from the Southern United States, 1910–70* (New York: Garland Publishing, Inc., 1979); William E. Vickery, *The Economics of the Negro Migration, 1900–1960* (New York: Arno Press, 1977), pp. 4–8; and Fligstein, *Going North*. Also see Ira Katznelson, *Black Men, White Cities: Migration*

154   The Great Migration in Historical Perspective

to Cities in the U.S., 1900–1930 and Britain, 1948–68 (London and New York: Published for the Institute of Race Relations by Oxford University Press, 1973).

14. For a recent discussion of the relationship between history and other social science disciplines, see John Modell, "A Note on Scholarly Caution in a Period of Revisionism and Interdisciplinarity," in *Social History and Issues in Human Consciousness: Some Interdisciplinary Connections*, Andrew Barnes and Peter N. Stearns, eds. (New York: New York University Press, 1989), pp. 41–64.

15. Vickery, *The Economics of the Negro Migration, 1900–1960*, p. 6.

16. See *Slavery and Freedom in the Age of the American Revolution*, Ira Berlin and Ronald Hoffman, eds. (Urbana: United States Capitol History Society by the University of Illinois Press, 1986); Allan Kulikoff, *Tobacco and Slaves: The Development of Southern Cultures in the Chesapeake, 1680–1800* (Chapel Hill, University of North Carolina Press, 1986); and August Meier and Elliott Rudwick, *Black History and the Historical Profession, 1915–1980* (Urbana: University of Illinois Press, 1986), especially chapter 4, "The Historiography of Slavery: An Inquiry into Paradigm-Making and Scholarly Interaction."

17. A. Kulikoff, "Uprooted Peoples: Black Migrants in the Age of the American Revolution, 1790–1820," in *Slavery and Freedom in the Age of the American Revolution*, pp. 143–71.

18. Eric Foner, *Reconstruction: America's Unfinished Revolution, 1863–1877* (New York: Harper and Row, 1988); Leon Litwack, *Been in the Storm So Long: The Aftermath of Slavery* (New York: Vintage Books, 1979); Armstead L. Robinson, "The Difference Freedom Made: The Emancipation of Afro-Americans," in *The State of Afro-American History: Past, Present, and Future*, Darlene Clark Hine, ed. (Baton Rouge: Louisiana State University Press, 1986), pp. 51–74; Nell Irvin Painter, *Exodusters: Black Migration to Kansas after Reconstruction* (1976; reprint, Lawrence, KA: University of Kansas Press, 1986), p. 260.

19. Gary B. Nash, "Forging Freedom: The Emancipation Experience in the Northern Seaport Cities, 1775–1820," in *Slavery and Freedom in the Age of the American Revolution*, pp. 3–48. Also see G. Nash, *Forging Freedom: The Formation of Philadelphia's Black Community, 1720–1840* (Cambridge: Harvard University Press, 1988); G. Nash, *The Urban Crucible: Social Change, Political Consciousness, and the Origins of the American Revolution* (Cambridge: Harvard University Press, 1979); and James O. Horton and Lois E. Horton, *Black Bostonians: Family Life and Community Struggle in the Antebellum North* (New York: Holmes and Meier Publishers, 1979).

20. Nash, "Forging Freedom," in *Slavery and Freedom in the Age of the American Revolution*, p. 4; Leonard P. Curry, *The Free Black in Urban America, 1800–1850: The Shadow of the Dream* (Chicago: University of Chicago Press, 1981), pp. 21–22.

21. Robinson, "The Difference Freedom Made," in *The State of Afro-American History*, p. 70. See also Howard Rabinowitz, *Race Relations in the Urban South, 1865–1890* (1978; reprint, Urbana: University of Illinois Press, 1989); and John Blassingame, *Black New Orleans, 1860–1880* (Chicago: University of Chicago Press, 1973).

22. Pete Daniel, *Breaking the Land: The Transformation of Cotton, Tobacco and Rice Cultures since 1880* (Urbana: University of Illinois Press, 1985); Jay R. Mandle, *The Roots of Black Poverty: The Southern Plantation Economy after the Civil War* (Durham: Duke University Press, 1978); Arnold R. Hirsch, *Making the Second Ghetto: Race and Housing in Chicago, 1940–1960* (Cambridge: Cambridge University Press, 1983); Harvard Sitkoff, *The Struggle for Black Equality, 1954–1980* (New York: Hill and Wang, 1981).

23. *Minority Report: What Has Happened to Blacks, Hispanics, American Indians and Other Minorities in the Eighties*, Leslie W. Dunbar, ed. (New York: Pantheon Books, 1984), p. 96; William J. Wilson, *The Declining Significance of Race: Blacks and Changing American Institutions* (Chicago: University of Chicago Press, 1978), and his *The Truly Disadvantaged: The Inner City, the Underclass, and Public Policy* (Chicago: University of Chicago Press, 1987).

24. See above, "Rethinking the Great Migration: A Perspective from Pittsburgh," by Peter Gottlieb.

CONTRIBUTORS

PETER GOTTLIEB, State Archivist, State Historical Society of Wisconsin, Madison, is the author of *Making Their Own Way: Southern Blacks' Migration to Pittsburgh.* His articles and reviews have appeared in *Labor History, Appalachian Review,* and *International Labor and Working Class History.*

JAMES R. GROSSMAN, Director of the Family and Community History Center at the Newberry Library, is the author of *"Land of Hope": Chicago, Black Southerners and the Great Nation.* He is currently working on a study of the relationship between race, class, ethnicity, and ideas of community in the restructuring of twentieth-century politics.

DARLENE CLARK HINE, John A. Hannah Professor of History at Michigan State University, East Lansing, is the author of *Black Women in White: Racial Conflict and Cooperation in the Nursing Profession; When the Truth Is Told: Black Women's Culture and Community in Indiana, 1875–1950;* and *Black Victory: The Rise and Fall of the White Primary in Texas.* Her articles have appeared in a variety of scholarly journals.

EARL LEWIS, Associate Professor of History and Afroamerican and African Studies at the University of Michigan, Ann Arbor, is the author of *In Their Own Interests: Race, Class and Power in Twentieth Century Norfolk.* He is currently working on a study of the social and cultural history of black school teachers.

SHIRLEY ANN MOORE, Assistant Professor of History at California State University, Sacramento, is completing her first book, *To Place Our Deeds: The Black Community in Richmond.*

JOE WILLIAM TROTTER, JR., Professor of History at Carnegie Mellon University, Pittsburgh, is the author of *Coal, Class, and Color: Blacks in Southern West Virginia, 1915–32* and *Black Milwaukee: The Making of an Industrial Proletariat, 1915–45.* He is currently working on a comparative study of blacks in three Alabama cities.

INDEX

Abbott, Robert, 91–93
Accoville, W.Va., 52
African Methodist Episcopal Church, 91
Africans: mentioned, viii, 1, 127, 150
Agricultural conditions in South, 71, 72, 76, 77
Alabama, ix, 5, 6, 48, 52, 53, 55, 57
Albion, Mich., 133
Albrier, Frances Mary, 119, 120
Alston, David, 26
Alston, Irene Johnson, 26
Amalgamated Meat Cutters and Butcher Workmen, 83
American Federation of Labor, 86, 92, 93, 94
Anderson, Ind., 127, 132
Anderson, Karen Tucker, 141
Anderson, S. R., 61
Anti-immigration laws. *See* Migration, black
Appalachia. *See* West Virginia
Archibald, Katherine, 118
"Armed March" of miners, 57
Armour, Phillip, 91
Auxiliary Unions, 119

Baldwin-Felts detectives, 54
Ballard, Allen B., 15
Baptist churches, 90
Batchan, Irene Malbrough, 109, 110
Bay Area (San Francisco): pre–World War II migration to, 106; employment for workers in, 107; 1906 earthquake and fire, 107; World War II migration to, 112; East Bay, 107. *See also* Richmond, Calif.
Beasley, Sam, 55
Bennett, George W., 22–23
Bethel, Elizabeth R., 15
Bigham, Darrel E., 148
Birmingham, Ala., ix, 6, 23, 53, 89, 110, 131
Black migration: culture transplant, 134. *See also* Migration
Bluefield, W.Va., 61
Bodnar, John, 111, 149
Boilermakers' Union, 119
Boling, Gus, 58
Boling, Lawrence, 58
Bolling, Nannie, 55
Bonaparte, Louis, Sr., 108, 114
Borchert, James, 13, 110, 128
Boston, Mass., 3, 6
Boykins, Jasper, 56
Broadnax, Elizabeth, 58
Brooks, Benjamin, 133

Brooks, Sara, 131, 133, 137
Brotherhood of Sleeping Car Porters, 91
Brotherhood of Timber Workers, 89
Burch, Arlena, 132–33
Burch, Elizabeth, 132–33, 138
Burch, Mattie Elizabeth, 133
Butcher Workmen, 92
Buxton, Iowa, 148

California: black population increase in, 107; pre-war black migration to, 107; reputation of, 108; African-American rights in, 109; wartime population increase, 112; black sailors in, 106; employment in, 109, 110. *See also* Richmond, Calif.; Bay Area (San Francisco)
Carey, Archibald J., 91
Cayton, Horace R., 11
Certainteed Manufacturing Company, 109
Chapmanville, W.Va., 62–63
Chase, John, 37
Chesapeake and Ohio Railroad, 48
Chicago, Ill.: blacks in, xii, 6, 8–9, 10, 11–12, 15, 83–105, 127, 128, 134, 136, 139, 140, 148–49
—religion: churches and unions, 90–91; links between churches and employers, 91; storefront churches, 90–91
—Stockyards Labor Council: black membership, 86–87, 89–90; organizing strategies, 84–85, 86, 95–96; racial policies, 84–85, 87; rallies, 83–84
—YMCA: antiunion activities, 90; ties to Chicago industrialists, 94
Chicago Commission on Race Relations, 4–5, 8, 98
Chicago Defender: influence among migrants, 88, 91–92; ties to Chicago industrialists, 90; on unions and strikes, 84, 91–92; race consciousness, 92–93
Chicago Federation of Labor, 83, 86–87, 95–96
Chicago Urban League: position on unionization, 83–84, 93–95; ties to Chicago industrialists, 90, 94; industrial program, 94; influence among migrants, 93–94; race consciousness, 94
Chicago *Whip*, 93
Cincinnati, Ohio, 127, 134
Civil War, 48, 127, 150, 151
Clark-Lewis, Elizabeth, 129
Class formation. *See* Proletarianization
Cleveland, Ohio, 127, 128, 130, 131, 132, 133, 137, 138, 139